THE NEW PSYCHOLOGY
OF LANGUAGE

Cognitive and Functional
Approaches to Language Structure

✳

Volume 2

THE NEW PSYCHOLOGY OF LANGUAGE

Cognitive and Functional Approaches to Language Structure

Volume 2

Edited by

Michael Tomasello
Max Planck Institute for Evolutionary Anthropology
Leipzig, Germany

 LAWRENCE ERLBAUM ASSOCIATES, PUBLISHERS
2003   Mahwah, New Jersey   London

Lawrence Erlbaum Associates, Inc., Publishers
10 Industrial Avenue
Mahwah, New Jersey 07430

Cover design by Kathryn Houghtaling Lacey

Library of Congress Cataloging-in-Publication Data

The new psychology of language : cognitive and functional approaches
to language structure (vol. 2) / edited by Michael Tomasello.
   p. cm.
   Includes bibliographical references and index.
   ISBN 0-8058-3428-1 (alk. paper). — ISBN 0-8058-3429-X (pbk. :
alk. paper).
   1. Psycholinguistics. I. Tomasello, Michael.
P37.N44   1998
401'.9—dc21   98-11415
                                                          CIP

Books published by Lawrence Erlbaum Associates are printed on acid-free paper,
and their bindings are chosen for strength and durability.

Printed in the United States of America
10 9 8 7 6 5 4 3 2 1

Contents

Introduction: Some Surprises for Psychologists   1

1   Concept Structuring Systems in Language   15
    Leonard Talmy

2   Discourse and Grammar   47
    John W. Du Bois

3   Human Cognition and the Elaboration of Events:
    Some Universal Conceptual Categories   89
    Suzanne Kemmer

4   Social Interaction and Grammar   119
    Cecilia E. Ford, Barbara A. Fox, and Sandra A. Thompson

5   Cognitive Processes in Grammaticalization   145
    Joan Bybee

6   Pronouns and Point of View: Cognitive Principles
    of Coreference   169
    Karen van Hoek

7 On Explaining Language Universals   195
       Bernard Comrie

8 The Geometry of Grammatical Meaning:
       Semantic Maps and Cross-Linguistic Comparison   211
       Martin Haspelmath

9 Regularity and Idiomaticity in Grammatical
       Constructions: The Case of *Let Alone*   243
       Charles J. Fillmore, Paul Kay, and Mary Catherine O'Connor

Author Index   271

Subject Index   277

Introduction:
Some Surprises for Psychologists

Michael Tomasello
Max Planck Institute for Evolutionary Anthropology

Linguistics can sometimes be a technical discipline, with a reality and a vocabulary all its own. For this reason, psychologists have often waited for linguists to tell them what language is—that is, give them a good description
according to the latest theory—so they can go on to study its comprehension, processing, and acquisition. But much of the theoretical framework
and vocabulary of modern linguistic theories relies on the categories and
terminology of traditional Western linguistics. Traditional Western linguistics arose historically in the Middle Ages (from Greek and Roman sources),
mainly for the teaching of Latin as a language of scholarship. Nouns and
verbs, subjects and objects, predicate adjectives and predicate nominals, are
manifestly not phenomena that were created by psychologists, or even linguists with a psychological bent, with the goal of describing how all the people of the world, speaking more than 5,000 different languages, actually
comprehend and use a natural language. Many of them are not applicable
at all to many non-European languages (Croft, in press; Dryer, 1997).

It may be that some of these categories are indeed useful for the explanatory purposes of psycholinguists. But some may not be; it is in each case an
empirical question. And that is one of the revolutionary aspects of the new
wave of linguistic theories that fly under the banner of Functional and/or
Cognitive Linguistics. Although they too use technical terminology—some
of it from the traditional vocabulary—in principle each linguistic entity is
defined with respect to the function it serves in real processes of linguistic
communication. In addition to this general functional orientation, Cogni-

1

tive–Functional (Usage-Based) linguists also make the "cognitive commitment" to couch their definitions and explanations as much as possible in theoretical constructs and terminology that are compatible with those of the other Cognitive Sciences (Lakoff, 1990). This makes the work more accessible to psychologists, and indeed it is even possible now that psychologists can share in the discussion and help to identify psychologically real linguistic entities involved in processes of linguistic communication.

This is the reasoning behind the title *The New Psychology of Language*, which is descriptive of the chapters both in Tomasello (1998) and in the current volume. Structural linguistics adopts many categories of traditional Western linguistics uncritically—indeed positing them as innate aspects of a supposed universal grammar—and then goes on to create new linguistic categories based not on their cross-linguistic applicability or on their psychological plausibility, but rather on their formal adequacy within the framework of a specific mathematical theory of language. (Thus, when a formal advance is made in the theory, as in the new minimalism [Chomsky, 1993], it is automatically assumed to be a part of universal grammar, with no empirical verification deemed necessary.) Cognitive–Functional Linguistics, on the other hand, adopts the categories of traditional Western linguistics only tentatively and provisionally based on their correspondence to the actual patterns of use of particular people using particular languages; when it creates new categories it justifies them on the basis of how people in a particular language, or set of languages, use them in acts of linguistic communication.

In the introduction to the first volume, I attempted to give an overview of Cognitive–Functional Linguists for psychologists and psycholinguists, in the hopes that this might provide them with some new perspectives for viewing basic processes of linguistic communication (Tomasello, 1998). In the more modest introduction to this the second volume, I simply wish to highlight, and to briefly explore, some of the discoveries—or in some cases, rediscoveries with modern reformulations—of modern Cognitive–Functional (Usage-Based) Linguistics, with special reference to those that seem to have most direct relevance for psychologists. Many of these discoveries—or at least the new light in which they are cast in modern Usage–Based theories—will be surprising to psychologists and psycholinguists who have not kept up with recent research on such things as grammatical analyses of non-Indo–European languages, grammaticalization in language history, the relation between written and spoken language, and the relation between language and human cognition and social interaction. In my opinion, a serious consideration of these new facts about language could change fundamentally the way psychologists and psycholinguists go about their business.

Spoken Language Does Not Work Like Written Language

Everyone agrees that the primary focus of Linguistics, and *a fortiori* Psycholinguistics, should be spoken language. Spoken language was primary by many tens of thousands of years in human history, and indeed, until quite recently, the majority of human beings on the planet have not used a written language at all. Today, spoken language is still primary by several long years in individual ontogeny, and the struggles of many children in learning to read—as compared with the relative ease with which they learn to speak—attests to the "unnaturalness" of written language.

The problem is that learning to use a written language—not to mention learning metalinguistic skills for talking about it, as in Western grammar schools—profoundly influences the way we think about language. Olson (1994, pp. 258–265) argued this point forcefully in a series of principles, some of which are: (a) Writing was responsible historically for bringing aspects of spoken language into conscious awareness, that is, for turning aspects of language into objects of reflection, analysis, and design; (b) No writing system brings all aspects of what is said in spoken language into awareness, and those aspects of spoken language that are not represented by written language are extremely difficult to bring into consciousness; and (c) Those aspects of spoken language represented by written language are felt by individuals, erroneously, to be a complete model of language, and once this model has been internalized, it is extremely difficult to unthink it and look at spoken language "naively."

The way to deal with this problem, of course, is to focus not on "grammatical sentences" found introspectively—as is common in much of Linguistics—but rather to actually observe, record, and analyze spontaneous spoken speech (see Ford, Fox, & Thompson, this volume). This is not as easy as it sounds, and indeed it is only with the invention of affordable recording equipment (and resources for paying transcribers) that it has become a possibility at all. With the invention of computational tools for tagging and searching transcripts of spoken language, a whole new world of corpus linguistics is opening up that allows for the analysis of decent-sized corpuses that represent what people actually do when they speak (e.g., Biber et al., 1998; Sinclair, 1991). Here is a partial list of some of the findings that emerge when one looks at spontaneous spoken speech (SSS) in comparisons with writing:

- There is very little in SSS that corresponds to a "sentence," as many people discovered when they first read transcripts of the informal conversations of politicians as recorded on the infamous Watergate tapes. People speak in "intonation units," which consist of prosodically and semantically coherent stretches of language typically containing only one new piece of information (DuBois, this volume). These intonation units are typically grammatical units of one sort or another (e.g., Noun Phrases, Adpositional Phrases, Clauses), but only sometimes are they entire "sentences" on the model of written language.

• What are often thought of as prototypical utterances in a language actually are not. For instance, utterances like the English "John bought a motorcycle," in which there are full nouns (i.e., noun phrases) designating both of the main participants, are extremely rare in SSS (but reasonably frequent in writing). In SSS, what people prefer to do mostly is to introduce the main referent in one intonation unit, and then predicate something about it in another (often using a pronominal reference to the just introduced entity), as in: "hey . . . ya know that guy John . . . down at the poolhall . . . he bought a Harley . . . if you can believe that." (Chafe, 1994, 1998).

• What are thought of as the prototypical uses of certain linguistic constructions often are not. For example, textbooks tell us that English relative clauses serve to "restrict" reference, as in "The motorcycle that he bought uses diesel fuel," and they often do do this in writing. But, it turns out, in English SSS people very seldom use a relative clause to restrict the reference of the primary participant (subject), which, as noted previously, is most often a pronoun. Also, people seldom use the word *that* to introduce a relative clause in SSS. This leads once again to more natural utterances like "ya know that motorcycle he bought . . . . [it uses diesel]" (Fox & Thompson, 1990).

• Utterances high in transitivity (an agent does something to cause a change of state in a patient), which are often used as the prototype of a sentence in many languages, are not so frequent in SSS. In one analysis, Thompson and Hopper (in press) found that only about one quarter of the clausal intonation units in SSS had two participants, and many of these were low in transitivity (primary participant not very agentive or secondary participant did not undergo change of state). There were also many dispersed verbal predicates instead of single lexical verbs (e.g., *have a hard time V-ing, go to all the trouble of V-ing, wander around V-ing Xs*, etc.).

• When one systematically compares such things as noun phrases, subordinate clauses of all types, focus constructions of all types, and many others, one finds that SSS and written language are very different grammatically (Miller & Weinert, 1998). Many constructions occur only or mainly in speech, for example, imperatives and interrogatives, or only in writing, for example, some types of complex nominals (e.g., "a rigorous and valid examination of Applied Economics that consists of three papers"), but not in both.

These are enough examples to make the point. The real thing—spontaneous spoken speech—has properties of its own that are different, in some cases very different, from the intuitive model of language that literate, educated people carry around in their heads. This internalized model may of course be used to generate hypotheses about the structure of SSS, but the fact is that SSS must be studied in its own right, by the normal processes of scientific observation and experimentation, however difficult and costly this may be.

Grammar Arises Historically From Language Use

Although it is not well known in the Cognitive Science community, the fact is that virtually all linguists who are involved in the detailed analysis of individual languages cross-linguistically—mostly known as linguistic typologists—now agree that there are very few if any specific grammatical constructions or markers that are universally present in all languages. There are many languages that simply do not have one or the other of relative clauses, sentential complements, passive constructions, grammatical markers for tense, grammatical markers of evidentiality, ditransitives, topic markers, *a copula* (to be), case marking of grammatical roles, subjunctive mood, definite and indefinite articles, incorporated nouns, plural markers, and on and on. Typological research has also established beyond a reasonable doubt that not only are specific grammatical constructions not universal, but basically none of the so-called minor word classes of English that help to constitute particular constructions (e.g., prepositions, auxiliary verbs, conjunctions, articles, adverbs, complementizers, and the like) are universal across languages either (Croft, in press; Dryer, 1997).

This does not mean that there are no language universals—there demonstrably are—but only that we must look for those universals in places besides particular linguistic items and constructions. One place to look is human cognition, and of course that is one of the central tenets of Cognitive Linguistics. Talmy (this volume) outlines four "concept structuring systems" that, by hypothesis, underlie all languages. Thus, all human beings conceptualize the world in terms of certain configurations of space and time, force dynamics and causality, perspective and attentional distribution; and so languages, as conventional symbolic systems designed to communicate about this world, obviously reflect these conceptualizations as well. Kemmer (this volume) analyzes how many different languages construe events and elaborate their participants, proposing a universal event model that then different languages instantiate differently in their various constructions. Haspelmath (this volume) illustrates graphically some of the interesting and complex ways in which universal forms of conceptualization get symbolized into languages cross-linguistically, with both some universal patterns and also a healthy dose of language–specific idiosyncrasies. Another place to look for universals is human communication in the sense of the communicative goals and needs of human beings—some of which are universal and some of which are particular to particular speech communities. Comrie (this volume) outlines some possible linguistic universals due to the kinds of things that humans need to talk about most urgently and the ways they need to talk about them in order to avoid ambiguities and achieve their communicative goals.

If grammatical items and constructions are not universally given to human beings, then where do they come from? Beginning in the last century, historical linguists have observed that many grammatical items in a language seem to come from more contentful lexical items. Some of the best-known European examples are as follows:

- The main future tense marker in English comes from the full lexical verb *will*, as in *I will it to happen*. At some point expressions arose of the form *It'll happen* (with the volitional component of *will* "bleached" out). Similarly, the original use of *go* was for movement (*I'm going to the store*) and this became *I'm gonna do it tomorrow* (with the movement bleached out).
- The English past perfective, using *have*, is very likely derived from sentences such as *I have a finger broken* or *I have the prisoners bound* (in which *have* is a verb of possession). This evolved into something like *I have broken a finger* (in which the possession meaning of *have* is bleached out).
- English phrases such as *on the top of* and *in the side of* evolved into *on top of* and *inside of* and eventually into *atop* and *inside*. In some languages relator words such as these spatial prepositions may also become attached to nouns as case markers (although not in English)—in this instance as possible locative case markers.
- In French, the main negative is the expression *ne . . . pas*, as in *Je ne sais pas*. Currently in spoken French, the *ne* is becoming less often used and *pas* is becoming the main negative marker. But the word *pas* was at one point the word for "step," with the expression being something like the English "not one bit" or "not one step further."

In addition, larger constructions themselves are products of grammaticalization processes, albeit these processes may be somewhat different and so they have been called *syntactitization* (Givón, 1979, 1995). The basic idea is that instead of sequences of words becoming one word, or a word changing from a more referential to a more grammatical function, or a word turning into a grammatical morpheme, in this case whole phrases take on a new kind of organization; that is, loose discourse sequences, often across intonation units, become tighter syntactic constructions. Some possible examples:

- Loose discourse sequences such as *He pulled the door and it opened* may become syntacticized into *He pulled the door open* (a resultative construction).
- Loose discourse sequences such as *My boyfriend . . . He plays piano . . . He plays in a band.* may become *My boyfriend plays piano in a band.* Or, similarly, *My boyfriend . . . He rides horses . . . He bets on them.* may become *My boyfriend, who rides horses, bets on them.*
- Similarly, if someone expresses the belief that Mary will wed John, another person might respond with an assent *I believe that,* followed by a repetition of the expressed belief that *Mary will wed John,* which become syntacticized into the single statement *I believe that Mary will wed John.*
- Complex sentences may also derive from discourse sequences of initially separate utterances, as in *I want it . . . I buy it.* evolving into *I want to buy it.*

Interestingly, along with plenty of idiosyncratic grammaticalization paths in individual languages, there would seem to be some universal, or nearly universal, grammaticalization and syntactitization paths as well. Among the most widely attested are such things as (a) main verb → auxiliary verb → tense-aspect-mood marker (e.g., a process begun by English *will* [future] and *have* [perfective]); (b) demonstrative → definite article (e.g., English *the* from *that*); (c) the numeral "one" → indefinite article (Spanish *uno/a,* French *un,* English *a*); and (d) demonstrative → complementizer (e.g., in English *I know that* → *I know that she's coming*). These happen separately in separate languages, presumably attesting to common processes of change based on universal principles of human cognition and linguistic communication (Croft, 2000).

Bybee (this volume) proposes some specific explanations for these common grammaticalization paths in terms of cognitive and communicative processes well known to psychologists, such as automatization, habituation, decontextualization (emancipation), categorization, pragmatic inferencing, and others. These processes occur as individuals use pieces of language in communication over time, with speakers constantly trying to say no more than is necessary and listeners trying to make sure that speakers say enough that they can understand adequately the intended message. Van Hoek (this volume) explains why certain processes of reference and anaphora across clauses and intonation units operate the way they do in language. Her explanation focuses on the way people package their conceptualizations for purposes of interpersonal communication.

The Units of Language Are Many and Various and Do Not Constitute "A Grammar"

In traditional Western linguistics we speak of "The Grammar" of a language, and Chomsky has followed in this tradition by speaking of children as working with "A Grammar." But languages as they are really spoken and used are very messy, and to maintain the myth of "The Grammar" of a language as a coherent entity many interesting structures must simply be ignored. For example, it is well known that in traditional terms English is an SVO (Subject–Verb–Object) language; subjects typically precede the verb and agree with it in number. Thus we say:

> She plays the piano.
> They play the piano.

But a class of the most frequent constructions in English does not work in this way (see Lakoff, 1987, for a thorough analysis). Thus, we say:

> There is my shoe.   Here is my shoe.
> There are my shoes.   Here are my shoes.

In this case, it is the element following the verb that agrees with it in number and so is, by that criterion, its subject. (Making matters even more complicated, the very similar looking utterance *It is my shoe* does not also have the form *It are my shoes*.) It is also well known that many so-called ergative languages have ergative organization in, for example, first and second person utterances, but accusative organization in third person utterances (there can also be split ergativity based on tense; DeLancey, 1981).

The point is that different constructions in a language often have their own idiosyncratic properties that do not fit neatly into the rules of "The Grammar." Fillmore, Kay, and O'Conner in their famous 1988 paper in *Language* (reprinted in abridged form in this volume) explore some of the many and various idiosyncratic constructions of English, focusing especially on the construction exemplified in utterances such as *She wouldn't live in New York, much less Boston.* Whereas it was always known that all languages have some idioms, metaphors, proverbs, and quirky constructions, what this paper underlines is the fact that many constructions in a language are in fact mixtures of more "regular" and more "idiomatic" subconstructions.

Subsequent studies on various other "odd" constructions have turned up many other similar examples, most famously:

- the nominal extraposition construction (Michaelis & Lambrecht, 1996), as in *It's amazing the people you meet here.*
- the WXDY construction (Kay & Fillmore, 1999), as in *What's my sister doing in a bar?*
- the way-construction (Goldberg, 1995), as in *He smiled his way into the meeting.*
- the twisting-the-night-away construction (Jackendoff, 1996), as in *He's sleeping his college career away.*
- the -er construction, as in *The richer they are, the nicer they are.*
- the incredulity construction, as in *Him be a doctor!*

These constructions are not just totally weird idioms, but rather they represent complex mixtures of regular and idiomatic components, and so in traditional Linguistics it is difficult to know what to do with them.

The theoretical move in traditional as well as Chomskian linguistics has always been to simply designate some items and constructions of a language as irregular or idiomatic; they are then relegated to the lexicon. This approach has been most clearly instantiated in Chomsky's (1980) distinction between the Core and the Periphery in The Grammar of a language. More recently, it is also evident in the Words and Rules approach of Pinker (1999) and Clahsen (1999), in which all irregular aspects of a language are in the lexicon—and so must be learned by rote—whereas all the regular aspects of a language are a part of its grammar and so fall under a rule that then generates its structural description. The problem again is that this tidy distinction is very difficult to maintain in the face of mixed constructions such as those listed, in which it is almost impossible to segregate the regular and idiomatic aspects. To look more closely at just one example, the incredulity construction (*My mother ride a motorcycle!*) is fully productive. A native speaker of English can generate new exemplars indefinitely. In some ways it is like other English constructions (e.g., it has SVO ordering, the NPs are regular), but of course the S is marked as an object pronoun (accusative case) and the verb is nonfinite (not marked for agreement). And so the question is: Is this a rule-based construction or an idiom? If it is an idiom, it must be called a productive idiom. The problem is that there are thousands and thousands of productive idioms in a language that are regular and idiomatic in myriad different ways—so that they merge into more regular constructions with no clear break (Nunberg, Sag, & Wasow, 1994).

The discovery—perhaps best credited to Bolinger (1977) but due mostly to the work of Fillmore, Kay, and colleagues—is that there is no clear distinction between the "core" and the "periphery" of a language, and this undermines the whole idea of The Grammar of a language as a clearly defined set of rules. It is interesting and important that when linguists who have worked for years in the Chomskian tradition look carefully at particular grammatical items and constructions, they find that many of them that were at one time considered members of the same category (e.g., complementizer) or construction (e.g., complement clause) turn out to be very different from one another in detail—and so not assimilable to the same rigid rule (Cullicover, 1999; Jackendoff, 1996).

The alternative is to conceive of a language as "a structured inventory of symbolic units," each with its own structure and function (Langacker, 1987). These units may vary in both their complexity and generality. For example, the one word utterance *Fore!* is a very simple and concrete construction used for a specific function in the game of golf. *Thank you* and *Don't mention it* are multiword constructions used for relatively specific social functions. Some other constructions are composed of specific words along with "slots" into which whole classes of items may fit, for example, *Down with __!* and *Hooray for __!* There are also constructions that are extremely general and abstract. Thus, the ditransitive construction in English prototypically indicates transfer of possession and is represented by utterances such as *He gave the doctor money*, abstractly described as NP+VP+NP+NP. Abstract linguistic constructions such as this have their own meanings, in relative independence of the lexical items involved, and indeed this is the source of much of the creativity of language (Goldberg, 1995). Abstract constructions are thus an important part of the inventory of symbolic resources that language users control—and they do much of the work that would be done by core grammar in more traditional accounts—but they are best seen as just one form that linguistic constructions may take.

In general, the breakdown of the distinction between linguistic "core" and linguistic "periphery" is a genuine scientific discovery about the way language works, and sorting out its implications will play a key role in creating a new psychology of language. When we conceive of linguistic constructions as cognitive schemas of the same type as we find in other cognitive skills, that is, as relatively automatized procedures for getting things done (in this case, communicatively), it is quite natural that they should not be of only two kinds (regular and idiomatic) but rather that they should vary from simple to complex and, independently, from concrete to abstract in many complex ways.

Frequency Counts

Individuals do not hear abstract constructions; they hear only individual utterances. To create abstract constructions, they must find patterns in the language they hear around them. Children begin with constructions based on concrete items and phrases; they then discover a variety of relatively local constructional patterns; and only later do they discover more general patterns among these local constructional patterns (Tomasello, 1992, 2000). But as children create more general constructions, they do not throw away their more item-based and local constructions. The idea that people operate always and only with the most abstract structures that linguists can find is what Langacker (1987) called the *rule-list fallacy*. It reflects a very deep difference in the theoretical goals of formal linguists and more psychologically oriented linguists.

In cognitively and functionally oriented (usage-based) approaches, people can possess abstract cognitive structures that they use in certain instances, but they still operate on some occasions with the more concrete structures that instantiate the abstraction. As just a handful of many thousands, or tens of thousands, of relatively concrete and fixed expressions that native speakers of English control (which may or may not instantiate more abstract constructions): *I'm simply amazed, I looked everywhere for it, You keep out of this, That was a close call, It's a matter of priorities, From time to time . . . , I'd do it all over again, I'm surprised to hear that, Do what you're told!, I see what you mean, I thought you'd never ask, Have some more, You can't be too careful, Where did you find it?, He's busy right now, You can't believe a word he says,* and on and on (Pawley & Syder, 1983).

Bybee and Scheibman (1999) provided evidence that people sometimes produce complex utterances—which they know at some level have internal structure—as single processing units. They analyze in some depth various uses of the English word *don't* and find that in highly frequent and relatively fixed expression like *I don't know* people tend to reduce the pronunciation of *don't*, in some cases so much that it is barely recognizable if listened to in isolation. Thus, the most common pronunciation of *I don't know* is actually something more like *Idunno*, and in some cases the expression is barely more than a characteristic intonation contour. This same reduction of the word *don't* does not occur in other, less frequent expressions and constructions. Although most adults can analyze this expression into its components—for example, if a questioner persists they can say each of the words slowly and emphatically, "I . . . DON'T . . . KNOW!"—from a processing point of view its great frequency has made it a production routine. Bybee (1995) argued that the token frequency of an expression serves to entrench it in a speaker's repertoire and make it a processing unit. Type frequency—repeated instantiations of the same pattern but with different concrete items—entrenches the pattern but also, at the same time, makes it more generally applicable to more items. Thus, young children initially form and use only very concrete and local constructional islands (based on specific lexical items) but with high type frequency in one or more slots, for example: *Where's the X?, I wanna X, More X, It's a X, I'm X-ing it, Put X here,*

Mommy's X-ing it, Let's X it, Throw X, X gone, I X-ed it, Sit on the X, Open X, X here, There's a X, X broken (Braine, 1976; Lieven, Pine, & Baldwin, 1997; see Tomasello, 2000, for a review of the evidence).

Frequency also plays a crucial role in grammaticalization and language change. Thus, it is well known that the linguistic constructions that are most resistant to change are those that are most frequent. That is why most irregular verbs in a language are typically highly frequent (e.g., in English the verbs *to be* and *to have*). Bybee and Thompson (in press) analyzed the example of the subjunctive mood in Canadian French, which has basically been lost. However, in a few highly frequent fixed expressions it lives on (as it also does in frequent English expressions like "If I were you . . . ."). At the same time, highly frequent expressions also in some contexts become grammaticalized, and so change their function, sometimes retaining the old function in other contexts (as in the English main verbs *have* and *go* and their more recent instantiations as auxiliary verbs as well). In the context of language acquisition, Brooks, Tomasello, Lewis, and Dodson (1999) argued and presented evidence that the entrenchment of particular verbs in particular constructions (in both comprehension and production) is a major factor preventing children from overgeneralizing their abstract constructions to inappropriate verbs. This finding (in combination with that of Brooks & Tomasello, 1999, who demonstrated the importance of two other usage-based factors) thus solves in large measure the puzzle of why children do not use their powerful grammatical rules indiscriminately with their entire lexicons, as they might be expected to if they possessed the abstract rules that formal grammar writers often attribute to them (e.g., Pinker, 1984, 1989).

Talk of frequency and entrenchment raises the specter of Behaviorism, which, as is well known, was exorcised from Linguistics once and for all by Chomsky (1959). But just because frequency and entrenchment were important concepts for behaviorists—who knew little of the structure of language—does not mean that they are useless in other, more cognitively and functionally sophisticated approaches. It turns out that both the type and token frequency with which particular constructions are used makes an enormous difference both in their historical fate and in the way they are understood, acquired, cognitively represented, and used by contemporary speakers of a language.

CONCLUSION

Linguistics as a discipline hovers between the Humanities and the Behavioral/Cognitive Sciences. For much of its history Linguistics consisted solely of the analysis of texts and the teaching of rules. Many linguists thus did not consider it their concern to worry about psychological reality, or to acquire expertise with the kinds of rigorous methods of data sampling and statistical analysis that are the foundation of the Behavioral/Cognitive Sciences. But, with the rise of Cognitive Science as an interdisciplinary enterprise, with the rise of new technologies that make possible the recording and analysis of real live linguistic communication, and with the rise of Cognitive–Functional (Usage-Based) approaches to linguistic theory, the balance is beginning to tip toward the side of science. In a utopian future, linguists and psychologists will work together to investigate the actual psychological processes by means of which human beings comprehend, produce, and acquire a natural language. The chapters in this volume—as well as those in the first volume—represent theoretical approaches that will help us to make progress toward that goal.

REFERENCES

Biber, D. (1988). *Variation across speech and writing.* Cambridge: Cambridge University Press.

Biber, D., Conrad, S., & Reppen, R. (1998). *Corpus linguistics: Exploring language structure and use.* Cambridge: Cambridge University Press.

Bolinger, D. (1977). *Meaning and form.* New York: Longman.

Braine, M. (1976). Children's first word combinations. *Monographs of the Society for Research in Child Development, 41*(No. 1).

Brooks, P., & Tomasello, M. (1999). How young children constrain their argument structure constructions. *Language, 75,* 720–738.

Brooks, P., Tomasello, M., Lewis, L., & Dodson, K. (1999). How children avoid argument structure errors: The entrenchment hypothesis. *Child Development, 70,* 1325–1337.

Bybee, J. (1995). Regular morphology and the lexicon. *Language and Cognitive Processes, 10,* 425–455.

Bybee, J., & Scheibman, J. (1999). The effect of usage on degrees of constituency: The reduction of *don't* in English. *Linguistics, 37,* 575–596.

Bybee, J., & Thompson, S. (in press). Three frequency effects of syntax. *Proceedings of the Berkeley Linguistic Society.*

Chafe, W. (1994). *Discourse, conciousness, and time.* Chicago: University of Chicago Press.

Chafe, W. (1998). Language and the flow of thought. In M. Tomasello (Ed.), *The new psychology of language: Cognitive and functional approaches* (pp. 111–150). Mahwah, NJ: Lawrence Erlbaum Associates.

Chomsky, N. (1959). A review of B. F. Skinner's "Verbal behavior." *Language, 35,* 26–58.

Chomsky, N. (1980). Rules and representations. *Behavioral and Brain Sciences, 3,* 1–61.

Chomsky, N. (1993). A minimalist program for linguistic theory. In K. Hale & S. Keyser (Eds.), *A view from Building 20* (pp. 1–53). Cambridge, MA: MIT Press.

Clahsen, H. (1999). Lexical entries and rules of language: A multidisciplinary study of German inflection. *Behavioral and Brain Sciences, 22,* 980–999.

Croft, W. (2000). *Explaining language change: An evolutionary approach.* London: Longman.

Croft, W. (2002). *Radical construction grammar.* Oxford: Oxford University Press.

Cullicover, P. (1999). *Syntactic nuts.* Oxford: Oxford University Press.

DeLancey, S. (1981). An interpretation of split ergativity and related patterns. *Language, 57,* 626–657.

Dryer, M. (1997). Are grammatical relations universal? In J. Bybee, J. Haiman, & S. Thompson (Eds.), *Essays on language function and language type* (pp. 115–144). Amsterdam, Netherlands: John Benjamins.

Fillmore, C., Kaye, P., & O'Connor, M. (1988). Regularity and idiomaticity in grammatical constructions: The case of let alone. *Language, 64*, 501–538.

Fox, B., & Thompson, S. (1990). A discourse explanation of "The Grammar" of relative clauses in English conversation. *Language, 66*, 297–316.

Givón, T. (1979). *On understanding grammar.* New York: Academic Press.

Givón, T. (1995). *Functionalism and grammar.* Amsterdam, Netherlands: John Benjamins.

Goldberg, A. (1995). *Constructions: A construction grammar approach to argument structure.* Chicago: University of Chicago Press.

Jackendoff, R. (1996). Twistin' the night away. *Language, 73*, 534–559.

Kay, P., & Fillmore, C. (1999). Grammatical constructions and linguistic generalizations. *Language, 75*, 1–33.

Lakoff, G. (1987). *Women, fire, and dangerous things: What categories reveal about the mind.* Chicago: University of Chicago Press.

Lakoff, G. (1990). The Invariance Hypothesis: Is abstract reason based on image schemas? *Cognitive Linguistics, 1*, 39–74.

Langacker, R. (1987). *Foundations of cognitive grammar* (Vol. 1). Palo Alto, CA: Stanford University Press.

Lieven, E., Pine, J., & Baldwin, G. (1997). Lexically-based learning and early grammatical development. *Journal of Child Language, 24*, 187–220.

Michaelis, L., & Lambrecht, K. (1996). Toward a construction-based theory of language function: The case of nominal extraposition. *Language, 72*, 215–247.

Miller, J., & Weinert, R. (1998). *Spontaneous spoken language.* Oxford: Oxford University Press.

Nunberg, G., Sag, I., & Wasow, T. (1994). Idioms. *Language, 70*, 491–538.

Olson, D. (1994). *The world on paper.* Cambridge: Cambridge University Press.

Pawley, A., & Snyder, F. (1983). Two puzzles for linguistic theory. In J. Richards & R. Smith (Eds.), *Language and communication* (pp. 185–209). New York: Longman.

Pinker, S. (1984). *Language learnability and language development.* Cambridge, MA: Harvard University Press.

Pinker, S. (1989). *Learnability and cognition: The acquisition of verb–argument structure.* Cambridge, MA: Harvard University Press.

Pinker, S. (1999). *Words and rules.* New York: Morrow Press.

Sinclair, J. (1991). *Corpus, concordance, and collocation.* Oxford: Oxford University Press.

Thompson, S., & Hopper, P. (in press). Transitivity, clause structure, and argument structure: Evidence from conversation. In J. Bybee & P. Hopper (Eds.), *Frequency and the emergence of linguistic structure.* Amsterdam: John Benjamins.

Tomasello, M. (1992). *First verbs: A case study in early grammatical development.* New York: Cambridge University Press.

Tomasello, M. (1998). Introduction: The cognitive–functional perspective on language structure. In M. Tomasello (Ed.), *The new psychology of language: Cognitive and functional approaches to language structure* (pp. 1–25). Mahwah, NJ: Lawrence Erlbaum Associates.

Tomasello, M. (2000). Do young children have adult syntactic competence? *Cognition, 74*, 209–253.

Chapter 1

Concept Structuring Systems in Language

Leonard Talmy
University of Buffalo

This chapter is built around a selection of topics within the framework of cognitive semantics set forth in Talmy (2000a, 2000b). The topics here have been selected (with the help of Michael Tomasello) for their specific relevance to psychology. The framework is governed by certain major organizing factors, and several of these are briefly sketched now as a background for the topics discussed in greater detail later.

A universal design feature of languages is that their meaning-bearing forms are divided into two different subsystems, the open-class, or lexical, and the closed-class, or grammatical (see Talmy, 2000a, ch. 1). Open classes have many members and can readily add many more. They commonly include (the roots of) nouns, verbs, and adjectives. Closed classes have relatively few members and are difficult to augment. They include such bound forms as inflections (say, those appearing on a verb) and such free forms as prepositions, conjunctions, and determiners. In addition to such overt closed classes, there are implicit closed classes such as the set of grammatical categories that appear in a language (say, nounhood, verbhood, etc., per se), the set of grammatical relations that appear in a language (say, subject status, direct object status, etc.), and perhaps also the grammatical constructions that appear in a language.

One crucial finding here is that the meanings that open-class forms can express are virtually unrestricted, whereas those of closed-class forms are highly constrained, both as to the conceptual category they can refer to and as to the particular member notions within any such category. For example, many languages around the world have closed-class forms in construction with a noun that indicate the number of the noun's referent, but no languages have closed-class forms indicating its color. And even closed-class forms referring to number can indicate such notions as singular, dual, plural, paucal, and the like, but never such notions as even, odd, a dozen, or countable. By contrast, open-class forms can refer to all such notions, as the very words just used demonstrate.

The total set of conceptual categories with their member notions that closed-class forms can ever refer to thus constitutes a specific approximately closed inventory. Individual languages draw in different ways from this inventory for their particular set of grammatically expressed meanings. The inventory is graduated, progressing from categories and notions that appear universally in all languages, through ones appearing in many but not all languages, down to ones appearing in just a few languages.

In accordance with the different semantic constraints on them, a further major finding is that the two types of classes have different functions. In the conceptual complex evoked by any portion of discourse, say, by a sentence, the open-class forms contribute most of the *content*, whereas the closed-class forms determine most of the *structure*. Thus, the inventory of conceptual categories and individual concepts that closed-class forms can ever express amounts to the fundamental conceptual structuring system used by language.

The concepts and conceptual categories in the inventory can be seen to cluster together so as to form several distinct extensive and integrated groupings, termed *schematic systems*. Each of these handles a certain portion of the concept structuring function of the whole inventory. One such schematic system—that of *configurational structure*—includes the schematic (often geometric) delineations that partition scenes, structure entities, and relate separate entities to each other within space or time or other qualitative domains. A second schematic system—that of *force dynamics*—covers the forces that one entity delineated by the first schematic system can exert on another such entity. This force dynamic system thus also covers all the various forms of causation. A third schematic system—that of *perspective*—governs where one places one's "mental eyes" to look out over the scene whose delineations and force interactions have been determined by the first two schematic systems. And a fourth schematic system—that of *distribution of attention*—directs one's attention differentially over the structured scene that one regards from one's perspective point. The next four sections illustrate these four schematic systems.

SPACE–TIME CONFIGURATION

Several fundamental properties of the first schematic system, configurational structure, are sketched here. A further pervasive property of conceptual organization in language—a homologous structuring of space and time—is also demonstrated for this schematic system.

Figure–Ground Organization

In language, the spatial disposition of any focal object in a scene is largely characterized in terms of a single further object, also selected within the scene, whose location and sometimes also "geometric" properties are already known (or assumed known to an addressee) and so can function as a reference object (see Talmy, 2000a, ch. 5). The first object's site, path, or orientation is thus indicated in terms of distance from or relation to the geometry of the second object. The sentences in (1) can illustrate. For their apparent relation, if not identity, to the figure and ground concepts in Gestalt psychology, these first and second scene objects are respectively termed the *Figure* and the *Ground*—capitalized to mark their specific function in language.

(1) a. The bike stood near the house.
    b. The bike stood in the house.
    c. The bike stood across the driveway.
    d. The bike rolled along the walkway.

The bike's site is characterized in (1a) by *near*, in terms of distance from the house's location ("proximal"). The bike's site is characterized in (1b) by *in*, in terms of the house's location *and* geometry ("colocational" + "part of interior"). The bike's site *and* orientation are characterized in (1c) by *across* in terms of the driveway's location and geometry ("colocational" + "one's length perpendicular to the other's length"). And the bike's *path* is expressed in (1d) by *along* in terms of the walkway's location and geometry ("colocational" + "colinear with the long axis"). The bike functions as the Figure in all four sentences, while the house functions as the Ground in the first two sentences and the driveway does so in the last two. Throughout characterizations of this sort, it remains implicit that the Ground object can be used as a reference only by virtue, in a recursive manner, of its own known spatial disposition with respect to the remainder of the scene. That is, those spatial characterizations that are expressed overtly (as with prepositions) ultimately rest on certain further spatial understandings that are unexpressed.

The definitional functions that have here been isolated for a scene's Figure and Ground are represented by the top entry in (2). These definitional functions are seen generally, though not absolutely, to correlate with other associated property differences between the two objects. The alignment is shown in (2):

(2)

	Figure	Ground
definitional characteristics	has unknown spatial (or temporal) properties to be determined	acts as a reference entity, having known properties that can characterize the Figure's unknowns
associated characteristics	• more movable	• more permanently located
	• smaller	• larger
	• geometrically simpler (often point-like) in its treatment	• geometrically more complex in its treatment
	• more recently on the scene/in awareness	• more familiar/expected
	• of greater concern/relevance	• of lesser concern/relevance
	• less immediately perceivable	• more immediately perceivable
	• more salient, once perceived	• more backgrounded, once Figure is perceived
	• more dependent	• more independent

It might be argued for cases like (1) that language simply relates two objects in space without any inequality of status, that is, without one object serving as reference for the other. But the semantic reality of their functional difference can be demonstrated simply by interchanging the nominals, as in a sentence-pair like the following:

(3) a. The bike is near the house.
    b. The house is near the bike.

One could have expected these sentences to be synonymous on the grounds that they simply represent the two inverse forms of a symmetric spatial relation. But the obvious fact is that they do not have the same meaning. They *would* be synonymous if they specified *only* this symmetric relation, that is, here, the small quantity of distance between two objects. But in addition to this, (3a) makes the nonsymmetric specification that the house is to be used as a fixed reference point by which to characterize the bike's location, itself to be treated as a variable. These nonsymmetric role assignments conform to the exigencies of the familiar world, where in fact houses have locations more permanent than bikes and are larger landmarks, so that (3a) reads like a fully acceptable sentence. The sentence in (3b), on the other hand, sounds quite odd, and is thereby well flagged as semantically distinct from (3a). As the assertion of nearness is unchanged, the reason for the difference can only be that (3b) makes all the reverse reference assignments, ones that in this case do not happen to match the familiar world.

It might at first be thought that certain grammatical constructions, for example, the reciprocal, are means available in a language specifically to avoid assigning different referencing roles, which otherwise are inescapably imposed on a basic proposition in formulations like (3). But in fact, the reciprocal does not abstract the symmetric relation common to the inverse asymmetric forms, but rather *adds* the two together. This is shown by the fact that the reciprocal for the preceding example:

(4) The bike and the house are near each other.

sounds odd in just the same way as (3b) itself, that is, because of the implication that the house is somehow a floating entity to be fixed with respect to a stable bike.

As they specifically function in language, the Figure and Ground concepts can be characterized as follows:

(5) *The general conceptualization of Figure and Ground in language*
The Figure is a moving or conceptually movable entity whose site, path, or orientation is conceived as a variable, the particular value of which is the relevant issue.
The Ground is a reference entity, one that has a stationary setting relative to a reference frame, with respect to which the Figure's site, path, or orientation is characterized.

In a linguistic context, the Figure and Ground notions amount to semantic roles or "cases," in the sense of Fillmore's (1968) "Case Grammar." The present notions, in fact, compete with those of Fillmore, and certain advantages can be claimed for them. Full comparison aside, one main difference is that four Fillmorian cases, "Locative," "Source," "Path," and "Goal," because they incorporate particulars of direction, fail to capture the crucial spatial factor they have in common: their function as reference object for a figural element, a function specifically delegated to our Ground notion. Further, because it names separate cases for several different incorporated directionals, Fillmore's system is open to question over how it can handle novel directional distinctions that some language might mark or directions that do not clearly fit one of his four established cases. For example, should the directionals represented by the prepositions in *The ball rolled across the crack./past the TV./around the lamp* all be classed as Fillmore's "Path"? By identifying a distinct Ground notion, our system can set up a separate Directional component for the various attendant path types—one that can, within universal constraints, expand or contract and exhibit somewhat different structurings as appropriate for each particular language. This separation, moreover, corresponds to the usually encountered division of morpheme classes, where the Ground notion is expressed by a noun root (plus any modifiers) and the Directional notions by grammatical elements such as noun affixes or adpositions.

As part of a system of spatio-temporal homology extensively found in language, the reference of Figure and Ground to the relative location of objects in space is generalized to the relative location of events in time. Paralleling their characterization earlier for spatial objects, the categories of Figure and Ground can be given the following more specific characterization for temporal events:

(6) *The temporally specific conceptualizations of Figure and Ground in language*
The Figure is an event whose location in time is conceived as a variable, the particular value of which is the relevant issue.
The Ground is a reference event, one that has a stationary setting relative to a reference-frame (generally, the one-dimensional time line), with respect to which the Figure's temporal location is characterized.

The fact that these semantic categories also apply to temporal structures can be seen in a complex sentence like

(7) He exploded after he touched the button.

This sentence seems to assign a Ground interpretation to the button-touching event—setting it up as a fixed, known reference point—and to assign a Figure interpretation to the explosion event—establishing the temporal location of this more salient event with respect to the other event. As with the earlier demonstration for the "bike/house" example, we can confirm that these different functions have been assigned here simply by noting that the inverse sentence

(8) He touched the button before he exploded.

is different in meaning. To me, in fact, it sounds comical, and acquires a suitable seriousness only after one imagines special circumstances, such as an official search into the possible causes of a known death.

Topological Properties of Space–Time Schemas

The prepositions and conjunctions of the earlier examples are closed-class forms that specify spatial and temporal structure with their "geometric"-type schemas. Such schemas abstract away from the bulk of physical objects and the activity of events, idealizing them down to particular configurations of points, lines, and planes. Further, such schemas abstract away from any specificity as to shape (curvature) or magnitude for these points, lines, and planes—and hence, also from any specificity as to angles or distances between them as they relate within the schema. This sort of further abstraction is characteristic of the relations defined within the mathematical field of topology. Euclidean geometry, by contrast, distinguishes shape, size, angle, and distance. Distinctions of this latter sort are mostly indicated in languages by open-class forms, for example, *square*, *huge*, *right*, and *inch*. But closed-class forms show greater affinity with topology (see Talmy, 2000a, ch. 1). (One might further postulate that it was this subsystem—and its counterparts in other cognitive systems—that gave rise to intuitions from which the field of topology was developed.) I illustrate linguistic topology here with respect to two of its characteristics.

Irrelevance of Magnitude. Possibly without exception, the spatial closed-class forms of languages specify the same schemas for small objects and distances as for great ones. This is not some necessary fact to be taken for granted. It would be easy to imagine that, say, objects capable of fitting in one's hand and broad geographic terrains might have different spatial characteristics of relevance to humans and that closed-class forms would reflect such differences. Yet, the evidence is that much the same spatial structures are recognized all along the size spectrum, a fact that points to a unified cognitive system for structuring space in language. To illustrate, consider these two sets of sentences:

(9) a. The lamp stood in the box.
 The man stood in the barn.
 The building stood in the valley.
 b. The ant crawled across my palm.
 The man walked across the field.
 The bus drove across the country.

Here, the range in the size of a Reference Object, from a box to a valley for the static cases, or from a palm to a country, with the corresponding range in the length of the path traveled, is irrelevant to the choice of the schema-specifying prepositions *in* and *across*. Such closed-class forms are *magnitude neutral*.

Comparably, the use of the closed-class demonstratives *this* and *that*—indicating objects relatively nearer and farther from the speaker—can be equally used in the two sentences in (10).

(10) This speck is smaller than that speck.
 This planet is smaller than that planet.

Again the difference in size between a speck and a planet, and the difference in the distances involved—from millimeters to parsecs—is irrelevant to the use of the spatial terms.

Magnitude neutrality is also seen in closed-class forms referring to time. Thus, the English past tense inflection *-ed* can be used in the sentence *Alexander died with dignity* with equal felicity whether the time referred to was last year, in speaking of an acquaintance, or over two millenia ago, in speaking of Alexander the Great. As before, this closed-class form refers to a particular schematic arrangement in time—in idealized form, that of a point event located within the period leading up to the point of the present moment—and is neutral to temporal magnitude.

Irrelevance of Shape.   Spatial closed-class forms generally also permit wide ranges of shape variation. For example, the use of *in* requires that a Ground Object be idealizable as a surface so curved as to define a volume. But that surface can be squared off as in a box, spheroidal as in a bowl, or irregular as in a piano-shaped swimming pool (*The ball is in the box / bowl / pool*). It can be open over some area as in the preceding examples, or wholly closed to form a complete enclosure, as in a silo. And it can be an unbroken solid as in the previous examples, or have gaps, like a birdcage or a house with its doors and windows open. As we see, none of these variations of shape affect the use of *in*. Likewise, whereas the *across* schema may prototypically specify a strip-shaped Ground object, like a street, the Ground can readily diverge from having parallel edges or even a strip shape. Thus, one can swim "across" a lake with irregular curved "edges" that join to form a rough circle.

This property of *shape neutrality* applies not only to the Ground Object itself but also to the path the Figure takes with respect to it. Thus, I could have swum along an irregular path "across" the irregular lake. Similarly, the closed-class spatial form *through*, in its use referring to a linear path within a medium, can apply to a path of any shape:

(11) I arced/zigzagged *through* the woods.

Fictive Motion

I posit the extensive occurrence in cognition of a certain pattern in which an individual concurrently has two discrepant representations of the same entity. The individual holds one of these representations, the *factive* one, to be more veridical than the other representation, the *fictive* one. It is assumed that the two representations are the products of two different cognitive subsystems, and that the veridicality assessment itself is produced by a third cognitive subsystem. This *general fictivity pattern* may occur in several cognitive systems including visual perception (see Talmy, 2000a, ch. 2), but is here considered only for language. Perhaps the commonest form of fictivity in language is that of *fictive motion*, in which a factive representation of an object as stationary is held in cognition concurrently with a fictive representation of the same object as moving.

Of the many categories of fictive motion, the one best known in the linguistic literature—here termed *coextension paths*—involves the conceptualization of a fictive entity that moves fictively along or over the extent of a factive entity in a way that can characterize its contour or location. This category has most often been illustrated by forms like *This road goes from Modesto to Fresno* or *The cord runs from the TV to the wall.* But a purer demonstration of this type of fictive motion would exclude reference to an entity that supports the actual motion of other objects (as a road guides vehicles) or that itself may be associated with a history of actual motion (like a TV cord). The "mountain range" example in (12) avoids this problem.

(12) a. That mountain range lies (longitudinally) between Canada and Mexico.
 b. That mountain range goes from Canada to Mexico.
 c. That mountain range goes from Mexico to Canada.

Here, (12a) directly expresses the more veridical static spatial relationships in a stative form of expression, without evoking fictive motion. But (12b) and (12c) represent the static linear entity, the mountain range, in a way that evokes a sense or a conceptualization of something in motion—respectively, from North to South and from South to North. These latter two sentences manifest the general fictivity pattern. They each involve two discrepant representations of the same object, the mountain range. Of these two representations, the fictive representation, that is, the one that is assessed and experienced as less veridical, consists of the literal reference of the words, which directly depict the mountain range as moving. The factive representation, the one assessed and experienced as more veridical, consists of our belief that the mountain range is stationary.

The Phenomenology of Fictive Motion. Most observers can agree that languages systematically and extensively refer to stationary circumstances with forms and constructions whose basic reference is to motion. We can term this *constructional fictive motion.* Speakers exhibit differences, however, over the degree to which such expressions evoke an actual sense or conceptualization of motion, what can be called *experienced fictive motion.* Thus, for the same instance of constructional fictive motion, some speakers will report a strong semantic evocation of motion, whereas other speakers will report that there is none at all. What does appear common, though, is that every

speaker experiences a sense of motion for *some* fictive-motion constructions.

Where an experience of motion does occur, there appears an additional
range of differences as to what is conceptualized as moving. This conceptualization can vary across individuals and types of fictive motion. A single individual may even deal with the same example of fictive motion differently
on different occasions. Included in the conceptualizations of this range,
the fictive motion may be manifested by the named entity (e.g., by the
mountain range in [12]); by some unnamed object that moves with respect
to the named entity (e.g., a car or hiker relative to the mountain range); in
the mental imagery of the speaker or hearer, by the imagistic or conceptual
equivalent of their focus of attention moving relative to the named entity;
by some abstracted conceptual essence of motion moving relative to the
named entity; or by a sense of abstract directedness suggesting motion relative to the named entity. The strength and character of experienced fictive
motion, as well as its clarity and homogeneity, are a phenomenological concomitant of the present area that will need more investigation.

Categories of Fictive Motion.   Many further categories of fictive motion
exist. The following sketch of several of these will provide a fuller sense of
the phenomenon.

The category of *emanation paths* involves the fictive conceptualization of
an intangible line emerging from a source point and terminating on a target point, where factively nothing is in motion. Three types within this category are illustrated in (13).

(13) a. demonstrative paths
          The arrow points toward / past / away from the town.
      b. sensory paths
          I looked toward / down into / past the valley.
      c. radiation paths
          The light shone from the sun into the cave. / onto the back wall
          of the cave.

In the *pattern paths* category of fictive motion, some material factively
moves, with the result that some pattern or configuration changes and is
conceptualized as moving fictively. Thus, in (14), the drops of paint
factively move vertically downward, but the pattern of spots on the floor
moves fictively in a horizontal direction.

(14) pattern paths
          As I painted the ceiling, (a line of) paint spots slowly progressed
          across the floor.

With respect to a global frame of reference, an observer can be factively represented as moving relative to the stationary surroundings, as in (15a). But by the fictive motion category of *frame-relative motion*, the observer can be reconceptualized as being at the center of a local stationary frame, relative to which the surroundings are fictively moving, as in (15b).

(15) frame-relative motion
  a. *global frame: fictive motion absent*
     I rode along in the car and looked at the scenery we were passing through.
  b. *local frame: fictive motion present*
     I sat in the car and watched the scenery rush past me.

Finally here, the category of *access paths* depicts a stationary object's location in terms of a path that some other entity might follow to the point of encounter with the object. What is factive here is the representation of the object as stationary, without any entity traversing the depicted path. What is fictive is the representation of some entity traversing the depicted path, whether this is plausible or implausible. Though it is not specified, the fictively moving entity can often be imagined as being a person, some body part of a person, or the focus of one's attention, depending on the particular sentence, as can be seen in the examples of (16).

(16) access paths
  a. The bakery is across the street from the bank.
  b. The vacuum cleaner is down around behind the clothes hamper.
  c. That quasar is 10 million light-years past the North Star.

Distinguishing Features. The several distinct categories of fictive motion as indicated differ from each other with respect to a certain set of conceptual features. Each category of fictive motion exhibits a different combination of values for these features, of which the main ones are shown in (17).

(17) *Principal features distinguishing categories of fictive motion in language*
  1. factive motion of some elements need not / must be present for the fictive effect
  2. the fictively moving entity is itself factive / fictive
  3. the fictive effect is observer-neutral / observer-based
     —and, if observer-based:
     a. the observer is factive / fictive
     b. the observer moves / scans
  4. what is conceived as fictively moving is an entity / the observation of an entity

FORCE AND CAUSATION

Some basic properties of the second schematic system, force dynamics—
which also includes causation—are presented next.

Illustrating the Category of Force Dynamics

Because force dynamics is a novel category in linguistics, it would be best to
give it immediate illustration (see Talmy, 2000a, ch. 7). The minimal pairs
in (18) mostly contrast force-dynamically neutral expressions with ones that
do exhibit force-dynamic patterns, showing these in a succession of semantic domains.

(18) 1. be VPing / keep Vping   —physical
        a. The ball was rolling along the green.
        b. The ball kept (on) rolling along the green.
     2. not VP / can not VP   —physical/psychological
        a. John doesn't go out of the house.
        b. John can't go out of the house.
     3. not VP / refrain from Vping   —intrapsychological
        a. He didn't close the door.
        b. He refrained from closing the door.
     4. polite / civil   —intrapsychological: lexicalized
        a. She's polite to him.
        b. She's civil to him.
     5. have (got) to VP / get to VP   —sociopsychological
        a. She's got to go to the park.
        b. She gets to go to the park.

Illustrating the purely physical realm, (1a) depicts a force-dynamically
neutral event. The use of the word *keep* in (1b), however, brings in either of
two force-dynamic patterns: either the ball has a tendency toward rest that
is being overcome by some external force acting on it, say, the wind, or the
ball presently has a tendency toward motion that is in fact overcoming external opposition to it, say, from stiff grass.

In (2) a psychological force factor joins the physical one. The force-
dynamically neutral expression in (2a) merely reports an objective observation, John's not going out. But (2b), in addition to the same observation,
also sets forth a full force-dynamic complex: that John *wants* to go out (conceivable as a force-like tendency toward that act), that there is some kind of
force or barrier opposing that tendency, and that the latter is stronger than
the former, yielding a net resultant of no overt action.

Example (3) illustrates that language can depict a force opposition as wholly psychological, and in fact as occurring within a single psyche. Again, both (3a) and (3b) refer to the same overtly observable situation, an agent's non-action. But (3b) in addition represents this situation as the resultant of an intrapsychological conflict, one between the agent's urge to act and the same agent's stronger inhibition against acting.

Example (4) exhibits the same type of force dynamic contrast as (3), but demonstrates that this can be lexicalized. Whereas the *polite* of (4a) is neutral, (4b)'s *civil* indicates that the subject's basic tendency here is to be impolite but that she is successfully suppressing this tendency.

Example (5) demonstrates that language extends force-dynamic concepts as well to interpsychological—that is, social—interactions. Here, both of the expressions exhibit force-dynamic patterns, but of different types, ones that yield the same overt resultant for different reasons. In (5a), the subject's desire (= force tendency) is not to go to the playground, but this is opposed by an external authority who does want her to do so, and prevails. In (5b), the subject's desire *is* to go to the playground, and stronger external circumstances that would be able to block her from doing so are reported as either disappearing or not materializing, thus permitting realization of the subject's desire.

Steady-State Force-Dynamic Patterns

Underlying all more complex force-dynamic patterns is the steady-state opposition of two forces, and we now examine the factors that comprise it. The primary distinction that language marks here is a role difference between the two entities exerting the forces. One force-exerting entity is singled out for focal attention—the salient issue in the interaction is whether this entity is able to manifest its force tendency or, on the contrary, is overcome. The second force entity, correlatively, is considered for the effect that it has on the first, effectively overcoming it or not. Borrowing the terms from physiology where they refer to the opposing members of certain muscle pairs, I call the focal force entity the *Agonist* and the force element that opposes it the *Antagonist*.[1]

In the system of diagraming used to represent force-dynamic patterns, the Agonist (Ago) will be indicated by a circle and the Antagonist (Ant) by a concave figure, as shown in (19a).

---

[1]As they function within language, Agonist and Antagonist can be regarded as semantic roles. The roles that they represent for force interactions, moreover, are parallel to the Figure and Ground roles within spatial and temporal relations.

(19) Force Entities   Intrinsic force tendency

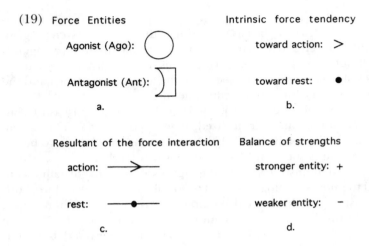

    Agonist (Ago):   toward action: >

    Antagonist (Ant):   toward rest: ●

       a.   b.

  Resultant of the force interaction   Balance of strengths

    action: ────>────   stronger entity: +

    rest: ────●────   weaker entity: −

       c.   d.

As language treats the concept, an entity is taken to exert a force by virtue of having an intrinsic tendency toward manifesting it—the force may be constant or temporary, but it is in any case not extrinsic. In an entity's force tendency, language again marks a two-way distinction: The tendency is either toward motion or toward rest—or, more generally, toward action or toward inaction. Diagrammatically, an Agonist's tendency toward action will be represented by an arrowhead, and a tendency toward rest by a large dot, as seen in (19b), placed within the Agonist's circle. No tendency marker is shown within the Antagonist symbol, as it is here understood to be opposite that of the Agonist.

A further concept in association with opposed forces is their relative strengths. As language treats this, the entity that is able to manifest its tendency at the expense of its opposer is the stronger. In the diagrams, a plus is placed in the stronger entity.

Finally, according to their relative strengths, the opposing force entities yield a resultant, an overt occurrence. As language schematizes it, this resultant is one either of action or of inaction, and it is assessed solely for the Agonist, the entity whose circumstance is at issue. The resultant will be represented as a line beneath the Agonist, one bearing either an arrowhead for action or a large dot for inaction, as in (19c).

With these distinctions in hand, we are able to characterize the four most basic force-dynamic patterns, those involving steady-state opposition, as diagrammed and exemplified in (20). To describe these in turn, (20a) involves an Agonist with an intrinsic tendency toward rest that is being opposed from outside by a stronger Antagonist, which thus overcomes its resistance and forces it to move. This pattern is one of those to be classed as "causative," in particular involving the extended causation of motion. The sentence in (20a) illustrates this pattern with a ball that tends toward rest but that is kept in motion by the wind's greater power. In (20b), the Agonist still tends toward rest, but now it is stronger than the force opposing it, so it is able to manifest its tendency and remain in place. This pattern belongs to the "despite" category, in this case where the Agonist's stability prevails despite the Antagonist's force against it. In (20c), the Agonist's intrinsic tendency is now toward motion, and although there is an external force opposing it, the Agonist is stronger, so that its tendency becomes realized in resultant motion. This pattern, too, is of the "despite" type, here with the Antagonist as a *hindrance* to the Agonist's motion. Finally, in (20d), although the Agonist again has a tendency toward motion, the Antagonist is this time stronger and so effectively *blocks* it, rather than merely hindering it: The Agonist is kept in place. This pattern again represents a causative type, the extended causation of rest.[2]

(20) The basic steady-state force-dynamic patterns

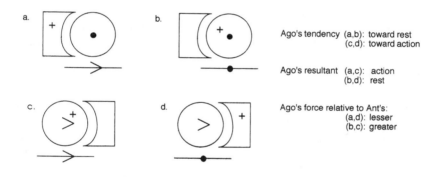

		Ago's tendency (a,b): toward rest
		(c,d): toward action
		Ago's resultant (a,c): action
		(b,d): rest
		Ago's force relative to Ant's:
		(a,d): lesser
		(b,c): greater

(a) The ball kept rolling
    because of the wind blowing on it.
(b) The shed kept standing
    despite the gale wind blowing against it.
(c) The ball kept rolling
    despite the stiff grass.
(d) The log kept lying on the incline
    because of the ridge there.

Of these four basic force dynamic patterns, each pair has a factor in common. As the diagrams are arranged in the matrix in (20), each line captures a commonality. In the top row, (20a, 20b), the Agonist's intrinsic tendency is toward rest, whereas in the bottom row (20c, 20d), it is toward action. In

---

[2]For clarity, the illustrative sentences here contain explicit mention of both force elements. But more colloquial sentences mentioning only one element can equally represent the same force-dynamic patterns. Thus, *The shed kept standing.* can, in context, represent the same (20b) pattern that the fuller sentence given in the illustration represents unambiguously.

the left column, (20a, 20c), the resultant of the force opposition for the Agonist is action, whereas in the right column, (20b, 20d), it is rest. More significantly, the diagonal starting at top left, (20a, 20d), which represents the cases where the Antagonist is stronger, captures the factor of extended causation. These are the cases in which the resultant state is *contrary* to the Agonist's intrinsic tendency, results *because of* the presence of the Antagonist, and would otherwise *not occur*. And the diagonal starting at top right, (20b, 20c), which gives the cases where the Agonist is stronger, captures the "despite" factor. In fact the very concept of "despite/although" can be characterized in terms of the common factor in this subset of force-dynamic patterns. Here, the resultant state is *the same* as that toward which the Agonist tends, results *despite* the presence of the Antagonist, and would otherwise *also occur*. Thus, the force-dynamic analysis—even in the portion excerpted here—captures certain basic general concepts, for example, "despite" as counterposed to "because of," as well as certain particular concepts, for example, "hindering" and "blocking." In doing so, an advantage of the present analysis becomes evident: It provides a framework in which a set of basic notions not usually considered related are brought together in a natural way that reveals their underlying character and actual affinity.

Because schematic systems are established on the basis of the meanings of extant closed-class forms, such forms with force-dynamic meaning should be pointed out. Some forms of this sort appear in (20). With the Agonist appearing as subject, the role of a stronger Antagonist can be expressed by the conjunction *because* or the prepositional expression *because of* (which in other languages often appears as a simple adposition). The role of a weaker Antagonist can be expressed by the conjunction *although* or the preposition *despite*. Force dynamic opposition in general can be expressed by the preposition *against,* as seen in (20b) or in such sentences as *She braced herself against the wind / They drove the ram against the barricade.* Perhaps the single form most indicative of the presence of force dynamics in English is the regular verb *keep* (*-ing*), currently an open-class form. However, in the course of language change, *keep* is likelier than other verbs to become grammaticalized into an auxiliary, as its equivalents have done in other languages and much as *use to,* which stems from a syntactically regular verb, is now partially grammaticalized in its limitation to a single form. And in any case, the force-dynamic role of *keep* can be seen as well in other forms that are unimpeachably closed-class. Examples are the adverbial particle *still* and the verb satellite *on,* as illustrated in (21).

(21) a. The ball kept rolling
b. The ball was still rolling } despite the stiff grass.
c. The ball rolled on

Elaborations of Causality

As just seen, a cognitive–semantic analysis can treat causativity as a part of force dynamics, but it can further treat it as a whole with its own parts. The analysis in Talmy (2000a, ch. 8) discerns within this whole a number of distinct types of causative situations of varying complexity. It resolves the types into basic semantic elements and the ways these combine. This analysis is conceived in terms of a step-by-step buildup in accordance with the way greater numbers of basic semantic elements combine in increasingly complex semantic causative situations.

The semantic elements and situations discerned are taken to be fundamental, figuring in the semantic basis of all languages. That is, they are taken to constitute a part of universal semantic organization, deeper than those respects in which individual languages differ from each other. For the semantic notions brought forth in this analysis, such differences would involve mainly where, how explicitly, and how necessarily the notions are expressed at the surface.

As a guide to this analysis, the distinct types of causative (and related) situations are listed here in an overall order of increasing complexity.

autonomous events	onset causation	Undergoer
basic causation	serial causation	self-agentive causation
event causation	enabling causation	"purpose"
Instrument causation	Agent causation	caused agency
point-/extent-durational	Author causation	chain of agency
causation		

To exemplify these types, we present the following sets of sentences, grouped to demonstrate particular causative distinctions.

Ordered according to complexity and differing as to the element foregrounded (appearing initially) are:

(22) a. *(autonomous event)*
        The vase broke.
     b. *(resulting-event causative [basic causative])*
        The vase broke from (as a result of) a ball('s) rolling into it.
     c. *(causing-event causative)*
        A ball's rolling into it broke the vase.
     d. *(Instrument causative)*
        A ball broke the vase in (by) rolling into it.
     e. *(Author causative—i.e., with unintended outcome)*
        I broke the vase in (with my/by) rolling a ball into it.

f. *(Agent causative—i.e., with intended outcome)*
   I broke the vase by rolling a ball into it.

Differing as to the number of links in a serial causative chain are:

(23) a. *(autonomous events)*
        The aerial toppled.
        The branch fell down upon the aerial.
        The wind blew on the branch.
     b. *(2-event causative chain)*
        The branch's falling down upon it toppled the aerial.
     c. *(3-event causative chain)*
        The wind's blowing the branch down upon it toppled the aerial.

Differing as to the degree of continuity in a causal chain are:

(24) a. *(continuous causative chain)*
        I slid the plate across the table by pushing on it with a stick.
     b. *(discontinuous causative chain)*
        I made the plate slide across the table by throwing a stick at it.

Differing as to the coextensiveness of the causing event with the resulting event are:

(25) a. *(extended causation)*
        I pushed the box across the ice of the frozen pond.
        [I kept it in motion, going along with it].
     b. *(onset causation)*
        I pushed the box (off) across the ice of the frozen pond.
        [I set it in motion and stayed put].

Differing as to the overcoming of resistance versus the removal of blockage are:

(26) a. *(effectuating causation)*
        I emptied the tub by dipping out the water.
        [I emptied the tub with a dipper].
     b. *(enabling causation)*
        I emptied the tub by pulling out the plug.
        [*I emptied the tub with a plug].

Differing as to the scope of intention on the part of a sentient entity are:

(27) a. *(Agent causation)*
    I hid the pen somewhere in the kitchen.
  b. *(Author causation)*
    I mislaid the pen somewhere in the kitchen.
  c. *("Undergoer" situation [not causative])*
    I lost the pen somewhere in the kitchen.

Differing as to knowledge of outcome are:

(28) a. *(Agent causation)*
    I killed the snail by hitting it with my hand.
  b. *("purpose" situation)*
    I hit the snail with my hand in order to kill it.

Differing as to the presence of internal self-direction are:

(29) a. *(autonomous event)*
    The log rolled across the field.
    (Motion event conceptualized as internally simple and as excepted from any causal continuum.)
  b. *(self-agentive causation)*
    The girl rolled across the field.
    (Through internal neuromusculature, the girl volitionally causes her body to roll.)

Differing as to the presence of self-directedness in mid-causal chain are:

(30) a. *(Agent causation)*
    They threw him into the room.
    (Purely physical chain: they throw him; he sails through air; he enters room.)
  b. *(inducive causation [caused agency])*
    They sent him into the room.
    (They speak instruction to him; he chooses to comply and causes self to move into room.)

Differing as to the number of occurrences of self-directedness along a causal chain are:

(31) a. *(2-member chain of agency)*
    The king sent for his pipe.
    (King commands; servant goes and brings)

    b. *(3-member chain of agency)*
       The king sent for his daughter (to come).
       (King commands; servant goes to fetch; daughter comes)
    c. *(4-member chain of agency)*
       The king had his daughter sent for.
       (King commands; servant 1 relays message; servant 2 goes to
       fetch; daughter comes)

In consonance with this study's findings that there is no single situational notion of causation, as many linguistic treatments have it, but a number of types, there is accordingly no use made here of a single deep verb "CAUSE," but, rather, of as many deep verbs as there are types. To provide an immediate idea of this, we can consider the main verbs of the sentences in (22b–f): The five appearances of *broke* are each taken to represent distinct causative types, being the homophonous product of conflation of the autonomous *break* of (22a) with five different deep causative verbs:

(32) a. . . . RESULTed-to-break   . . . $_R$broke
      b. . . . EVENTed-to-break   . . . $_E$broke
      c. . . . INSTRUMENTed-to-break . . . $_I$broke
      d. . . . AUTHORed-to-break   . . . $_{Au}$broke
      e. . . . AGENTed-to-break   . . . $_A$broke

PERSPECTIVE

As previously indicated, the third schematic system, perspective, establishes a conceptual perspective point from which a referent scene is cognitively regarded (see Talmy, 2000a, ch. 1). Whereas this schematic system is presumably neutral to particular sensory modalities, it is most readily characterized in visual terms as, in effect, pertaining to where one places one's "mental eyes" to "look out" on a referent structure. The perspective system includes such schematic categories as: a perspective point's spatial (or temporal) positioning within a larger frame; its distance away from the referent entity; and its change or lack of change of location in the course of time and the path it follows with change. These three schematic categories are characterized next.

Perspectival Location

The first schematic category, *perspectival location*—a perspective point's spatial positioning within a larger frame—can be illustrated by the sentences in (33) (adapted from a Fillmore example used for another purpose). The first sentence induces the listener to locate her perspective point inside the room, whereas the second sentence is conducive to an external perspectival location (or perhaps to a non-specific one). How is this accomplished? The cognitive calculations at work appear to combine a rule of English with geometric knowledge. Though often breached, an apparent general rule in English is that if the initiator of an event is visible, it must be included in the clause expressing the event, but if not visible, it must be omitted. Thus, in (33a), no initiator of the door's opening is mentioned, hence none must have been visible. But the second clause indicates that the apparent initiator, the two men, moved from outside to inside the lunchroom. Assuming opaque walls and door, the only way that an entering initiator could not be visible to an observer during the door's opening is if that observer were located inside the lunchroom. In (33b), by contrast, the initiator is mentioned, hence must be visible. The only way a door-opening initiator who moves from the outside to the inside can be visible to an observational perspective point is if that perspective point is outside. Note that the example sentences use the verb *walk* rather than *come* or *go* to eliminate the confounding perspectival information that such deictic verbs would add.

(33) position of perspective point
  a. interior: The lunchroom door slowly opened and two men walked in.
  b. exterior: Two men slowly opened the lunchroom door and walked in.

Perspectival Distance

A second schematic category that closed-class forms can specify for a perspective point is that of *perspectival distance*. The main member notions of this category are a perspective point's being *distal*, *medial*, or *proximal* in its relative distance away from a regarded entity.

Perspectival distance tends to correlate with another schematic category, an object's or event's *degree of extension*. Typically a distal perspective correlates with a reduced degree of extension, a medial perspective with a median degree of extension, and a proximal perspective with a magnified degree of extension. Now, a lexical referent that is perhaps most basically conceived as regarded from one particular perspectival distance and as comprising one particular degree of extension can, by various grammatical specifications that induce a shift, be reconceptualized with some other perspectival distance and degree of extension. Consider the event referent of *climb a ladder*. This referent seems to be basically associated with a medial perspective and with a median degree of extension in the temporal domain. These values appear in (34) in conjunction with the closed-class form "*in* + NP$_{extent-of-time}$":

(34) She climbed up the fire-ladder in 5 minutes.

With a different accompanying grammatical form, like the "$at + \mathrm{NP}_{\text{point-of-time}}$" in (35) (as well as different contextual specifications), the event referent of the preceding can be shifted toward another conceptual schematization: that of being regarded from a distal perspective and of comprising a point of time—that is, as being point-durational.

(35) Moving along on the training course,
     she climbed the fire-ladder at exactly midday.

This shift in the cognizing of the event can be thought to involve a cognitive operation of *adoption of a distal perspective*, as well as one of *reduction* in degree of extension. The shift can also go in the other direction. The event referent can be conceptually schematized as being viewed proximally and as being an unbounded extent by the effect of closed-class forms like *"keep -ing," "-er and -er,"* and *"as + S,"* as in (36).

(36) She kept climbing higher and higher up the fire-ladder as we watched.

Here there would seem to have taken place a cognitive operation of *adoption of a proximal perspective*, as well as one of *magnification* in degree of extension. By these operations, a perspective point is established from which the existence of any exterior bounds falls outside of view and attention—or, at most, are asymptotically approachable.

It is not clear whether perspectival distance *necessarily* correlates with degree of extension, or with certain other categories. But it seems to be a frequent concomitant and, in any case, it can, on the basis of the visual analogy, function as an organizing aegis to coordinate conceptual phenomena pertaining to the scope, size, and granularity of a referent. Thus, *as with* a distal perspective, there occurs a conceptual correlation of larger scope of attention, apparent reduced size of entities, coarser structuring, and less detail, whereas *as with* a proximal perspective, there occurs a conceptual correlation of smaller scope of attention, apparent magnified size, finer structuring, and greater detail.

Perspectival Motility

A third schematic category pertaining to perspective point is *perspectival motility*, that is, whether a perspective point is *stationary* or *moving*. Rather than treating this category in isolation, we observe that its members generally function together with members of the category of perspectival distance.

The member notions of these two categories tend to align thus: the stationary with the distal and the moving with the proximal. In addition, these conceptual alignments are generally further linked to two different scopes of attention—that is, with a factor from the next schematic system—respectively, with a global scope of attention and with a local scope of attention. Finally, these two associational complexes can be deemed to make up a larger schematic category, that of *perspectival mode*, whose two main members can be termed the *synoptic* mode and the *sequential* mode, as summarized in (37).

(37) perspectival mode:
    a. synoptic mode: the adoption of—
       a stationary distal perspective point with global scope of attention
    b. sequential mode: the adoption of—
       a moving proximal perspective point with local scope of attention

Different types of referent situations may tend to correlate with one or the other perspectival mode. In particular, there may tend to be a basic association on the one hand between a static situation and the synoptic mode of cognizing it, and on the other hand between a progressional situation and the sequential mode of cognizing it, and realizations of such correlations with appropriate closed-class forms are readily evident. In addition, though, often an alternative set of closed-class forms can direct the cognizing of a referent situation with the opposite perspectival mode.

Sequentializing. For illustration, consider first an example with a static referent, namely, objects in location. The synoptic (37a) type of perspectival mode—the one more congruent with such a referent—is invoked in (38a). It is multiply specified there by the set of grammatical forms shown underlined, namely, plural number and agreement, an adverbial expression of spatial dispersion, and the locative preposition *in*. But these forms can be replaced by other grammatical forms coding for the sequential (37b) perspectival mode, as in (38b) with singular number and agreement, an adverbial expression of temporal dispersion, and the motion preposition *through*. Thereby, the evoked cognitive representation is converted to one where one's perspective point and attention—or one's own projected location—shift in turn from object to object. In effect, a static multiplexity of objects has been converted into a sequential multiplexity of events consisting of conceptualized encounters with each of the objects in turn. Here, a cognitive operation of *sequentializing* has been carried out.

(38) a. There <u>are</u> houses <u>at some points</u> <u>in</u> the valley.
     b. There <u>is</u> <u>a</u> house <u>every now and then</u> <u>through</u> the valley.

Synopticizing. The reverse of the preceding circumstances also exists. A referent that most basically is in fact sequential, for example, a multiple succession of occurrences, can be represented in association with the more congruent mode for cognizing it, the sequential perspectival mode, as in (39a). The sequential mode is triggered by the presence of certain closed-class forms: singular number, an adverbial of iteration, and a preposition (or prepositional complex) expressing temporal progression. But essentially the same referent can also be presented as the object of a fixed global perspective point, that is, of the synoptic perspectival mode, as in (39b). Here, the conceptual effect is that the entirety of the sequence is regarded together simultaneously for an integrated or summational assessment, as if the sense of progression that is associated with the temporal dimension were converted into a static co-presence. Here, a cognitive operation of *synopticizing* has been carried out. The closed-class forms in the present example that trigger this operation are: the perfect auxiliary, a quantifier complex indicating aggregation, plural number, and a preposition of static containment.

(39) a. I took <u>an</u> aspirin <u>time after time</u> <u>during</u> / <u>in the course of</u> the last hour.
     b. I <u>have</u> taken <u>a number of</u> aspirins <u>in</u> the last hour.

DISTRIBUTION OF ATTENTION

The fourth schematic system, distribution of attention, consists of the various patterns of different strengths with which one's attention is directed over a referent object or scene in accordance with the specifications of closed-class forms (see Talmy, 2000a, ch. 1 and ch. 4). Three factors in the attentional system govern the distribution of attention over a referent scene. The first factor is the *strength of attention*, which can range from faint to intense. Closed-class forms can set attentional strength with respect to either of two scales. They can set it at some value from low to high on an absolute, or zero-based, scale—a cognitive operation for which, of the terms in current linguistic use, "salience" or "prominence" seems the most apt. Or they can set it comparatively lower or higher than some reference value on a relative, or norm-based, scale—a cognitive process for which the terms "backgrounding" and "foregrounding" are apt.

The second factor is *pattern of attention*, by which attentions of different strengths are combined and arranged in particular patterns. We can identify a number of patterns that closed-class forms designate. One such pattern is *focus of attention*—a center–periphery pattern in which greater attentional strength is placed in a central region and lesser attentional strength is placed in a surrounding region. This focusing pattern applies, for example, to Figure–Ground organization (see earlier section, "Figure–Ground Organization"). In a second pattern, *level of attention*, either greater attention is assigned to a higher level of organization within a referent scene, and lesser attention goes to a lower organizational level, or the reverse allocation occurs. A third pattern is *window of attention*, in which one or more (discontinuous) portions of a referent scene are foregrounded in attention, or "windowed," by their explicit mention, and the remainder of the scene is backgrounded in attention (or "gapped") by their omission from mention. In the present overview, only this windowing type is shown and, within that, only "path windowing" is discussed.

The third factor is *mapping of attention*, by which the particular parts of an attentional pattern are mapped onto particular regions of the referent scene. By the operation of this factor, a single attentional pattern can be overlaid in different ways onto the same referent scene. To illustrate with the center–periphery pattern applied variously to a single commercial scene, focal attention can either be mapped onto the seller, with lesser attention on the remainder, as in *The clerk sold the vase to the customer*, or focal attention can be mapped onto the buyer, with lesser attention on the remainder, as in *The customer bought the vase from the clerk*.

Path Windowing

Language can apply attentional windowing to particular subevents within a causal chain or to particular phases within a cycle, among other possibilities, but here we discuss only the windowing of particular portions of a path, that is, *path windowing*. Within this type, an *open path* refers to a path that is described by an object physically in motion in the course of a period of time, that is conceptualized as an entire unity—thus having a beginning and an end—and whose beginning point and ending point are at different locations in space. To illustrate open path windowing, the example in (40) pertains to a single particular instantiation of the open path type but with various patterns of windowing and gapping imposed on it. Thus, (1a) presents the event with maximal windowing over the whole of the conceptually complete path, whereas (2) presents three forms of gapping over one portion of the path, and (3) presents three forms of windowing over one portion of the path. It is understood here that the gapped portions are attentionally backgrounded relative to the foregrounded windowed portions but that, given sufficient context, a hearer would reconstruct each of the partially gapped paths in (2 and 3) into the same conceptualization of a complete path.

(40) The crate that was in the aircraft's cargo bay fell—
  1. with maximal windowing over the whole of the so-conceived entire path:
      —out of the plane through the air into the ocean.
  2. with gapping over one portion of the path:
      a. medial gapping = initial + final windowing
          —out of the plane into the ocean.
      b. initial gapping = medial + final windowing
          —through the air into the ocean.
      c. final gapping = initial + medial windowing
          —out of the airplane through the air.
  3. with windowing over one portion of the path:
      a. initial windowing = medial + final gapping
          —out of the airplane.
      b. medial windowing = initial + final gapping
          —through the air.
      c. final windowing = initial + medial gapping
          —into the ocean.

We can suggest factors that may play a role in the putative cognitive processes by which an open path becomes conceptualized as an *event-frame*, that is, as a unitary event bounded off from surrounding material of space, time, or other qualitative dimensions. One such factor might be the *scope of perception* that one might imagine as being normatively or canonically available at the referent scene. For instance, in generating or in interpreting the sentences of the preceding example, a speaker or a hearer might imagistically locate a viewpoint for themselves at a canonic position between the aircraft and the ocean from which the crate's path from the plane to the ocean would fall within the available scope of perception and thereby be treated as a unity. From such a viewpoint the crate would not be visible either in its prior motion while in the cargo bay nor in its subsequent motion through the water to the ocean floor, thus such additional surrounding paths of motion would be excluded from the event-frame in the operation of the putative scope-of-perception factor.

Another possible cognitive factor would function to frame together a sequence of phenomena that was assessed as having one qualitative character and separate that off from otherwise adjoining sequences assessed as being qualitatively different. One form of this factor, involving stationary boundary periods, would treat a period of stationariness as qualitatively distinct from a period of motion, so that the attribute of unitary entityhood could be cognitively ascribed to a period of continuous motion that was bounded by two stationary periods. Although perhaps otherwise frequent, this form of the factor would not play a role in the preceding aircraft example as the crate is in fact in motion both before and after the path represented in the sentences.

However, the factor of qualitative difference may have other forms, ones that would apply to the example. One such form might be the treatment of a conceivedly abrupt shift in path direction as marking the distinction between two qualitatively distinct paths and the conceivedly sharp-angled point of the shift as marking the boundary between the two paths. Such a *path singularity* form of the factor could be at work in the aircraft example to mark the beginning-point of the crate's fall. Another form of the qualitative factor might address any abrupt shift in the character of the space surrounding a path, for example, a change in the ambient medium. This form of the factor could then apply in the example to the passage of the crate's path from air to water, treating that as the endpoint of the preceding portion of motion.

When they have the requisite character, certain qualitative shifts in a path complex may lead to a conceptual reanalysis of the path into an embedded structure consisting of one smaller distinct path nested within a larger path that can then act as a background reference frame. Thus, though the crate in the aircraft example may be assumed to have objectively traced out a complex path consisting of a horizontal segment followed by a descending parabola, a hearer of the example sentence would probably reconceptualize the motion situation as involving an attentionally salient straight downward vertical path that is abstracted out as separate from an attentionally backgrounded horizontal forward path that preceded the vertical plummet and that the aircraft maintains after dropping the crate. The simpler parts of such a conceptually nested path structure would tend to be demarcated by the so-conceived singularity points located at qualitative shifts.

EVENT STRUCTURE: COMPONENTS
OF MOTION EVENTS CODED IN LANGUAGE

This final section returns to the first schematic system, configurational structure, but with two points of difference. It was observed in the Introduction that the meanings of closed-class forms considered across languages establish the existence and the conceptual makeup of the various schematic systems. Earlier we focused on such closed-class forms. But here we see that open-class forms can also express some of these same structuring concepts in a systematic way, and can do so in interaction with closed-class forms. Second, the principles treated previously were universalist in character: All languages realize them in the same way (although sometimes manifesting them in different places). Here we again present a universal pattern, but languages now fall into a typology with respect to how they realize the pattern.

An examination across diverse languages shows that, as they represent it, a Motion situation consists of certain semantic components in certain relations. Here, the capitalized "Motion" covers both motion and location. The Motion situation includes a Motion event proper. This, in turn, consists of four components: the Figure, the Ground, the "Path"—that is, the path followed or the site occupied by the Figure relative to the Ground—and the fact of Motion per se. Further within the Motion situation, a separate *Co-event* is present that bears a relation such as that of Manner or Cause to the Motion event proper.

While this semantic structure is apparently universal, languages fall into a typology on the basis of where the components of the semantic structure show up on the surface—that is, which syntactic constituents they characteristically appear in (see Talmy, 2000b, ch. 1, ch. 2, ch. 3). Most revealing is what shows up in the verb (or, more specifically, the verb root). Although the verb always includes the fact of Motion per se, languages basically fall into three typological categories on the basis of whether their verb also characteristically includes the Co-event, the Path, or the Figure. Here, "characteristic" means that: (a) it is *colloquial* in style, rather than literary, stilted, and so on; (b) it is *frequent* in occurrence in speech, rather than only occasional; and (c) it is *pervasive*, rather than limited, that is, a wide range of semantic notions are expressed in this type.

Co-event + Motion

In a Motion-sentence pattern characteristic of one group of languages, the verb expresses at once both the fact of Motion and a Co-event, usually either the manner or the cause of the Motion. A language of this type has a whole series of verbs in common use that express motion occurring in various manners or by various causes. There may also be a series of verbs expressing location with various Manners or Causes, but they are apparently always much fewer. The meaning-to-form relationship here can be represented as in Fig. 1.1. Language families or languages that seem to be of this type are Indo-European (except for post-Latin Romance languages), Finno-Ugric, Chinese, Ojibwa, and Warlpiri. English is a perfect example of the type. In the following examples, BE (or WAS) with a subscript LOC is an abstract morpheme representing the basic concept of locatedness; MOVE is the abstract morpheme for the basic concept of translational motion; a subscript A indicates that MOVE is agentive; and GO (or WENT) is the abstract morpheme for the concept of an Agent's self-propelled motion.

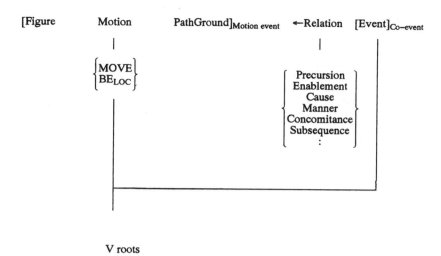

V roots

FIG. 1.1.   Co-event conflated in the Motion verb.

(41) *English expressions of Motion with Manner or Cause conflated in the verb:*
BE$_{LOC}$ + Manner
a. The lamp lay (stood / leaned) on the table =
   [the lamp WAS$_{LOC}$ on the table] WITH-THE-MANNER-OF
   [the lamp lay there]
b. The rope hung across the canyon from two hooks =
   [the rope WAS$_{LOC}$ (EXTENDED) across the canyon] WITH-
   THE-MANNER-OF [the rope hung from two hooks]
MOVE + Manner
c. The bottle floated (bobbed/glided) into the cave =
   [the bottle MOVED into the cave] WITH-THE-MANNER-OF
   [the bottle floated]
d. The gate swung (creaked) shut on its rusty hinges =
   [the gate MOVED shut (= to a shut position)] WITH-THE-
   MANNER-OF [the gate swung on its rusty hinges]
   comparably: The rock rolled/slid/bounced down the hill.
   The smoke swirled / rushed through the opening.
e. I bounced (slid/rolled) the keg into the pantry =
   I $_A$MOVED the keg into the pantry] WITH-THE-MANNER-OF
   [I bounced the keg]
   comparably: I twisted/popped the cork out of the bottle.
f. I ran (limped/jumped/stumbled/rushed/groped my way) down
   the stairs =
   [I WENT down the stairs] WITH-THE-MANNER-OF [I ran]

MOVE + Cause

g. The napkin blew off the table =
   [the napkin MOVED off the table] WITH-THE-CAUSE-OF
   [(something) blew on the napkin]

h. The bone pulled loose from its socket =
   [the bone MOVED loose from its socket] WITH-THE-CAUSE-
   OF [(something) pulled on the bone]
   comparably: The water boiled down to the midline of the pot.

i. I kicked (threw / pushed) the keg into the pantry =
   [I $_A$MOVED the keg into the pantry] WITH-THE-CAUSE-OF
   [I kicked the keg]

j. I chopped (sawed) the tree down to the ground at the base =
   [I $_A$MOVED the tree down to the ground] WITH-THE-
   CAUSE-OF [I chopped on the tree at the base]
   comparably: I blew/flicked the ant off the plate.

Here, the assessment of whether it is Manner or Cause that is conflated in the verb is based on whether the verb's basic reference is to what the Figure does or to what the Agent does. For example, in *I rolled the keg into the pantry*, the verb *rolled* basically refers to what the keg did and so expresses Manner, whereas in *I kicked the keg into the pantry*, the verb *kicked* refers to what I did, and so gives the Cause of the event.

Path + Motion

To a speaker of a language like English, sentences like the preceding may seem so straightforward that they offer little to ponder. How else might such propositions be colloquially expressed? But in fact there are languages with very different patterns of expression. Even a language as seemingly kindred as Spanish *can express virtually none* of these sentences in the way that English does. For example, to render the English sentence in (41c), Spanish must say something like *La botella entró a la cueva flotando*, literally, "The bottle entered to the cave floating." Thus, whereas English characteristically uses the verb to represent a Co-event of Manner or Cause (in combination with the fact of Motion), Spanish uses it to represent the Path. With the Spanish verb thus engaged, any Co-event of Manner or Cause is represented in a separate adjunct, often a verbal gerund (here, *flotando*, "floating"). For its part, because English has its verb taken up with Manner or Cause, the representation of Path must occur elsewhere, and in fact is characteristically in a satellite (i.e., a verb particle) and/or a preposition (here, *into*). Figure 1.1 can be modified to represent the characteristic Spanish pattern by removing the line leading down from the Co-event component and inserting a line that leads down from the Path component.

A language of the Spanish type thus has a whole series of verbs in common use that express motion along one or another path. Such verbs in Spanish, for example, include: *entrar* "MOVE in," *salir* "MOVE out," *subir* "MOVE up," *bajar* "MOVE down," *pasar* "MOVE past," *cruzar* "MOVE across," and *volver* "MOVE back." Language families or languages that seem to be of this type are Romance in general, Semitic, Japanese, Korean, Turkish, Tamil, Polynesian, Nez Perce, and Caddo. Note that although English does have a number of such path verbs—for example, *enter, exit, ascend, descend, pass, cross, return*—these are less colloquial nonnative forms that have been borrowed from Romance languages where they are the native type.

Figure + Motion

Yet a third pattern is exhibited by Navajo and by Atsugewi, a Hokan language of northern California that I worked on extensively. What characteristically appears here in the verb root is neither the Co-event as in English nor the Path as in Spanish, but the Figure. Figure 1.1 can accordingly be modified to represent languages of this type by removing the line leading down from the Co-event component and inserting a line that leads down from the Figure component. Such languages thus have a whole series of verb roots referring to one or another kind of object or material as moving or located. Atsugewi, for example, has such verb roots as *qput* "for dirt to move or be located," *lup* "for a small, shiny, spherical object (e.g., a hailstone, a round candy, an eyeball) to move or be located," and *swal* "for a linear flexible object suspended by one end (e.g., a sock on a clothesline, a killed rabbit hanging from a hunter's belt, a flaccid penis) to move or be located." With the verb root in Atsugewi taken up by the Figure, the other semantic components of the Motion situation are expressed elsewhere. Thus, Path and Ground are expressed together in some 50 individual verb suffixes with meanings like "out of liquid" and "into an aggregate (e.g., a crowd or bushes)." And a Co-event of Cause is represented by a set of some two dozen verb prefixes with meanings like "as a result of the wind blowing on the Figure" and "as a result of one's foot acting on the Figure."

CONCLUSION

This chapter has sketched some of the properties of conceptual organization in language as this is understood within the approach of cognitive semantics. One such property involved the division between open- and closed-class forms and between their respective functions: contributing conceptual content and determining its structure. Another property was the severe limit on closed-class meanings and the fact that they constitute an approximately closed graduated inventory. This inventory constitutes the fundamental conceptual structuring system of language. A third property was that the meanings in this inventory cluster into several schematic systems, each of which deals with a certain portion of the total system of conceptual structuring.

As part of its next phase of investigation, cognitive semantics has begun to compare the structuring system found in language with those found in other cognitive systems, such as perception, reasoning, affect, and motor control. One can find such comparisons of language with visual perception in Talmy (2000a, ch. 2), of language with a posited cognitive culture system in Talmy (2000b, ch. 7), and of language with a posited cognitive system for pattern formation in Talmy (2000b, ch. 8). In my view, the long-range goal in the research program of cognitive semantics is to integrate the linguistic and the psychological perspectives on cognitive organization in a unified understanding of human conceptual structure.

REFERENCES

Talmy, L. (2000a). *Toward a cognitive semantics: Vol. I. Concept structuring systems.* Cambridge: MIT Press.
Talmy, L. (2000b). *Toward a cognitive semantics: Vol. II. Typology and process in concept structuring.* Cambridge: MIT Press.

Chapter 2

Discourse and Grammar

John W. Du Bois
University of California, Santa Barbara

Differences that separate grammar from discourse are not hard to find. Grammar describes sentences; discourse goes beyond the sentence. Grammar limits options by rule; discourse is what speakers do with the freedom that is left. Grammar is general; discourse varies at the will of its speakers and whim of their topics. Grammar is meaningless,[1] proudly so; meaning and pragmatic force lie at the heart of discourse. Grammar is pointless in a sense, possibly a good sense; discourse realizes the ends, whether communicative, cognitive, interactional, ideological, aesthetic or otherwise, that its producers seek to attain. It is no surprise that the study of grammar and the study of discourse are so often seen as worlds apart, pursued with different goals and different methodologies by different people. And yet language itself, in its actual occurrences, would seem to display at once the characteristics that attract both the grammarian and the discourse specialist. If language responds to either approach taken, can the distance between grammar and discourse be so great as the dichotomies imply?

Perhaps this perceived gulf makes it needlessly difficult to reach a full understanding of language. If we hope to learn how language works we will need to pursue multiple vantage points, while encompassing grammar and discourse within a single field of view. We need to exploit a stereoptical vision to integrate the two into one unified domain of phenomenal inquiry,

---

[1]This and the following point about grammar are associated with the approach of Zellig Harris (1951) and his intellectual offspring in the formalist tradition of generative syntax.

even as our theoretical constructs retain the character distinctive of their separate origins. Indeed, a potent trend has become evident in recent attempts to illuminate the foundations of linguistic structure and language function (Ariel, 1998; Chafe, 1987, 1994, 1998; Du Bois, 1985, 1987; Fox & Thompson, 1990; Givon, 1979, 1992, 1998; Hopper, 1998; Hopper & Thompson, 1980; Nichols & Timberlake, 1991; Thompson, 1997, this volume). We propose to study grammar and discourse together in order to understand how language comes to be what it is.

In this chapter I illustrate this trend with reference to a particular pattern lying at the intersection of discourse and grammar, what I have termed *Preferred Argument Structure* (Du Bois, 1985, 1987; Du Bois, Kumpf, & Ashby, in press). Preferred Argument Structure represents neither a discourse structure nor a syntactic structure per se, but a preference in discourse for a particular syntactic configuration of linguistic elements, both grammatical and pragmatic. Roughly, the claim is that in spontaneous discourse, the distribution of nominal referential forms (such as full lexical noun phrases or pronouns) across the various syntactic positions (subject, object, oblique) is systematically skewed. Speakers freely realize full lexical noun phrases in intransitive subject position or transitive object position, but strongly avoid placing them in transitive subject position. In a pragmatic parallel to this, new information (typically expressed by full lexical noun phrases) freely appears in intransitive subject or transitive object roles, but not in transitive subject role. This strong tendency—not a categorical rule—is evidenced widely in the spontaneous discourse of virtually all languages investigated to date (Du Bois, 1987; Du Bois et al., in press). In the following, I illustrate this pattern via its linguistic consequences, presenting short excerpts from English conversations, supplemented by a brief summary of the quantitative evidence from several languages. Along the way I try to point out some of the general implications of this work for the mutual connection and influence—even co-evolution—of discourse and grammar.

We have been used to thinking of grammar as the preserve of whatever generality and systematicity can be extracted from the phenomena of language. Such a conception leaves us with an inconvenient residue of randomness, to be disposed of in the lap of some field of language study or other. Lexicon used to be the dumping ground of irregularity. But the once-despised lexicon has now been cleaned up, its reputation refurbished as it becomes a bright new field of generalization. We recognize that the fine-grained patterning that permeates the field of lexical organization can become a foundation upon which generalizations of grammar are built. The social sphere has served its time on scapegoat duty, too. Linguistic variation between one social group or one society and the next could be dismissed as a mere surface perturbation—instigated by haphazard influences from local cultures—of the otherwise tidy picture of rule-bound normative grammar. Psycholinguistic processing could be tapped to supply exculpating performance factors that would allow competence to remain pure and unaccountable. Pragmatics could be counted on to tie up any loose ends that grammar couldn't sort out, an all-too-convenient passing of the buck that should be considered suspect unless it's accompanied by delivery of the pragmatic goods in the form of specific working analyses.

But in the end it is discourse that has remained as the final stronghold of random fluctuation, if only because it stands as the domain of the speaker's ultimate personal prerogative. Here the freedom to express one's unique, unconstrained intention—what the self unfathomably wishes to say—would appear to preclude any generalization. At best the discoursist is limited to narrow claims of form–function symbolization: If what you want to say is a (certain) thing then say that (certain) thing using this form. A repressive tolerance for the untrammeled individualism of speaker intention leads us to assume that once grammar has skimmed its generalizations off the top there will remain no linguistic pattern of any consequence to be found among the whimsy products of talk.

The surprising thing, then, is that powerful trends of systematicity do remain to be discovered within discourse, even granting first-born grammar its due. If we know how to look—with a theoretical framework that helps us to see the patterning for what it is—we can recognize the systematicity of discourse, appreciating both its distinctive character and its critical impact on grammar. The real story of discourse and grammar research is that there is a place for pattern, and generalization, in both domains. Discourse and grammar each claim a distinctive type of patterning, neither of which is reducible to the other. And yet—here's the challenge—grammar and discourse interact with and influence each other in profound ways at all levels, so that in real life neither can even be accessed, not to mention explained, without reference to the other.

I make three theoretical assumptions about discourse and grammar. First, speakers exploit available grammatical structure to realize their goals in speaking. Second, the aggregate sum of what speakers do in discourse exhibits recurrent patterning beyond what is predicted by rules of grammar. Third, grammatical structure tends to evolve along lines laid down by discourse pattern: Grammars code best what speakers do most. From this perspective, forged through investigations of grammar and discourse-pragmatic function in typologically diverse languages, we are led to seek out cross-linguistically recurrent patterns of grammar on the one hand, and of discourse on the other. If we learn that a certain distinctive pattern of grammatical relations turns up in a variety of unrelated languages around the world, we take this wide occurrence of similar grammatical structure, arrived at through independent historical development, to be evidence of a fundamental pattern: something that needs to be explained. What we have found is that wherever there is fundamental patterning in grammatical structure, we are likely to discover parallel, yet not identical, fundamental patterning in discourse function. One such discourse-and-grammar parallel is to be found in Preferred Argument Structure. But first we cast a brief glance at another approach, which assumes a rather different role for discourse in the description and explanation of grammar.

WHAT IS DISCOURSE?

Even where the value of discourse as a locus of grammatical research is granted, there may remain differences regarding what goals are to be pursued and what methods established. How one conceives the nature of discourse has much to do with how one conceives the nature of language itself. It will be instructive to briefly consider some alternative approaches, without any pretense to surveying the rich diversity of viewpoint that characterizes the present intellectual ferment in the arena of discourse.

One longstanding role for discourse is represented in the Americanist tradition of grammatical description (Boas, 1911), in which linguists and ethnographers of unfamiliar languages are urged to document the trilogy of grammar, lexicon, and text. The approach flourishes to this day and remains useful and valid for the goals it sets. Here the role of discourse ("text") relative to grammar becomes, in a sense, to substantiate the claims made in the grammar. Once a text in the language (usually a narrative) has been elicited from a native speaker, transcribed, and glossed, sentence tokens are culled from it and displayed to exemplify the grammatical types posited for the grammar of the language (cf. Aissen, 1987). The practice of culling individual examples from texts indeed goes back much further, to the traditions of historical linguistics and comparative philology, where it has long proved indispensable for documenting the facts of languages known only from older written sources. The hallmark of the approach is its use of discourse as a data source for documenting grammatical types.

Saussure, who as a historical linguist was well versed in such uses of texts as evidence about grammar, held that parole—in effect the aggregate of tokens of speaking (or writing)—could not be studied directly (Saussure, 1916). Only language, conceived as a system of types, was an accessible and viable object of study. On this approach the discourse data, however invaluable, remain transparent in a sense, almost invisible. They are taken as representative instantiations of types, the types constituting the actual focus of interest. Aside from its useful supporting role as a source of evidence for linguistic types, discourse as such is not seen. One does not look there for pattern, generality, or explanation; these rather remain the purview of the language as system. Yet even Saussure recognized a most intimate connection between discourse and grammar, when he acknowledged that language is both instrument and product of speaking.

In one modern variant of this approach, pragmatics and even discourse may be usefully described in terms of types. In place of the type categories of sentence grammar, it is now discourse-pragmatic types whose function is to be described via evidence drawn from discourse. To characterize a discourse particle like *anyway* or *well* whose impact extends beyond the sentence, a discourse-pragmatic function is invoked—*anyway* signaling, for example, "end of off-topic excursion," whereas *well* might be said to mark "dispreferred speaker response." In effect, the function of a word (*anyway, well*) is stated as the pairing of a form type with a meaning type. Of course the discourse data in this case cannot be invisible, because they must be analyzed to apprehend the pragmatic meaning of the particle or structure in question. But after the discourse tokens have yielded their service to the types, they may remain elusive in themselves. This approach is on target for analyzing specific forms bearing well-defined meanings in the realm of discourse-pragmatics. The classic case is discourse particles (Schiffrin, 1987), whose meanings often commingle semantic and pragmatic components, the latter being difficult or impossible to discover without an astute analysis of extended stretches of natural discourse. The success of the method lies in its ability to recognize an extended discourse pattern, associate it with a specific linguistic form, and reduce the whole complex of use to a compact description of the form's meaning. This is the familiar linguistic sign of Saussure (1916)—what could be called the "sign function," to be contrasted with what I describe later as the "structure function" of grammar.

The temptation, though, is to extend this potent method beyond its effective range. Because so much of language is describable in terms of form–meaning pairings, one can be led to see all of language in this light. (For an approach that seeks to take the symbolizing role of grammar as far as it will go, see Langacker, 1987, 1998.) But the form–meaning method as applied to discourse may reach its limit once one undertakes to analyze the more abstract and highly grammaticized roles such as subject and object (as we see later).

Where some methodologies treat discourse tokens as a mere means of arriving at, or confirming evidence of, a type description, the present approach to discourse has no wish to efface the tokens, neither in the process of analysis, nor in the summation of generalizations, nor even in the framing of explanation for why the type system of grammar is as it is. To achieve the explanatory goals we have set ourselves, the body of utterance tokens necessarily becomes an object of study in its own right. If the goal is to understand language, even in its aspect as a system of grammatical types, we find it essential to simultaneously seek knowledge of the fundamental patterning of the mass of instances of language use, what I have called the *token aggregate* (Du Bois, 1987). The accumulated linguistic experience of a lifetime amounts to a body of utterances encompassing form, meaning, and contextualization. This aggregate of realized tokens of language use exhibits patterning that in its broad outlines, allowing for a certain degree of analytical and statistical abstraction, remains remarkably constant from one speaker to the next and even from one language to the next. The challenge is to probe the patterning of discourse in a way that speaks to the language as a whole: to discover how talk shapes grammar as much as grammar shapes talk.

Why pursue specifically speaking, if writing equally constitutes discourse? Speaking has several key features to recommend it, despite the admitted convenience of working with written material. What, after all, is discourse? What do we hope to find in it? Natural discourse encompasses any authentic instance of language use in all its manifestations, which is to say, any organically motivated act of producing or apprehending language, via any medium, spoken, written, or otherwise, subsuming the full scope of the situated utterance in all aspects of form, meaning, and contextualization. Leaving aside artificial discourses, such as might be constructed for purposes of experimental control, we face an almost unlimited variety of genres or types of language use: newspaper editorials, novels, horoscopes, comics, boilerplate legalese, grocery lists, love letters, lectures, credos, religious rituals, roll call, sporting news, enthusiastic recitations of bad poetry, long-winded jokes, chit-chat, put-downs, the clipped commands of workplace talk. For natural discourse there can be no a priori requirement of truth, sincerity, beauty, respectability, coherence, or even grammaticality in the normative sense. Each of these uses of language is natural discourse, and each merits study on its own terms. Yet amidst the diversity there is one kind of use that is often singled out as worthy of special attention, that of face-to-face conversation. Not so much a genre as a matrix within which particular genres may be invoked, conversation, while exhibiting far-reaching variability within itself, can be characterized as pervasive, spontaneous, interactional, and contextualized. It is pervasive, constituting the commonest use of language for virtually all language users, the first learned by children, and one of the few forms of language use found in all languages, at all stages of human history (Chafe, 1994, 1998).[2] No written genre can stake such a broad claim, even for today. Conversation is typically spontaneous, giving us the opportunity to witness on-line planning and other processes that attend the unfolding of discourse as it is produced. Conversation oc-

---

[2]Ironically, one of the other forms of discourse most pervasive in human life is one that is the opposite of conversation in many respects: ritual language, which appears in all human cultures (Du Bois, 1986). Arguably it has been with us from the earliest stages of humanity.

curs in an environment of dialogic interaction between speakers, where give and take among interlocutors affords us additional clues as to how the discourse is being interpreted and evaluated by the participants themselves. And finally, conversation is highly contextualized, filled with subtle cues at all levels marking the relation of utterances to contexts of prior discourse, to situational and cultural contexts, to contexts of social relations between speech event participants, and even to the mutual cognitive context within which the dialogic interaction is embedded. Spontaneous discourse reflects the speaker's cognitive frames and processes, as when a pause reflects a stage of planning for the next utterance (Chafe, 1987, 1994; McNeill, 1992); and it reflects the speaker's cognitive model of the hearer's cognitive model, as when a referential form is selected that takes into account what the listener does and doesn't know (Ariel, 1990, 2001; Chafe, 1994, 1998; Clark, 1996). To be sure, cognitive processing takes place whenever we write for others to read, too. But if we do our writing alone in a room, all evidence of cognitive processing that would be carried by pauses, ruminations, restarts, rephrasings, corrections, rhythm, and more is carefully and deliberately effaced through successive waves of editing, as we strive to present our audience with a seamless piece of prose. To the extent that we would hope to access the cognitive processes that underlie discourse and ultimately grammar, we need to be present to witness the innumerable cues that attend its actual moment-by-moment coming into being. This wealth of information is most fully available in spontaneous spoken discourse. In all, spoken language, and specifically conversation, remain closest to the living embodiment of language. If we seek to understand the system of grammar, and if grammars code best what speakers do most (Du Bois, 1985), then it is to spoken language that we must devote our most scrupulous attentions.

There are additional reasons for preferring authentic discourse data over inspecting one's intuitions about invented discourse. There is reason to believe that native speakers simply lack reliable intuitions about linguistic patterning on a scale as large as that of extended discourse. Whatever ability individuals may have to judge grammaticality or acceptability at the sentence level (and of course the reliability of such claims is controversial even at the sentence level) seems to desert them when the higher level patterning of discourse is broached. For example, decades of work on the syntax of isolated sentences failed to elicit any articulate awareness of a key patterning of grammar, Preferred Argument Structure, which is apparently followed quite regularly by all speakers. On the other hand, certain sentence structures that appear perfectly unproblematic in isolation are nevertheless strongly avoided in spontaneous discourse. Evidently it takes a systematic, theoretically conscious assessment of a mass of authentic spontaneous discourse data to discover the fundamental organization of discourse.

In summary, spoken discourse most transparently reveals grammar in use. Crucially, this use is use in context. Discourse and grammar research undertakes to analyze grammatical elements and structures in their ecological relationship to each other and to overall functional patterns of use in the total context. By context we understand no less than the sum of the salient situation, prior discourse, interlocutors' actions, models of mutual knowledge, cultural frames, and even the publicly visible processes of marshaling cognitive resources in acts of communication. The ecological perspective on grammar (Du Bois, 1980, 1985) becomes especially important once we undertake to examine the strategic use of grammar across extended sequences in discourse (see "Constraint and Strategy" later).

DATA

The data in this chapter are drawn from naturally occurring conversations and other speech events in the Santa Barbara Corpus of Spoken American English (Du Bois, 2000). For reasons of space, most examples cited are very brief, usually just a line or two, without the larger discourse context. In some cases the transcription has been slightly simplified for the sake of conciseness and accessibility.[3] At the start of each example, the citation includes the short title (e.g., ATOMS, denoting the discourse whose full title is "Atoms Hanging Out"), followed by the line number in the transcript. The published corpus (Du Bois, 2000) is available for consulting the larger discourse context and full transcription detail for many of these examples, if desired.

A key aspect of the selection and presentation of discourse examples in this chapter concerns the intonation unit: Most excerpts constitute exactly one intonation unit, no more and no less. The intonation unit can be defined as a stretch of speech occurring under a single coherent intonation contour, as reflected in several specific prosodic cues including initial pause and final lengthening (Chafe, 1987, 1998; Du Bois, Schuetze-Coburn, Paolino, & Cumming, 1992). In the transcription system used here (Du Bois et al., 1992; Du Bois, Schuetze-Coburn, Cumming, & Paolino, 1993), each line represents one intonation unit. Intonation units play an important role in much of current research on spoken discourse and grammar, because of their status as perhaps *the* fundamental unit of cognitive processing, social interaction, and other domains (Chafe, 1987, 1994, 1998;

[3]The main simplification pertains to cited utterances in which the speaker's words overlap with another utterance, not included in the citation, by a second speaker. Had both utterances been cited, each would contain square brackets [ ] marking the point where overlap begins and ends. But wherever only one of a pair of overlapping utterances is cited in the excerpt, all overlap notations are left out, to avoid confusion.

Du Bois et al., 1992; Ford & Thompson, 1996; McNeill, 1992). Intonation units tend to show a fairly close correspondence with simple clause structure; consequently, in many of the examples cited, the intonation unit is roughly coextensive with a clause (e.g., a verb plus its nominal arguments).

Because the type of discourse and grammar research represented here makes claims about recurrent tendencies in discourse, its verification ultimately requires a numerical accounting of the commonest ("preferred") configurations in a body of discourse data. Such counts have long been a hallmark of discourse and grammar studies (Ariel, 1990, 1998; Clancy, 1980; Du Bois, 1980; Fox & Thompson, 1990; Givon, 1979, 1983, 1992; Hopper & Thompson, 1980; Thompson & Mulac, 1991), particularly in those establishing a common Preferred Argument Structure across a wide range of languages (Du Bois, 1987; Du Bois, Kumpf, & Ashby, in press; and references therein). Though an explication of the quantitative methodology is outside the scope of this chapter, the results of some of the relevant quantitative studies in several languages will be briefly summarized in Tables 2.1 to 2.5.

The observable pattern that concerns us most in this chapter involves the differential distribution across the clause of full lexical noun phrases versus pronouns. To make this contrast more visible to the reader, I adopt two supplementary formatting conventions for the examples cited: (a) full lexical noun phrases are boldfaced, and (b) pronouns (and ellipted "zeros") are underlined.

PREFERRED ARGUMENT STRUCTURE: WHERE GRAMMAR MEETS DISCOURSE

The verb is often accorded a dominant role in the grammatical structuring of its clause, which it realizes principally via its argument structure. In one popular view of clause structure, a given verb's argument structure grammatically specifies how many nouns will accompany it, and which roles they will play, within the clause (Chafe, 1970; Fillmore, 1977, this volume; McNeill, 1992, p. 253ff). From a cognitive point of view, an argument structure is nothing more than a structure of expectations triggered by a verb. Specifically, each use of a particular verb token raises the reliable expectation that a certain predictable configuration of nominal roles will occur in meaningful relation to it. The verb *enjoy*, for example, can be predicted to co-occur with a subject argument and an object argument, corresponding to the experiencer of enjoyment and the thing enjoyed, respectively. The particular nominal roles and their configurations will vary from verb class to verb class. Though subject to certain qualifications (Goldberg, 1998), this account will suffice for present expository purposes.

Among the arguments of a verb, some are core (subject, direct object, indirect object) and some are not (obliques, such as locative or temporal adverbials). The core arguments tend to be those most central to the clause structure. They are highly grammaticized, which is to say, obligatory rather than optional and relatively bleached of specific semantic meaning. For Preferred Argument Structure it is the clause core that is the primary unit of analysis, that is, the verb with its core arguments. To this must be added a discourse perspective: We are interested in the clause core as bounded by the intonation unit. In general all clause core elements tend to fit within the unified intonation contour that demarcates a single intonation unit.[4]

Referential Form

The noun phrase, considered as a structural position within a clause, can be realized by a wide variety of forms, such as a full lexical noun phrase with or without various modifiers, a personal pronoun, and so on. Grammarians would normally leave the selection among these realizations to factors outside the domain of syntax. Recognizing that discourse-pragmatic considerations such as referential continuity, information status, accessibility, and so on influence the choice of referential form (Ariel, 1990; Clancy, 1980), nevertheless from a narrowly structural perspective the variation counts as optional. As far as the grammar is concerned, apparently, the speaker of a clause like the following is free to choose whether to realize the subject of the verb *speeding up* with either a full lexical noun phrase or a pronoun:

  (1) {ATOMS 682}
      PHIL: ... **the molecules** are speeding up,

In (grammatical) principle, the full lexical noun phrase *the molecules* could be substituted by the pronoun *they* with no ill consequences (at least for grammaticality). Conversely, any pronoun should in theory be substitutable by a full noun phrase.[5]

Of course, once we take into account discourse-pragmatic factors (such as those involved in information management) as opposed to merely structural factors, the noun–pronoun alternation is demonstrably not free:

---

[4]Clausal elements may also exceed the boundaries of one intonation unit, spilling over into the next. Although this phenomenon is of considerable interest in its own right as evidence of the limited information-carrying capacity of the intonation unit, and of important cognitive processes of verbalization, consideration of this topic would carry us well beyond the scope of this chapter.

[5]We leave aside phenomena known as binding, where some current discussions treat so-called pronominals (as opposed to anaphors) as subject to grammatical limitations of a very different order from those treated here.

(2) {DEADLY 1354}
     JOANNE: **His tail** is curved like that.
                  Does <u>it</u> always get curved like that?

This first mention in discourse of the tail of a turtle (visible in context) is realized by the full lexical noun phrase *his tail*, whereas its second mention, in syntactically similar environment, is realized by the pronoun *it*. Taken in isolation from its discourse context, either sentence could in theory be realized with either noun or pronoun. But within the authentic discourse context, substitution of the grammatically alternative form cannot be treated as inconsequential: It could change the conveyed meaning or even induce incoherence. Speakers in discourse are careful about keeping track of which referents have been previously introduced and which are only now being introduced for the first time, mindful as they are of their interlocutors' current state of shared knowledge (or lack of it). Strategies for information management partly govern linguistic choices like that between lexical noun and pronoun, a phenomenon subsumed under the rubric of discourse pragmatics.

In the next example there appears a grammatical alternation between a proper noun (*Harold*) and a first person pronoun (*me*) in parallel syntactic contexts:

(3) {LAMBADA 1269}
     PETE: Without even telling **Harold**?
     HAROLD: . . Without telling <u>me</u>?

From the isolated-sentence syntactic perspective, the selection between noun and pronoun here would again count as free, as evidenced by (nearly) equivalent syntactic environments. (The appearance of two distinct words in nearly the same syntactic context precludes formulation of a syntactic rule predicting which must occur.) But from the discourse perspective the choice is evidently not free, being governed rather by pragmatic factors (including interactional criteria for self- and other-reference that need not concern us here).

So when we ask whether the selection of referential form (noun, pronoun, etc.) is *optional*, we need to add: With respect to what governing theoretical domain? If we take care to distinguish between syntactic and discourse-pragmatic determinants of referential form, we note that in each of these cases, syntactic structure seems to have no determining influence on the selection. Grammar is neutral about the choice between noun and pronoun. As long as there is an argument role available, as defined by the argument structure of a given verb, either noun or pronoun may equally occur, without preference. The discourse-pragmatic perspective, on the other hand, is not neutral, treating the selection as governed by factors in the total context of use such as referential continuity, degree of accessibility, speaker self-reference, and other information management factors. In these cases we conclude that there exist discourse-pragmatic, but not syntactic, determinants of referential form.

To ask where *in a syntactic clause structure* a full noun phrase can occur would seem therefore to be mixing up theoretical domains, or at best inviting a trivial answer: anywhere. That is, anywhere an argument role (say, subject) has been licensed by the argument structure of a verb (say, a transitive verb), a full noun phrase could supposedly occur.

But there is another perspective, in which this kind of question can hope to receive a more meaningful answer. Preferred Argument Structure carves the matter up a little differently, not necessarily respecting the traditional division of labor between discourse and grammar. Although recognizing the influence of discourse-pragmatic factors on the choice of referential form, it proposes an additional influence mediated by the syntactic structure itself. This comes not in the form of a syntactic rule categorically determining grammaticality, but rather in the form of an enabling influence: The syntactic role within the argument structure of a verb constitutes a factor influencing the probability of a lexical noun (as opposed to a pronoun) occurring there. For this reason we are especially interested, in what follows, in the question of where in the clause a given referential form occurs. In the end this will lead us to a conception of syntactic configurations as not merely classified into grammatical and ungrammatical, but as fulfilling specific structural roles in the cognitive management of information processing.

To prefigure my direction of argument, I propose that the grammatical structure of the clause contributes a kind of architectural framework for the management of cognitive processing tasks. Relatively demanding tasks (like processing the introduction of a new referent into the discourse) are largely confined to specific grammatical environments within the clausal architecture. Non-demanding tasks (like tracking an accessible referent already introduced), on the other hand, may occur anywhere in the clause. But we are getting ahead of ourselves. In order to build toward a picture of the grammatical ecology of information management, we must first lay out a survey of the available linguistic resources: the architectural repertoire of basic grammatical structures employed by speakers in discourse.

One-Place Predicates

We begin with the most basic configuration of arguments, that defined by a one-place predicate. An intransitive verb like *run* or *come* articulates an argument structure specifying that it will be accompanied by a single core argument noun phrase, typically functioning as its subject. By convention we label this the S role (a label that applies specifically to *intransitive* subjects, not to subjects in general). For clarity's sake, the first example of each set will be labeled for the argument roles S, A, and O, and subsequent examples repeating the same pattern will be left unlabeled.

(4) {CONCEPT 416}
　　MARILYN:　. . **The fish** are running,
　　　　　　　　　S

(5) {RUNWAY 637}
　　RANDY:　**The Caravan**'s coming across,

(6) {DOLLARS 629}
　　DAN:　. . **policies** change.

The intransitive subject or S role may be filled by a noun phrase of almost any shape, size, and meaning. These examples represent relatively modest full noun phrases, with just an article plus noun (*the fish, the Caravan*), or even a bare noun alone (*policies*). But the S role can easily accommodate more substantial noun phrases, containing adjectives and all kinds of other modifiers including relative clauses. (See later examples for a wider range of lexical noun phrase types.) In all, we can say that the S role is *free*, allowing noun phrases of any form and size without constraint.

　　The array of verbs and other predicates that invoke a single core argument is semantically diverse, as is the semantic relation that obtains between subject and predicate. This relation can range across agent, actor, source, recipient, theme, patient, and others. What remains constant is a syntactic argument structure that reserves a place for a single core argument.

Two-Place Predicates

A transitive verb, like *enjoy* or *eat,* invokes two core arguments: its transitive subject (termed the A role) plus its direct object (the O role). Hence there is the possibility of two full lexical noun phrases. But is this grammatical potential fully exploited in discourse? The evidence of discourse patterning suggests not:

(7) {HOWARDS 1102}
　　JANICE:　(H) But I enjoyed . . **the movie.**
　　　　　　　　A　　　　　O

(8) {ZERO 489}
　　NATHAN:　. . . She's eating **that bu=g**.

(9) {TREE 519}
    MARY: So <u>I</u> stopped **the car**,

(10) {JURY 871}
    REBECCA: <u>you</u> called . . **the police**.

The first thing to note about this highly characteristic transitive pattern
is that in discourse there regularly appears just one full lexical noun phrase.
The other argument, in contrast, is represented by just a pronoun (or other
such reduced form). The prevalence of this pattern in discourse is what
originally led me to formulate a constraint on grammatical quantity in core
argument positions, termed the *One Lexical Argument Constraint* (Du Bois,
1987):

(11) Avoid more than one lexical core argument

That is, even if a transitive verb provides two core argument positions, only
one of them is to be exploited to introduce a lexical noun phrase. The
other argument position will sustain only a pronoun, or ellipted "zero."
Note that this is a soft constraint, not a categorical grammatical rule. The
pattern is followed generally but not without exception.

The second aspect of this pattern pertains to grammatical role. Lexical
nouns do not appear with equal likelihood in all roles. In the direct object
(O) role, lexical nouns occur freely, but within the transitive subject (A)
role, we find that pronouns are used far more frequently. Put another way,
the single lexical argument allotted by the first constraint tends to favor the
O role but avoid the A role. Based on counts confirming this pattern as pervasive in spoken discourse, I have formulated a constraint on the syntactic
role of lexical arguments:

(12) Avoid lexical A

This preference, dubbed the *Non-Lexical A Constraint*, represents a very
strong tendency in discourse across numerous languages (Du Bois, 1987;
Du Bois et al., in press; see following). But again, this is a soft constraint
rather than a categorical grammatical rule, and exceptions do occur.

Three-Place Predicates

Ditransitive verbs like *give*, *tell*, and *show* raise the number of core argument
positions to three: subject (A), direct object (O), and indirect object (I).
But the question remains as to whether they thereby raise the actual capac-

ity of the spontaneously uttered clause to carry full lexical noun phrases. The evidence from discourse suggests not (Schuetze-Coburn, 1987). We see a pattern reminiscent of that for transitive verbs, in which some argument positions are left underexploited (in the sense of not carrying full noun phrases). The question is, how many?

(13) {LAMBADA 1126}
    MILES: I told you **that story**,
               A   I   O

(14) {DEADLY 1561}
    JOANNE: You have to buy em **feeder fish**.

(15) {HOUSEHOLD 1245}
    RON: Yeah she showed me **all that stuff**.

Despite the three possibilities (grammatically speaking) for lexical noun phrases in each ditransitive clause, in the prevailing discourse pattern only one is realized. The other two arguments are regularly realized as pronouns. Ditransitives thus dramatically confirm the One Lexical Argument Constraint. Even with three opportunities, only one is taken.

Moreover, ditransitives in discourse are consistent as to where the single lexical argument falls. As with transitives, it falls predominantly in the direct object role, as seen in the previous examples. The transitive subject role is avoided, conforming to the Non-lexical A Constraint. In a related constraint, lexical noun phrases also tend to be avoided in the indirect object role (though not, apparently, as strongly as for A role).

Quantitative Overview of Lexical Argument Distribution

Though a full quantitative justification of the claims of Preferred Argument Structure goes well beyond the scope of this chapter, we may offer a brief glimpse into some of the numerical evidence that has been adduced in studies over the last several years, based on analyses of spontaneous spoken discourse in a small sampling of geographically, historically, and structurally diverse languages of the world. All the studies summarized here specifically undertook to address the claims of Preferred Argument Structure, testing its viability within the language in question by amassing quantitative evidence on the distribution of lexical (and new) mentions relative to clauses and their argument structure roles. All the studies employ some variant of the methodology initiated by Du Bois (1987), usually using narrative discourse data.[6] Even so, differences arise in the specific analytical choices made, so caution should be exercised in comparing across studies. As each language represents a somewhat distinct grammatical ecology, the implementation in context of even so seemingly straightforward a category as "lexical noun phrase" can vary subtly, or substantially, from one language to the next. This requires each analyst to make coding decisions on the ground, as it were. Moreover, the particular discourse genres and even subgenres employed in the various studies often differ in potentially significant ways, with consequences that are not yet fully understood.

With all these caveats, the similarities across languages still manage to shine through. Apparently the pattern of Preferred Argument Structure is robust enough that even differences of method, language, and grammatical type cannot obscure it. Evidence from five languages on lexical quantity within the clause is presented in Table 2.1. In all the languages, clauses containing two lexical core arguments are much rarer than clauses with one or zero lexical arguments, thus providing evidence for the One Lexical Argument Constraint.

TABLE 2.1
Lexical Argument Quantity: Frequency
of Clauses by Quantity of Lexical Arguments[7]

Quantity:	0		1		2		Total	
Language	n	%	n	%	n	%	n	%
Hebrew	261	(50)	252	(48)	9	(2)	522	(100)
Sakapultek	211	(46)	240	(53)	5	(1)	456	(100)
Papago	430	(57)	307	(40)	22	(3)	759	(100)
English	252	(47)	241	(45)	39	(7)	535	(100)
Gooniyandi	2318	(62)	1305	(35)	114	(3)	3737	(100)

[6]In making comparisons across languages, it is important to compare similar genres. Most studies of Preferred Argument Structure published to date report on narrative, so that is mostly what I present in the tables that follow. The data for Sakapultek, Brazilian Portuguese, English, Hebrew, Papago, and Gooniyandi are narrative, of which the first three (and part of the fourth) are narratives elicited from viewers of a short film known as the Pear Film (Chafe, 1980). The Spanish and French data are relatively monologic sociolinguistic interviews. The Japanese data are conversation. (Conversational discourse is documented more extensively in the studies to appear in Du Bois, Kumpf, & Ashby, in press.)

[7]The sources for each language are: Hebrew: Smith (1996); Sakapultek: Du Bois (1987); Papago: Payne (1987); English: Kumagai (2001); Gooniyandi: McGregor (1999). Papago counts include all overt (i.e., not just lexical) mentions, but due to Papago's grammar this is not likely to greatly affect the results. Note that English counts reported by Kumagai include two instances of 3-argument intransitives and one instance of 3-argument transitives (not included in Table 2.1), suggesting that the counts include some non-core arguments.

TABLE 2.2
Lexical Argument Role: Syntactic Role of Lexical Core Arguments[8]

Role:	A		S		O		Total	
Language	n	%	n	%	n	%	n	%
Hebrew	18	(8)	103	(44)	111	(48)	232	(100)
Sakapultek	11	(5)	126	(58)	81	(37)	218	(100)
Papago	37	(10)	169	(47)	152	(42)	358	(99)
English	21	(8)	90	(35)	146	(57)	257	(100)
Spanish	35	(6)	215	(36)	341	(58)	591	(100)
French	32	(5)	290	(45)	324	(50)	646	(100)
BrPortuguese		(8)		(39)		(53)		(100)
Japanese	48	(7)	320	(48)	293	(44)	661	(100)

If the typical clause has at most one lexical core argument, the question arises as to where in the clause it will go. Table 2.2 shows evidence from eight languages suggesting that lexical arguments occur freely in the S role (35%–58%) or the O role (37%–58%), although tending to avoid the A role (5%–10%). The Non-Lexical A Constraint is thus supported across an array of very diverse languages.

Table 2.3 makes the simple point that the scarcity of lexical A's is not explained by a scarcity of A's in general, as there are plenty of transitive clauses in discourse (although intransitives almost always dominate). In these studies, from a third to a half of all clauses are transitive.[9]

Although this brief numerical interlude can only be suggestive, it does provide some idea of how pervasive the cited argument structure configurations are. For full quantitative analysis the reader is referred to the original sources cited, as well as to Du Bois (1987) and the studies in Du Bois et al. (in press).

Summary: Free and Constrained Roles in Argument Structure

How can we characterize the prevailing discourse patterns? Consider the transitive clause. With respect to allowing lexical noun phrases in transitive

---

[8]The sources for each language are as listed in the note for Table 2.1, plus: Spanish: Ashby and Bentivoglio (1993); French: Ashby and Bentivoglio (1993); Brazilian Portuguese: Dutra (1987); Japanese: Matsumoto (1997). Non-core lexical noun phrases (e.g., obliques) are not included in this table (but see Table 2.7). Note that the numbers for "intransitive" S combine all S role arguments of one-place arguments, including S of copular/equational clauses. For Japanese, Matsumoto's figures combine all overt forms including overt pronouns, not just lexical nouns. (This is presumably justified by the fact that most Japanese "accessible" reference is actually accomplished by zeros.)

[9]Note also that by definition we expect to see as many instances of A roles as of O roles, as each transitive verb token normally has one argument position of each type.

TABLE 2.3
Clause Type: Frequency of Intransitive Versus Transitive Verbs[10]

Language	Intransitive		Transitive		Total	
	n	%	n	%	n	%
Hebrew	256	(47)	286	(53)	542	(100)
Sakapultek	277	(61)	179	(39)	456	(100)
Papago	523	(69)	236	(31)	759	(100)
English	309	(58)	226	(42)	535	(100)
Spanish	979	(63)	571	(37)	1550	(100)
French	1025	(68)	481	(32)	1506	(100)
Japanese	764	(68)	357	(32)	1121	(100)

clauses, the O role can be said to be *free*, whereas the A role is *constrained*. "Free" means that the lexical argument *may* appear, not that it must. We can represent the argument configuration schematically using a capital letter to represent a free role, and a small letter for a constrained role. Thus the typical array of core arguments in a transitive clause in spoken discourse is:

(16) a O

As for one-place predicates, we saw that the single core argument position (S role) is free, in that it allows full lexical noun phrases. Applying the same notation to intransitives, the argument pattern for a one-place predicate is represented simply as:

(17) S

For ditransitive clauses, which introduce an additional core argument (the indirect object, or I role), the typical argument pattern is schematically:

(18) a i O

Here only the direct object is shown as a free role; the other two are constrained. Putting it all together, we can summarize the patterning of free and constrained roles for the three clause types. The arguments of one-, two-, and three-place predicates, respectively, are represented schematically as follows:

[10]The sources for Table 2.3 are the same as those for Table 2.2.

(19) S
   a O
   a i O

Note that, even as the number of core argument positions is increased, the number of allowed lexical arguments remains constant at one.

REFERENTIAL PRAGMATICS
AND INFORMATION MANAGEMENT

There is more to the distribution of lexical and pronominal arguments than just a patterning in grammar, of course. Referential pragmatics, with its intimate connection to processes of information management, plays a role that cannot be overlooked. An aspect of information flow in discourse, referential pragmatics refers specifically to the pragmatic factors influencing selection of the form, structure, role, and interpretation of referential forms such as noun phrases.[11] For example, when there is a new entity to be introduced into a discourse, this will characteristically motivate the use of a full lexical noun phrase of some kind. (The precise size and shape of the nominal reference can vary tremendously, in response to several additional referential-pragmatic factors including the scale of cognitive accessibility [Ariel, 1990, 2001].)[12] Once the entity has been introduced, in subsequent discourse it will generally be tracked by a reduced form such as a pronoun. These linguistic choices reflect the speaker's assumptions regarding the listener's cognitive processing cost for accessing the intended referent. A full noun phrase, characteristically deployed when new information is being introduced, is thus taken to be an index of relatively high effort in accessing the referent (Ariel, 1990, 2001). A pronoun, invoked when the referent is more or less obvious from context, is interpreted as an index of relatively low cognitive effort to access.

It might seem that we are putting things backward. Shouldn't a full noun phrase be easier to process, since it carries within itself more complete information spelling out explicitly who or what the intended referent is? Isn't

---

[11]Noun phrases are labeled referential forms because they are of a type typically used to refer, not because they always refer. Ironically, the first challenge faced by the student of referential pragmatics is to separate out those uses of noun phrases that are *not* referential, in order to mount a coherent analysis of the remaining, truly referential cases.

[12]The concept of "accessibility" articulated by Ariel (1990, 2001) differs from Chafe's (1994) "accessible" in several significant respects. Ariel's term denotes the entire range of a continuous scale of accessibility, whereas Chafe's refers to the middle term of a three-way contrast among discrete cognitive activation statuses: given, accessible, new. In this chapter, the term "accessible" is used for the range from mid accessibility through high accessibility on Ariel's scale.

a pronoun harder to process, since it carries so little information that it requires the listener to infer the referent from other cues? This logic might be applicable if speakers selected their referential forms at random or uncooperatively; for example, thrusting a pronoun upon an unprepared addressee. But speakers are not so cavalier. Once we acknowledge the implicit contractual commitments that bind the collaborating participants in a conversation (Clark, 1996), we can understand the cooperative exchange of information in a different light. In general speakers use pronouns precisely when warranted, that is, when the contextual ground has been sufficiently prepared in advance that no more than a hint is needed to point the listener toward the right referent. That hint is the pronoun. More generally, speakers consistently take care to assess just how much help their addressee will need to access the intended referent, so as to select a referential form that will provide precisely the right amount of information: neither too little nor too much. Am I introducing a new referent that my addressee has never encountered before? Or is it obvious who I'm talking about because it's the same person I just mentioned in the previous clause? The first case will call for a full noun phrase of some kind, more or less elaborated, whereas the second will generally call for a pronoun (or even an ellipted "zero" if the cognitive context is right).

Yes, a speaker in the heat of conversation could make a mistake, misjudging the listener's difficulty of access for a particular referent and consequently selecting an inappropriate form. But such miscalculations are few and far between, as long as we are dealing with natural spontaneous discourse, in which speakers speak freely from their own motivations and can draw on their own situated awareness of the interactional and informational context they are embedded in. In general a speaker's choice of referential form can be counted on as a sensitive and reliable indicator of the perceived cognitive cost of accessing a referent. Supporting the reliability of this methodological assumption, we note that it is relatively rare for a listener to halt the flow of interaction in order to request clarification for a pronominal reference.

This brief account of the cognitive processes and costs attending the exchange of information between discourse participants, though necessarily simplistic, must suffice for present purposes. We might mention, however, that the emphasis on the hearer's cost of access—as judged by the speaker—is not meant to preclude a role for the speaker's own immediate cost in developing the conceptualization and its verbal formulation in the first place (Chafe, 1994, pp. 71ff, 1998; McNeill, 1992, pp. 218ff). The growth process of the speaker's emerging utterance carries significant cognitive costs, too, which I suggest will again correlate with the selection between nominal reference forms of greater or lesser elaboration, and their distribution across argument structures. All that is required at this point for our analysis of discourse patterning is that lexical noun phrases reflect greater cognitive cost than pronouns, whether the cost accrues to the speaker, the hearer, or both; and that these costs can be consistently localized in relation to grammatical structures.

In the next three sections I revisit the available grammatical repertoire of intransitive, transitive, and ditransitive argument structures in order to consider what role referential pragmatics plays in their patterning and use, as speakers and hearers strive to systematically manage the cognitive costs of information exchange in discourse.

Intransitive Pragmatics

In speaking of *intransitive pragmatics* I purposely juxtapose a structural term (*intransitive*) with a functional one (*pragmatics*). But how could these two belong together? We have already noted a certain patterning of grammar in discourse, whereby one-place predicates freely admit lexical mentions in the S role. We can now ask whether there is a functional basis for this distribution. What kind of pragmatic function is responsible for the use of all those noun phrases? Consider the following clause:

(20) {CUZ 995}
    ALINA: .. **this new wa=ve of people** comes in.
               S

A new referent is here introduced into the discourse for the first time, via *this new wave of people*, as subject of the predicate *come in*. Presumably this new introduction is accompanied by a certain amount of initial cognitive processing, as a new cognitive file (Du Bois, 1980) is opened for its referent. In the next example, similarly, the first mention of a particular child appears in the S role as an indefinite noun phrase:

(21) {VETMORN 351}
    HEIDI: ... **a little kid** answered,

Information introduced in intransitive clauses is not limited to humans or other topically salient referents. In the next example (from a narrative about a car accident), *glass* is mentioned for the first time, in the S role:

(22) {FEAR 587}
    WALT: (H) **g=lass** is flying everywhere,

One-place predicates, with their unconstrained S role, can be counted on to allow the speaker unhampered fulfillment of the more demanding cognitive tasks, such as introduction of a new referent. They provide the simplest available clausal structure for information management. (In light of this role among adults, it is instructive to consider Tomasello's [1992] finding for children that one-place predicates play a critical role in the early development of verbal argument structure. In the earliest phases of development, even verbs that adults treat as two-place are subsumed into the congenial frame of one-place predicates.)

Transitive Pragmatics

With transitive verbs like *hire* and *devise* the presence of a second core argument role gives rise to a functional contrast between one free role, the O, and one constrained role, the A. The free role is where new entities are (optionally) introduced. In the following example, the O role lexical noun phrase *another voice* represents the first mention of its referent in the discourse, whereas the A role pronoun *they* refers back anaphorically to a previously mentioned referent.

(23) {NOTIONS 87}
     JIM: they hired **another voice**.
             A   O

The same pattern appears in the following two examples:

(24) {VISION 359}
     DANNY: (H) .. and so she devised **a plan**.

(25) {DEATH 818}
     PAMELA: ... I certainly miss **my do=g**.

The lexical noun phrases *a plan* and *my dog* each represent first mentions in their respective discourses. In contrast, the pronouns *she* and *I* refer to referents that are cognitively accessible based on prior discourse mention (plus, in the case of first person *I*, presence in the interactional context).

We can discern in this patterning of new information a set of pragmatic constraints parallel to those identified earlier for the distribution of grammatical elements across argument structures. The first I formulate as the *One New Argument Constraint*:

(26) Avoid more than one new core argument

Beyond this pragmatic constraint on *quantity*, there is a further pragmatic constraint on *role*:

TABLE 2.4
New Argument Quantity: Frequency of Clause Types
by Quantity of New Core Arguments[13]

Quantity:	0		1		2		Total	
Language	n	%	n	%	n	%	n	%
Sakapultek	336	(73)	122	(27)	0	(0)	458	(100)
English	463	(87)	72	(13)	0	(0)	535	(100)

(27) Avoid new A

This may be called the *Accessible A Constraint* (a slight revision of what I previously formulated as the *Given A Constraint* [Du Bois, 1987]).

As with intransitives, the transitive argument structure can be seen as providing an architectural framework for information management. But with two available roles, transitives introduce a sharp differentiation of pragmatic function between them. The free O role admits the demands of new information, whereas the constrained A role avoids them.

Ditransitive Pragmatics

The distribution of new versus accessible information in the ditransitive clause follows a by now predictable pattern. The direct object (O) readily accommodates new information whereas the other two core arguments, the transitive subject (A) and indirect object (I), do not.

(28) {RETIREMENT 163}
    SAM: .. I gave <u>him</u> **a red pepper.**
            A   I   O

Ditransitive verbs provide a particularly compelling confirmation of the One New Argument Constraint. With as many as three slots available, still only one is exploited for the heavier information management demands.

Cross-Linguistic Evidence for Pragmatic Constraints

The studies summarized in Tables 2.4 and 2.5 show that the previously cited patterns of new information distribution within the clause represent the prevailing ones in other languages as well. Table 2.4 confirms that clauses

---

[13]Sources are as for Table 2.1. Fewer languages are cited because fewer studies report the relevant data on new argument quantity in a comparable format.

TABLE 2.5
New Argument Role: Syntactic Role of New Core Arguments[14]

Role:	A		S		0		Total	
Language	n	%	n	%	n	%	n	%
Hebrew	6	(6)	40	(43)	47	(51)	93	(100)
Sakapultek	6	(6)	58	(55)	42	(40)	106	(101)
English	0	(0)	15	(21)	57	(79)	72	(100)
Spanish	2	(1)	56	(28)	142	(71)	200	(100)
French	0	(0)	75	(34)	143	(66)	218	(100)

with two new core arguments are very rare (or, within these two studies, nonexistent). Table 2.5 shows that the one allowable item of new information appears relatively rarely in A role, whereas no comparable avoidance characterizes the S or O roles.

Summary: A Discourse-and-Grammar Parallel

We have seen that Preferred Argument Structure has two parallel dimensions, a grammatical and a pragmatic. The grammatical dimension is expressed as a soft constraint on the quantity and the grammatical role of full lexical noun phrases relative to argument structures. The pragmatic dimension represents a soft constraint on introducing more than one item of new information (as opposed to accessible information, which suffers no such limitation) within the clause core, plus a constraint on the specific role within which this information may appear. (See Chafe, 1994, pp. 108–119 for a related constraint against more than one new idea per intonation unit.) Full noun phrases and new information both tend to be avoided in the transitive subject position, yet occur freely within intransitive subject and direct object positions. The quantity and role constraints on the distribution of grammatical and pragmatic elements across argument structures together constitute Preferred Argument Structure. These are summarized in Table 2.6.

How do the Quantity and Role constraints relate to each other? We can surmise that general cognitive limitations on information processing amount to an overall constraint on the quantity of new information that can be handled within a single processing unit. What the Role constraints add to this picture is a predictable locus for the heaviest cognitive demands. By segregating high-demand tasks from low-demand tasks and confining the former to a distinct, specified locus within the argument structure, us-

---

[14]Sources, and comments, are as in the note for Table 2.2. Fewer languages are cited because fewer studies report the relevant data on new argument role in a comparable format.

TABLE 2.6
Preferred Argument Structure Constraints: Quantity and Role

	Grammar	*Pragmatics*
Quantity	Avoid more than one lexical core argument	Avoid more than one new core argument
Role	Avoid lexical A	Avoid new A

ers of grammar are given a predictive advantage as to where they should direct their limited attentional resources.

Low Information Density

I have been emphasizing the challenge of managing the introduction of new information into discourse, and noting the link between such relatively heavy processing tasks and certain grammatical roles within the clause. But discourse is not always so demanding. The fact is, in some kinds of discourse there is relatively little new information to introduce, a situation we may describe as low information density.[15] When this situation obtains there may be no need to use full noun phrases at all to introduce new entities, if each of the entities relevant to what the speaker wants to say has already been introduced into the discourse.

Consider the one-place predicate. Despite its information-carrying privileges, there is no requirement that the S role's full processing capacity be exploited at every instance, whether needed or not. The intransitive S role cannot be reliably predicted to bear a lexical noun phrase, nor the pragmatic statuses that go with it. Often enough, the S role will be filled by a personal pronoun. In the following examples, each pronoun corresponds to an accessible referent previously introduced:

(29) {LUTHER 471}
    FOSTER: <u>He</u> wavers.
              S

(30) {CUTIEPIE 919}
    JILL: And <u>we</u> started laughing,

(31) {RAGING 365}
    SHARON: <u>she</u> gets real embarrassed,

---

[15]In Du Bois (1987) I spoke of low "information pressure." I now prefer the more neutral term "information density," modeled on Durie's congenial phrases "referential density" and "lexical density," which denote similar discourse measures (Durie, in press).

If the event that is being described calls unequivocally for a semantically one-place predicate (*waver, laugh, get embarrassed*), the S role will routinely be called into play regardless of whether there is a need for it to carry any new information. Verbs and their argument structures, like so many elements in grammar, are multifunctional: they are capable of serving both semantic and pragmatic functions. Despite the focus in this study on the most demanding aspects of information management, we should not be surprised to see that sometimes a particular argument structure (e.g., that of a one-place predicate like *waver* or *laugh*) is selected for its semantic function alone, even when its full information-carrying potential is not needed.

The same holds for transitive verbs. Whereas the O role is free to accommodate new information, it is perfectly compatible with accessible information as well. There is no *lower* limit on the number of new entities to be introduced within a transitive clause. In the following examples, all argument positions are filled by pronouns for the simple reason that all the referents are accessible (due to prior discourse mention plus the situational context):

(32) {CUTIEPIE 969}
    JEFF: .. (H) <u>she</u> didn't see <u>me</u>.
               A   O

(33) {RAGING 218}
    CAROLYN: Oh <u>I</u> believe <u>it</u>.

At such times it may happen that the only really new information carried in a clause is that expressed in the verb (*see, believe*) or in another element like a negative (*didn't*). Sometimes even the verb is already known and the only thing remaining to be specified is who did what to whom. In the next example, the concept of *kiss* as well as the kissing event's two participants have all been previously introduced. What remains is the selection of which referent goes into the subject role and which into the object, and the past-tense timing of the event itself:

(34) {HOWARDS 1124}
    LORI: <u>He</u> kissed <u>her</u>,
        A   O

Even ditransitive verbs entail no lower limit on the introduction of new nominal information. When pragmatically appropriate, all three argument roles may contain accessible information expressed by pronouns, as in the following example:

(35) {RETIREMENT 880}
    DORIS: <u>You</u>'ve told <u>us</u> <u>that</u>.
            A   I O

Clearly, speakers have good reasons to utter clauses that contain very little new information, at least of the sort encoded in lexical noun phrases.

Under conditions of low information density it will matter little whether the verb has one, two, or three core arguments available. We are likely to find that none of the argument roles is filled with a lexical noun phrase. It is not uncommon, and indeed entirely natural, for both the A and the O roles of a transitive clause, or the A, I, and O roles of a ditransitive clause, to be realized with pronouns.

It is important to point out that such all-pronoun clauses do *not* constitute violations of any of the Preferred Argument Structure constraints. These constraints posit only *upper* limits on the introduction of new and lexical information within the clause. True, if low density discourse was the norm, it would be hard to justify the constraints empirically, since it is only in high density discourse that the constraints become fully evident. As the density of new introductions increases, available S and O roles are more and more filled up with new lexical noun phrases. Meanwhile, it becomes more noticeable that the A role is not contributing much to managing the influx of new information. In contrast, low density discourse neither supports nor refutes the constraints.

But there is one important lesson to be learned from low density discourse. It reminds us that even a relatively frequent association of a particular discourse function with a particular grammatical role need not rise to the level of predictiveness we expect of a linguistic sign. Despite their critical contribution to the management of new information, neither the S nor the O role can be said to *stand for* new information. No matter how much linguists love signs, there is simply no justification for a Saussurean sign function here, by which a form (say, the O role) symbolizes a discourse-pragmatic function (say, "new information," or even "lexical noun phrase"). The all-pronoun clauses, which are by no means aberrant or exceptional, preclude this. Rather, what the S and O roles do is to enable or facilitate. They reserve a place in a structural configuration that allows, but does not require, the performing of demanding processing functions. In my terms, the S and O roles lack a sign function, but do fulfill a structure function: They provide a predictable locus for unpredictable work.

THE IMPORTANCE OF BEING STRUCTURED

Although the discourse pattern identified here is not reducible to a rule of grammar, neither is it without structure. We are not dealing with some crude constraint on overall quantity of nouns or items of new information, but rather a well-articulated preference that is systematically sensitive to the specific syntactic structuring of the surface clause. In particular, all the constraints identified apply precisely to *core argument* roles of the clause (subject, object, indirect object), and not to just any nouns in a clause—not even to nouns embedded within the core argument nouns themselves.

For example, prepositional phrases contain noun phrases, but insofar as these represent oblique rather than core roles within the clause, they are not governed by the accounting of quantity applicable to core arguments. Hence the oblique full noun phrases may occur freely, without heed of the limit that core arguments are held to:

(36) {DEADLY 1903}
    KEN: (TSK) (H) <u>He</u> drops **the goldfish** into **the tank**,
                             A   O   Obl

(37) {BANK 342}
    FRED: and then <u>he</u> borrowed **some money** from **his uncle**,

Here the prepositional objects *the tank* and *his uncle* happily coexist in the same clause with the direct objects *the goldfish* and *some money*, respectively. Only the direct objects are core arguments subject to constraint. In fact, it is not uncommon to see multiple oblique roles, each non-core and each bearing a full lexical noun, without any violation of the Preferred Argument Structure constraints.

(38) {DEADLY 894}
    LENORE: <u>0</u> take uh **one of those a day** on **an empty stomach**,
               A   O   Obl   Obl

Here we see three full noun phrases within one clause—and within one intonation unit—but two of these nominals (*a day* and *an empty stomach*) are in oblique roles, and hence not subject to constraint. Speakers have no trouble verbalizing all three noun phrases within a single intonation unit, even if more than one contains new information.

Bringing obliques into the overall picture of information management introduces some new complexities, which are mostly beyond the scope of this article. (Compare Table 2.7, which includes all lexical mentions, with Table 2.2, which includes only those in core argument roles.) I merely mention here that obliques, by falling outside the clause core and hence outside the scope of the Preferred Argument Structure constraints, represent another prime opportunity, beyond the S and O roles, for the introduction of new information. But the information introduced obliquely tends to be of a substantially different character, less topical and more ephemeral (Du Bois, 1980; Thompson, 1997), as the examples in this section suggest.

2. DISCOURSE AND GRAMMAR

TABLE 2.7
Lexical Argument Role: Syntactic Role of All Lexical Mentions

Role:	A		S		O		Oblique		Other		Total	
Language	n	%	n	%	n	%	n	%	n	%	n	%
Sakapultek	11	(3)	126	(33)	81	(21)	118	(31)	48	(12)	384	(100)
English	21	(5)	90	(23)	146	(37)	120	(31)	16	(4)	393	(100)

Another piece of evidence that the Preferred Argument Structure constraints are sensitive to specific syntactic structure concerns internally structured noun phrases:

(39) {RISK 98}
    JENNIFER: Yeah <u>you</u> get **a percentage** of **the amount** of **countries**
                        A   O
       you own,

Although this clause could be said to contain at least three lexical *noun phrases* (e.g., *a percentage, the amount,* and *countries you own*), a more perspicuous analysis would discern just one lexical *argument*, namely the complex noun phrase *a percentage of the amount of countries you own*, which as a unit fills the role of direct object of the verb *get*. The noun phrases *the amount* and *countries you own* do not fill verbal argument roles of their own, but are subsumed under the direct object role within the complex noun phrase that has *percentage* as its head.

We conclude that the internal syntactic structuring of the clause has precise consequences for the cognitive processing of lexical information. It will not do to formulate a syntactically naive or agnostic constraint like "Avoid more than one lexical noun phrase in an intonation unit" or even "Avoid more than one lexical noun phrase in a clause." Such claims are readily refuted by the pervasiveness in discourse of configurations like those cited in this section. The constraints on distribution of referential form are sensitive to a finer specification of syntactic structure, specifically to the argument structure of the surface clause, rather than to a gross unit-as-container organization, whether the unit proposed is the clause or the intonation unit. Similarly for information management, which is equally sensitive to surface syntactic configuration of the clause.

CONSTRAINT AND STRATEGY

Putting narrow limits on how much new information may be introduced within a clause, and where it may go, poses a certain puzzle. How do speakers manage to say what they need to say? Particularly confining, it seems, would be the constraint against introducing new information in the transitive subject role. Humans assuredly like to talk about humans. Often enough what attracts our interest is a human engaged in agentive action. When it comes time to verbalize such a content, we find that this would normally entail the human referent taking the role of agent of an active verb, hence implicating the transitive subject role. Must we forgo expressing such meanings due to obstacles thrown up by Preferred Argument Structure? Not at all. The way to fulfillment is via a simple principle of discourse: Speakers need not say everything in one clause. Facing cognitive constraints that could frustrate their expressive goals, speakers can simply mobilize their planning capacity to organize a series of successive clauses. In the following example, the narrator relates how a psychotherapist told him something interesting about herself. This state of affairs is most naturally conceived in terms of the psychotherapist playing the role of semantic agent of the telling event, which in verbal form would tend to place the *teller* in the role of syntactic subject of the verb *tell*. And there's the rub. To introduce the psychotherapist as new information in (di-)transitive subject role would be problematic, if we take seriously the constraints thus far identified. Fortunately there is another way:

(40) {LAMBADA 1284}
    MILES: .. I meet **this psychotherapist**.
            A   O
            ... who tells me she's addicted to **this dance**.
                A   O S   Obl

The verb *meet* nicely fills the bill of taking the pressure off, by breaking down the task at hand into a sequence of manageable subtasks. First, *meet* takes the newly introduced psychotherapist as its direct object—an unconstrained role—and so deftly evades the strictures of the Accessible A Constraint. Then, once the new referent has been properly introduced, it immediately becomes eligible to fill the role of subject of *tell*, because by now it already constitutes accessible information, expressible by a pronoun (*who, she*).

   Speakers show a certain ingenuity in developing strategies for maintaining a full expressive range of propositional semantics while accommodating constraints on discourse pragmatics. Many of these strategies appear to be routinized, memorized for reuse—even grammaticized as specialized constructions in the language. Like *meet*, the transitive verb *see* is handy in that it readily takes a human referent in O, thus supplying a free role that allows unconstrained introduction of new referents. Observe how *this girl* is introduced in the next example:

(41) {CONCEPT 1315}
      MARILYN: .. <u>we</u>'re pulling up,
                  .. and <u>I</u> see **this gir=l**.
                  A   O
                  <u>Who</u> <u>I</u>'d never seen before,
                  <u>0</u> sort of d=art out of **our driveway**.
                  ((4 LINES OMITTED))
                  and <u>0</u> watch <u>us</u> pull in,

I suggest that one of the things speakers know about the verb *see*, as about the verb *meet*, is that it fulfills a strategic function of introducing a new human referent without running afoul of the Accessible A Constraint. There may be semantic motivations for using the verb *see* here, but most of our reported experiences involve seeing, and yet we don't feel compelled to continually verbalize this information explicitly in every instance. I would argue that the choice to verbalize a verb like *see* (or *meet*) that takes humans in O role is often motivated more by information management factors than by semantic ones.

This motivation surely holds for certain intransitive predicates, whose bleached semantic content leaves little to motivate their use *except* for information management. There are numerous strategies that exploit the potential of the S role of intransitive and other one-place predicates. The key is not intransitive verb status per se, but simply avoiding transitive (and ditransitive) subjects. "Subjects" are perfectly compatible, it turns out, with the high cost of introducing new information—but only if the subject is that of a one-place, rather than a two- or three-place, predicate.

One class of intransitive verbs that has strategic significance beyond its propositional semantics is that of verbs expressing "existence or appearance on the scene" (Du Bois, 1987, pp. 830ff; Firbas, 1966; Kuno, 1972, p. 319), which are often called on to introduce new information. One much-analyzed construction is the so-called "existential" *there*-construction. This certainly qualifies as being bleached of semantic meaning, and yet it is very much in demand for its discourse-pragmatic properties. Note that introducing a new referent via *there*, as in the next example, successfully evades the constrained transitive subject position.

(42) {CUZ 400}
      ALINA: ... and there's **a car** in front of <u>me</u>,

Once this new car is introduced into the discourse, it allows definite mention of its driver, first as *the guy* and then *he*:

(43) {CUZ 399}
    ALINA: (H) So I'm driving up to **the house**,
           . . . and there's **a car** in front of me,
           and **the guy** is just like sitting there,
           <VOX> in **the middle of the roa=d**,
           and he's not moving,
           and,
           . . you know I wanna park **the car** </VOX>.

Similarly, an intransitive verb like *come*, semantically denoting motion toward the speaker, frequently fulfills the additional pragmatic function of
providing a framework for introducing a new referent "appearing on the
scene." The discourse-pragmatic function may even come to dominate over
the semantic one. Consider the example presented earlier, repeated here,
in which the first-mention heavy noun phrase *this new wave of people* serves to
introduce a new referent into the discourse (after which it becomes the
topic of subsequent discourse):

(44) {CUZ 995}
    ALINA: . . **this new wa=ve of people** comes in.

The choice of an intransitive verb for the introduction is no accident. Beyond the specific semantics of *come in*, the verb's intransitivity has the advantage of defining a single core argument position, which, lacking competi-
tors, is unconstrained. Verbs like *come* are useful in part because they are
free to welcome full lexical noun phrases of all shapes and sizes, along with
the cognitive cost of introducing new information.

PATTERN WITHOUT RULE

We noted earlier that presenting accessible information where new is allowed does not constitute a violation of any Preferred Argument Structure
constraint. But there are real exceptions, as Tables 2.1–2.5 document and
the examples in this section will portray. Exceptions are not always a bad
thing. In this case, they make it clear that despite its systematicity, Preferred
Argument Structure cannot be reduced to a grammatical rule. It must remain within the domain of discourse, as a patterning *of* grammar with consequences *for* grammar.
    It is noteworthy that when a departure from Preferred Argument Struc-
ture does occur in natural discourse, the resulting utterance bears not a
hint of ungrammaticality. For example, speakers sometimes do put a full

lexical noun phrase in transitive subject position, with no ill consequences
for grammaticality:

(45) {CUZ 1282}
    ALINA: **turtlenecks** don't hide <u>everything</u>.
              A   O

The A role sometimes even accommodates new information not previously
introduced, as in this first mention of (generic) *turtlenecks*. In the next example, the A role *cats* is a first mention in the discourse, also generic, while
the O role pronoun *those* represents an accessible referent (some vitamin
pills that are visible in the situational context):

(46) {CUZ 688}
    LENORE: **Cats** love <u>those</u>.
                A   O

Sometimes a transitive clause will contain even two full noun phrases, in
both A and O roles, thus violating both of the Preferred Argument Structure constraints on lexical mentions.

(47) {LAMBADA 78}
    HAROLD: .. **little kids** usually don't break **their legs** anyway.
              A   O

Each of these two noun phrases expresses a referent that is accessible in discourse context (there was prior talk of a specific child breaking his leg), so
this particular example may not present a significant violation of the *pragmatic* side of Preferred Argument Structure. But on occasion even new information full lexical nouns appear in both A and O roles. In the following
example, each of the two core argument noun phrases represents a first
mention in the discourse.

(48) {FEAR 580}
    WALT: (H) **trailer truck** hits **his brakes**,
              A   O

    To be sure, one might seek extenuating circumstances for all of these
cases,[16] and it must be said that in various ways the offending noun phrases

---

[16]For example, none of the "exceptional" A role lexical mentions cited in this section contains an article or other determiner, raising the question of just how "full" these full noun
phrases really are. This points to the important issue of a continuous scale of accessibility
(Ariel, 1990, 2001), which is beyond the scope of this chapter. See also Chafe (1994, pp.
108–119, 1998, p. 109) for exegesis of some applicable mitigating factors.

do not elicit the heaviest cognitive demands. But for the present it seems prudent to conclude that the discourse preferences so far identified constitute *soft* constraints: They may be violated without precipitating either ungrammaticality or processing failure.

It should be no surprise that the constraints are soft, to the extent that the discourse preferences are cognitively based. It would be risky to operate always at the outer limits of cognitive capacity. Better to set a routine limit lower than the maximum; under special circumstances one may then momentarily exceed this flexible limitation.

Of course, if exceptions like these were frequent, there would be no reason to posit a preferred argument structure in the first place. But in all they are relatively rare, as is attested by the evidence from a number of languages (cf. Tables 2.1–2.5). Even infrequent occurrences, however, are sufficient to preclude a categorical rule of grammar. Whereas models that depend entirely on categorical rules might take such an outcome as a failure to be regretted, from a discourse perspective the interpretation is quite different. We see it as noteworthy that a pattern of behavior so consistent across speakers and across languages can emerge in discourse and be sustained in the absence of any mechanical rule. And we go on to seek for deeper explanations.

The exceptions to the Accessible A Constraint, however rare, have another important theoretical consequence. They argue against interpreting the A role as *signifying* "accessible information." We cannot justify a sign function here, because new A's are encountered regularly, if not very frequently. (With a true sign function like the word *white*, we don't find that 5% of the time speakers mistakenly use it to mean *black*.) Even less plausible is treating S or O as a sign. As we saw earlier, half or more of the S and O positions may contain accessible information, making it impossible to reliably interpret S or O as signifying "new information." I say this despite the fact that S and O together clearly constitute *the* place to put new information within the clause core: If you have new information to introduce, that's where you nearly always put it. But the implication in the opposite direction does not hold, because S and O do not even come close to consistently predicting the presence of new information. The Saussurean construct of the sign function is of no help in our attempt to model the discourse phenomena underlying Preferred Argument Structure.

THE GRAMMATICAL ARCHITECTURE
OF COGNITIVE COST

If Preferred Argument Structure is not a rule of grammar and not a sign function, what can it be?

We began by identifying a curiously skewed patterning of full versus re-duced noun phrases within the grammatical frame articulated by argument structures in discourse. We went on to observe a parallel patterning of new versus accessible information. But if we probe still further, we soon see that these discourse patterns are not ultimately about noun phrases, nor even new information, but about cognitive cost. Specifically, they point to a sys-tematic exploitation of syntactic structure as a frame for organizing and man-aging cognitive costs in speech production and understanding. Some aspects of speech processing invoke high cognitive cost, whereas others are relatively undemanding (Ariel, 1990, 2001; Chafe, 1994, pp. 71–81). Other things be-ing equal, new referents are costly, accessible referents are cheap. But there are other costs as well, like those associated with processing relative clauses—which have been shown to follow a Preferred Argument Structure pattern, preferring S or O role over the constrained A role (Fox, 1987; cf. Fox & Thompson, 1990). The distribution of cognitive costs across the grammatical architecture of the clause is neither random nor constant, but systematically skewed. Speakers know where in a clause to produce, and hearers where to expect, the heavy processing demands such as those associated with the in-troduction of new information. Rather than leave this to chance, the role constraints of Preferred Argument Structure effectively enlist the syntactic structure of the clause to provide a consistent shape within which the more demanding tasks can be carried out: a predictable locus for unpredictable work. In this sense the surface grammatical structure of a clause, in particular its argument structure, can be seen as defining an architecture of cognitive cost, or more precisely, an architecture *for* cognitive processing, in which cer-tain locales are predictably specialized for high- or low-cost work.

The verbs of a language can be thought of as a diverse population of se-mantic-pragmatic-grammatical elements, each offering an argument struc-ture capable of managing some configuration of cognitive cost linked to a meaning frame. One-place predicates like intransitive verbs can handle their cognitive costs without special restrictions because in their simplicity they do not attempt to juggle more than one core argument slot for (noun-based) cognitive processing. Transitive verbs push the limits by introducing two slots, but at the cost of introducing constraints that limit the carrying capacity of one of them. Elaboration of still more complex structures, such as three-place ditransitive clauses, causatives, and certain complex clause structures, is attainable only through the trade-offs of historical evolution, that is, via the process of grammaticization. Grammaticization as an adap-tive process represents the crystallization of compromise between compet-ing motivations (Du Bois, 1985; see also Bates & MacWhinney, 1982). Due to limitations within a compact domain like the clause core or the intona-tion unit, new opportunities for semantic expression may be added only through the imposition of limits on old ones. Grammar is responsive to recurrent patterning in the aggregate of language use tokens, as it constitutes an adaptive architectural framework for cognitive function. Once crystallized as grammatical structure, the architecture becomes a cognitive resource available to all members of the speech community.

CONCLUSION

Roman Jakobson once quipped that "Grammar without meaning is meaningless" (1990, p. 332). In the context of his time this could be heard as a pointed critique of an approach that radically severed grammar from meaning. Since then a number of functional theorists have sought to restore meaning to a central place in language, offering a picture of grammar tightly integrated with it (Chafe, 1970; Fillmore, 1977, this volume; Langacker, 1987, 1998). If we wish to carry this understanding to its fullest development, then discourse pragmatics, too, will have to be accorded its distinctive place in the emerging grammatical synthesis.

It should be obvious by now that we do not accept the dichotomies between discourse and grammar that were recited at the outset of this chapter. More precisely, we do not accept the conclusion sometimes drawn from them, that the gulf between grammar and discourse is unbridgeable. Not only can apposite theory create productive links between discourse and grammar, but what at first glance seemed to be the freer, wilder, less constrained half of the equation—what we call spontaneous discourse—proves to embody some of the most pervasive, regular, profound, and cross-linguistically stable trends. And these well-grounded patterns in discourse have the power to shape the very foundations of grammar (Du Bois, 1987).

And yet the idea that syntax remains partly aloof from meaning retains a certain appeal. Could grammar, by showing some resistance to being directly semanticized, contribute something more than just another means of symbolizing what is meant? Could the lack of specific meaning free syntax to serve another role, more abstractly framing and organizing a crucial, if neglected, dimension of language use: its actual process of coming into being?

In the idealized cognitive world assumed in some versions of functional linguistics, there is no friction. A concept conceived is a concept verbalized, instantly and effortlessly rendered into words. But where is the process? In the world of natural spontaneous discourse, there is audible friction. Thought does not go gently into words. Wheels grind as we strive to speak, working to manage all the tasks that confront us at once. And some parts of the work are more demanding than others. Initializing a new cognitive file for a just-introduced referent takes more resources than updating an existing cognitive file for a highly accessible referent. A mix of easy and demanding tasks of speech production (or comprehension) are juggled simultaneously, in pursuit of the goal of verbalizing and conveying the idea striven for. All this takes place in real time as we strategically deploy limited cognitive resources. How do such real-time discourse processes impact grammar? The argument structure of a clause, although undoubtedly contributing to the expression of semantic roles like Agent, Patient, or Experiencer, is also called on to serve the demands of information management. Managing information and expressing a full range of propositional meanings are two functions that must be strategically integrated into the production of a single structured utterance. Thus discourse pragmatics takes its place alongside semantics as a driving force in language use and grammaticization, ultimately shaping the most fundamental structures of a language's grammar (Du Bois, 1987).

We recognize that there is no discourse without grammar. There is no raw speaking, nakedly expressing pure speaker intention or discourse function, without the imposition of grammatical category and structure. No pristine primordial world can be found in which discourse function operates on its own in splendid isolation, unhindered by grammatical form, its unique contribution transparently revealed. Perforce we take discourse as it comes, in its grammatical clothing. Conversely, no speaker ever encounters grammar except as it is manifested in discourse. For better or worse, discourse and grammar are inextricably linked. So it is that within discourse we analyze tangible grammar (noun phrases and their roles of subject, object, oblique) and, tipped off by the cross-linguistic patterns identified by grammatical typology (Comrie, this volume), we take the trouble to distinguish between subjects of transitive verbs and subjects of intransitive verbs—because we know that many languages treat this discrimination as fundamental even if English and most European languages don't. Simultaneously we note the discourse-pragmatic functions and cognitive processes realized via each nominal reference token (new vs. accessible information, high vs. low processing cost). The interwoven strands of data are tallied in tandem as we look for correlations between grammatical structure and discourse-pragmatic function. This program of discourse research probes into syntactic structures within the sentence, often at the clause level or smaller. Against the stereotype that the discourse analyst's proper domain lies beyond the sentence, I call this "discourse inside the clause." Of course what's happening inside the clause isn't really a world unto itself. Its discourse patterns have larger origins. The point is that there is massive interpenetration extending from sentence-internal structures at the level of noun phrase and clause up to the scale of the larger discourse units and the longest threads of referential continuity. The analysis crosses the lines between small and large, structure and function, token and type. The ultimate payoff is in understanding and explaining grammar. But the payoff doesn't come without a commitment to pursue grammatical and discourse-pragmatic patterns within an integrated frame of cross-disciplinary inquiry.

Surprises emerge from this approach to discourse and grammar. In principle, what the rules of grammars do not prohibit they should allow. Yet for all the freedom that their grammars afford them, speakers travel a straight and narrow path. Consider the free-willed speaker, who on each occasion of utterance is graced with the liberty—under the rules of grammar—to introduce a full noun phrase (perhaps one expressing an item of new information) into each and every argument position in a clause. Overwhelmingly, the speaker neglects this grammatical potential. Moreover the unused options are not random but consistent in their grammatical patterning. One specific syntactic position is avoided for new information while others are favored, even though none of this is demanded by grammatical rule. We are led to conclude that something is at work that goes beyond grammar. When we discover the same discourse regularity without grammatical obligation recurring in the spontaneous speech of different speakers, talking in diverse contexts about varied topics, and when we find this same pattern recurring across languages of distant regions, independent histories, and radically divergent grammatical types, then we have grounds to invoke a universal of discourse more broadly grounded, more stable, and more empirically confirmable than many that have been claimed for grammar. Such is the discourse universal of Preferred Argument Structure. It is a recurrent pattern of language use that cannot be reduced to grammatical rule. It stands in its own right as a generalization about discourse, one that involves grammar, in that it is defined over grammatical categories, and yet is not part of grammar.

If grammar is assumed to be a functioning part of the total system of language, it is necessary to ask what role it plays. The theory of discourse and grammar I have been advancing points to the conclusion that structure is functional. Meaningless grammar need not mean functionless grammar. Sometimes grammar serves function by refusing to mean. By decoupling from signification and escaping the narrow role of a specific sign function, core grammatical roles like A, S, and O are freed instead to support a broader structure function. What grammar contributes instead of meaning is an architectural framework within which cognitive processing is realized. In place of the sign function with its form–meaning pairing that well serves so much of language, grammar sometimes offers nothing more nor less than a structure function. If the emerging picture of language reveals a more complex relationship between structure and function than many might have wished for, it is nevertheless one that is more in keeping with that complexity which is now more and more recognized as characteristic of all evolved forms of life and culture.

ACKNOWLEDGMENTS

I thank Mira Ariel, Patricia Clancy, and Michael Tomasello for their very helpful input on an earlier version of this chapter. Any remaining mistakes are my own.

REFERENCES

Aissen, J. (1987). *Tzotzil clause structure.* Dordrecht, Netherlands: Reidel.

Ariel, M. (1990). *Accessing noun-phrase antecedents.* London: Routledge.

Ariel, M. (1998). Cognitive universals and linguistic conventions: The case of resumptive pronouns. *Studies in Language, 23,* 217–269.

Ariel, M. (2001). Accessibility theory: An overview. In T. Sanders, J. Schilperoord, & W. Spooren (Eds.), *Text representation: Linguistic and psycholinguistic aspects* (pp. 29–87). Amsterdam: Benjamins.

Ashby, W. J., & Bentivoglio, P. (1993). Preferred Argument Structure in spoken French and Spanish. *Language Variation and Change, 5,* 61–76.

Bates, E., & MacWhinney, B. (1982). Functionalist approaches to grammar. In E. Wanner & L. Gleitman (Eds.), *Language acquisition: The state of the art* (pp. 173–218). Cambridge: Cambridge University Press.

Boas, F. (1911). Introduction. *Handbook of American Indian languages, Part 1* (pp. 1–83). Bureau of American Ethnology, Bulletin 40. Washington, DC: Government Printing Office.

Chafe, W. L. (1970). *Meaning and the structure of language.* Chicago: University of Chicago Press.

Chafe, W. L. (Ed.). (1980). *The pear stories: Cognitive, cultural, and linguistic aspects of narrative production.* Norwood, NJ: Ablex.

Chafe, W. L. (1987). Cognitive constraints on information flow. In R. S. Tomlin (Ed.), *Coherence and grounding in discourse* (pp. 21–51). Amsterdam: Benjamins.

Chafe, W. L. (1994). *Discourse, consciousness, and time: The flow and displacement of conscious experience in speaking and writing.* Chicago: University of Chicago Press.

Chafe, W. L. (1998). Language and the flow of thought. In M. Tomasello (Ed.), *The new psychology of language: Cognitive and functional approaches to language structure* (pp. 93–111). Mahwah, NJ: Lawrence Erlbaum Associates.

Clancy, P. M. (1980). Referential choice in English and Japanese narrative discourse. In W. L. Chafe (Ed.), *The pear stories: Cognitive, cultural, and linguistic aspects of narrative production* (pp. 127–202). Norwood, NJ: Ablex.

Clancy, P. M. (in press). The lexicon in interaction: Developmental origins of Preferred Argument Structure in Korean. In J. W. Du Bois, L. E. Kumpf, & W. J. Ashby (Eds.), *Preferred Argument Structure: Grammar as architecture for function.* Amsterdam: Benjamins.

Clark, H. H. (1996). *Using language.* Cambridge: Cambridge University Press.

Du Bois, J. W. (1980). Beyond definiteness: The trace of identity in discourse. In W. L. Chafe (Ed.), *The pear stories: Cognitive, cultural, and linguistic aspects of narrative production* (pp. 203–274). Norwood, NJ: Ablex.

Du Bois, J. W. (1985). Competing motivations. In J. Haiman (Ed.), *Iconicity in syntax* (pp. 343–365). Amsterdam: Benjamins.

Du Bois, J. W. (1986). Self-evidence and ritual speech. In W. L. Chafe & J. Nichols (Eds.), *Evidentiality: The linguistic coding of epistemology* (pp. 313–336). Norwood, NJ: Ablex.

Du Bois, J. W. (1987). The discourse basis of ergativity. *Language, 63,* 805–855.

Du Bois, J. W. (2000). *Santa Barbara corpus of spoken American English, Part 1* [3 CD-ROMs]. Philadelphia: Linguistic Data Consortium, University of Pennsylvania.

Du Bois, J. W., Kumpf, L. E., & Ashby, W. J. (Eds.). (in press). *Preferred Argument Structure: Grammar as architecture for function.* Amsterdam: Benjamins.

Du Bois, J. W., Schuetze-Coburn, S., Cumming, S., & Paolino, D. (1993). Outline of discourse transcription. In J. A. Edwards & M. D. Lampert (Eds.), *Talking data: Transcription and coding in discourse research* (pp. 45–89). Hillsdale, NJ: Lawrence Erlbaum Associates.

Du Bois, J. W., Schuetze-Coburn, S., Paolino, D., & Cumming, S. (1992). *Discourse transcription. Santa Barbara papers in linguistics* (Vol. 4). Santa Barbara: Department of Linguistics, University of California, Santa Barbara.

Durie, M. (in press). New light on information pressure: Information conduits, escape valves, and role alignment stretching. In J. W. Du Bois, L. E. Kumpf, & W. J. Ashby (Eds.), *Preferred Argument Structure: Grammar as architecture for function.* Amsterdam: Benjamins.

Dutra, R. (1987). The hybrid S category in Brazilian Portuguese: Some implications for word order. *Studies in Language, 11,* 163–180.

Fillmore, C. J. (1977). Topics in lexical semantics. In R. W. Cole (Ed.), *Current issues in linguistic theory* (pp. 76–138). Bloomington: Indiana University Press.

Firbas, J. (1966). Non-thematic sentences in contemporary English. *Travaux linguistiques de Prague, 2,* 239–256.

Ford, C. E., & Thompson, S. A. (1996). Interactional units in conversation: Syntactic, intonational, and pragmatic resources for the management of turns. In E. Ochs, E. A. Schegloff, & S. A. Thompson (Eds.), *Interaction and grammar* (pp. 134–184). Cambridge: Cambridge University Press.

Fox, B. (1987). The noun phrase accessibility hierarchy reinterpreted: Subject primacy or the absolutive hypothesis? *Language, 63,* 856–870.

Fox, B., & Thompson, S. A. (1990). A discourse explanation of the grammar of relative clauses in English conversation. *Language, 66,* 297–316.

Givon, T. (1979). *On understanding grammar.* New York: Academic Press.

Givon, T. (Ed.). (1983). *Topic continuity in discourse: A quantitative cross-language study.* Amsterdam: Benjamins.

Givon, T. (1992). The grammar of referential coherence as mental processing instructions. *Linguistics, 30,* 5–55.

Givon, T. (1998). The functional approach to grammar. In M. Tomasello (Ed.), *The new psychology of language: Cognitive and functional approaches to language structure* (pp. 41–66). Mahwah, NJ: Lawrence Erlbaum Associates.

Goldberg, A. E. (1998). Patterns of experience in patterns of language. In M. Tomasello (Ed.), *The new psychology of language: Cognitive and functional approaches to language structure* (pp. 203–219). Mahwah, NJ: Lawrence Erlbaum Associates.

Harris, Z. S. (1951). *Methods in structural linguistics.* Chicago: University of Chicago Press.

Hopper, P. J. (1998). Emergent grammar. In M. Tomasello (Ed.), *The new psychology of language: Cognitive and functional approaches to language structure* (pp. 155–175). Mahwah, NJ: Lawrence Erlbaum Associates.

Hopper, P. J., & Thompson, S. A. (1980). Transitivity in grammar and discourse. *Language, 56,* 251–299.

Jakobson, R. (1990). *On language.* Cambridge, MA: Harvard University Press.

Kumagai, Y. (2001). Preferred Argument Structure and discourse ergativity in English. *Mulberry, 50,* 77–90.

Kuno, S. (1972). Functional Sentence Perspective: A case study from Japanese and English. *Linguistic Inquiry, 3,* 269–320.

Langacker, R. W. (1987). *Foundations of cognitive grammar: Vol. 1. Theoretical prerequisites.* Stanford, CA: Stanford University Press.

Langacker, R. W. (1998). Conceptualization, symbolization, and grammar. In M. Tomasello (Ed.), *The new psychology of language: Cognitive and functional approaches to language structure* (pp. 1–39). Mahwah, NJ: Lawrence Erlbaum Associates.

Matsumoto, K. (1997). NPs in Japanese conversation. *Pragmatics, 7,* 163–181.

McGregor, W. B. (1999). "Optional" ergative marking in Gooniyandi revisited: Implications to the theory of marking. *Leuvanse Bijdragen, 87,* 491–534.

McNeill, D. (1992). *Hand and mind: What gestures reveal about thought.* Chicago: University of Chicago Press.

Nichols, J., & Timberlake, A. (1991). Grammaticalization as retextualization. In E. C. Traugott & B. Heine (Eds.), *Approaches to grammaticalization: Vol. 1. Focus on theoretical and methodological issues* (pp. 129–146). Amsterdam: Benjamins.

Payne, D. L. (1987). Information structuring in Papago narrative discourse. *Language, 63,* 783–804.

Saussure, F. (1916). *Cours de linguistique generale [Course in general linguistics].* Paris: Payot.

Schiffrin, D. (1987). *Discourse markers.* Cambridge: Cambridge University Press.

Schuetze-Coburn, S. (1987). *Topic management and the lexicon: A discourse profile of three-argument verbs in German.* Unpublished master's thesis, University of California, Los Angeles.

Smith, W. (1996). Spoken narrative and preferred clause structure: Evidence from modern Hebrew discourse. *Studies in Language, 20,* 163–189.

Thompson, S. A. (1997). Discourse motivations for the core–oblique distinction as a language universal. In A. Kamio (Ed.), *Directions in functional linguistics* (pp. 59–82). Amsterdam: Benjamins.

Thompson, S. A., & Mulac, A. (1991). A quantitative perspective on the grammaticization of epistemic parentheticals in English. In E. C. Traugott & B. Heine (Eds.), *Approaches to grammaticalization: Vol. 2. Focus on type of grammatical markers* (pp. 313–329). Amsterdam: Benjamins.

Tomasello, M. (1992). *First verbs: A case study of early grammatical development.* Cambridge: Cambridge University Press.

Chapter 3

Human Cognition and the Elaboration of Events: Some Universal Conceptual Categories

Suzanne Kemmer
Rice University and
Max Planck Institute for Evolutionary Anthropology

One of the burning questions in cognitive science is how human beings conceptualize the world around them. How do we categorize experience, such that we can break it down for purposes of conceptual manipulation (i.e., thought) and communication? To what extent do all humans categorize experience in the same way? This leads to the second question: What conceptual categories are present in human cognition in general, as opposed to categories specific to individual languages, or that distinguish us from our primate relatives?

These questions have been approached from many different angles and with various types of methodology, including, for example, studies of infant cognition (Mandler, 1992, 2000), language acquisition (Bowerman, 1996; Slobin, 1985, 2000; Tomasello, 1992, 2000), and comparative primate cognition (Savage-Rumbaugh, Shanker, & Taylor, 1998; Tomasello & Call, 1997).

Two fields that have approached these questions using linguistic evidence from adult language are cognitive linguistics and language typology. Cognitive linguistics investigates how lexical and grammatical form express semantic content, relating such linguistic analyses to independently attested cognitive capacities and processes (Langacker, 1987; Talmy, 2000). Language typology also studies the relation of linguistic form and meaning, but specifically via the investigation of the range and the limits of cross-linguistic variation via broad-based samples of the world's languages (Comrie, 1981; Greenberg, 1978).

In this chapter I bring together the latter two kinds of investigation in an approach that can be called *cognitive typology*. The main claim in this research is the following: Recurrent typological patterns reveal the distinctness of a number of basic contrasting types of events to which human beings are sensitive. These categories are not purely perceptual, as they are not directly dependent on perceptual information; rather, they are conceptual categories, used in the chunking and organization of conceptual information for purposes of formulating, manipulating, and communicating thought. The categories I focus on are two basic categories of transitivity of the clause, as well as two other related categories, the reflexive and middle. I show that these four categories together define a restricted conceptual space that constrains the possible types of grammatical systems available for the expression of basic kinds of events. In the process I identify an important conceptual parameter, the degree of elaboration of events, which is not only fundamental for this semantic domain but has general ramifications for human conceptualization and language.

THE COGNITIVE-TYPOLOGICAL APPROACH

The approach of cognitive typology is to observe cross-linguistically recurrent patterns of linguistic expression, particularly grammatical expression. That is, we look at how languages systematically make distinctions in form to express differences in meaning, or, equally systematically, fail to make such distinctions. Thus we can find patterns in the ways that particular forms of expression are used in human languages to convey particular kinds of events or situations.

The idea is that if many languages are found to systematically distinguish between two similar meanings by means of a difference in grammatical coding, then such a difference is cognitively significant; the more widespread the differentiation is cross-linguistically, the more likely it is that there is a universal human propensity to pay attention to such a distinction. Conversely, if languages are recurrently found to subsume two meanings under a single form of expression, then this potential for lack of differentiation is also significant: it suggests that the meanings are cognitively closely related.[1]

For example, looking at how the notion of possession is treated in the languages of the world, we find that in many languages, in order to say that a person possesses something, one says literally that the thing possessed is

---

[1]The first proponent and explicator of this methodology and its theoretical basis that I am aware of is Charles Ferguson in his typological study of case (Ferguson, 1970).

"at" or "with" or "in the hand of," or "at the house of" the possessor (Heine, 1997). For example, in So, a language of East Africa, the predicative possessive construction is formed as in (1):

(1) *So*
    mek Auca eo-a   kus-in
    Neg Auca home-LOC skin-PL
    "Auca has no clothes." (Lit.: "Skins are not at Auca's home.")
    (Heine, 1997, p. 92, cited from Carlin, 1993, p. 68)

In this language, the construction used for expressing a possessive relation has the same structure as that used for talking about the actual location of an object or person. This formal relation between possession and location is extremely widespread in human languages.

In other languages, possession is treated formally differently from predication of location. In English, we say *I have a book* rather than **the book is at/ by/with me*, and similarly in many of the languages of Europe. In Guaraní, a South American language, there is a possessive construction that simply links an optional possessor subject with a possessive noun phrase, as in (2):

(2) *Guaraní*
    (Che) che-ajaka.
    (I)   my-basket
    "I have a basket." (Velazquez, 1996, p. 69)

Locational expressions in this language, in contrast, do not make use of possessive markers, but instead generally require adpositional phrases spelling out the location of an object.

Examining the relations of expressions for location and for possession cross-linguistically leads to the conclusion that these categories are related cognitively, and further, that of the two, location is the more fundamental category. Possessive constructions are often transparently locational in form and meaning, or else they are at least historically derived from locational expressions, whereas the opposite relation is rare or nonexistent. Given that we can compare and analyze the relation between the two meanings, and show a plausible link between them, it makes sense to hypothesize that the two categories frequently share the same forms of expression precisely because they are notions that are seen to be similar by humans. At the same time, the fact that some languages treat these same two semantic categories quite differently shows they are conceptually differentiable. In fact, the patterns of relation found suggest that each of these categories constitutes a separate conceptual archetype that can attract its own formal marking pattern; and that both are related to a third category, the predication of existence, which is also frequently based on locative expression (Clark, 1978).[2]

Using this basic methodology of comparing form–meaning relationships in the languages of the world for many different grammatical categories allows us to examine which kinds of situations human beings are likeliest to group together, and which they are likeliest to distinguish. In this way we can gain an insight into what kinds and properties of things and situations are significant for the human mind, and hence made the basis of conceptual categories. Further, it allows us, through semantic analysis, to work out the precise relations between the categories distinguished. The result of such an investigation is a network of relations among categories, a kind of "semantic map" of the conceptual domains investigated (Kemmer, 1993a).

The question arises why grammatical categories in particular should be examined, rather than, say, comparing lexical concepts across languages. And why focus on the structure of the clause and its components, rather than other linguistic units? I consider each of these issues in turn.

Typologists focus on grammar, that is, the categories associated with morphology and syntax, because the categories of grammar found in the languages of the world appear to be highly constrained in their meaning or function, compared to the meanings of ordinary lexical items, suggesting some cognitive limitations on the categories of grammar (cf. Talmy, 1988). Thus, for example, when it comes to encoding a function like tense, which (summarized simply) expresses the possible temporal relations between a described event and the moment of speech, there is a relatively small inventory of distinctions that tense morphemes or constructions are found to encode, compared with the infinite number of distinctions that are logically possible (Comrie, 1985). Similarly, for the case of locative and possessive predications considered earlier, which appear to represent universal functional categories in human language, there is only a rather limited number of types of such constructions found (Heine, 1997).

The meanings of ordinary lexical items, on the other hand, by no means fall into such small ranges of possible meanings. Unlike grammatical elements, ordinary words are to all appearances open-ended in regard to the concepts they can encode, and these concepts vary much more dramatically across languages as to how they are expressed (if at all). Lexical words typically convey rich and specific meanings that relate fairly directly to the physical, social, and cultural worlds of the speakers that use them. For example, a language might have words for particular recognized cultural concepts

---

[2]Clark (1978) used a diverse sample of 30 languages to demonstrate the cross-linguistic marking patterns linking locative, existential, and two predicative possessive types, possessor–topic and possessed–topic constructions. She did not speak of conceptual archetypes, or relate the semantic categories in significant detail, but her study foreshadows later cognitive–typological theory in many respects.

and artifacts like "the stillness of dawn" or "manioc beer strainer," for which other languages lack words. Sometimes such lexical items are paraphrasable by longer expressions in other languages, as in the examples just given, but quite often capturing the relevant concept in another language in even a minimally adequate way is quite difficult, especially if the cultures are very different. Even languages spoken by groups that are broadly socially and culturally similar (such as the linguistic populations of Europe) present innumerable cases of lack of lexical correspondences and of culture-specific lexical concepts, as any bilingual or translator knows.

One might think that perhaps comparing words expressing universally shared human experiences would reveal at least some universal human lexical categories. However, we run into difficulties even here. Words for apparently universal cultural experiences or entities such as "mother," "father," "hand," "eat," "sleep," and "die" certainly do share some conceptual content that presumably corresponds to aspects of universal human experience; yet on closer inspection the meanings of the words compared turn out to differ considerably from language to language. For example, even words meaning "mother" or "child" do not uniformly point to the same class of entities across languages. In some languages the same word is used for a biological mother of a particular child as well as for the sisters of that woman. Some languages have two words for "child," depending on whether the person described is being referred to as someone's offspring, or simply as a non-adult human. Lexical items in languages essentially represent the conventional cultural categories of entities and relations to which their speakers find it useful to make frequent reference. The vocabularies of languages vary from one another precisely to the extent that their cultures do.[3]

Grammatical meanings, on the other hand, are relatively abstract, sometimes extremely so, and are in general much less obviously relatable to cultural specificities. They are simply much more comparable across languages than the meanings of lexical items. Studying the more highly constrained systems of grammatical categories has allowed a good deal of progress to be made in identifying the range of possible conceptual categories expressed in grammar (cf. e.g., Talmy, 1988). Because these categories are in general abstract and hence not directly "given" in perceptual or other experience, and they recur in a relatively uniform way across lan-

---

[3]In a fascinating research program, Wierzbicka (1992, *inter alia*) has developed a "natural semantic metalanguage" that involves breaking down the meanings of lexical items (as well as grammatical categories) into a set of universal semantic lexical primitives. Differences among languages are seen in this program as being a matter of differences in the conventional combinations of the primitives. Although the analyses produced within this program are very insightful, identifying the set of primitives needed for the vast and open-ended range of lexical concepts found in human languages has proven to be an elusive task. It is at any rate clear that a great deal more generally accepted progress has been made on the grammatical front.

guages, we must conclude that such categories are highly significant from a human, cognitive standpoint.[4]

The second question raised is why the linguistic structures compared across languages by typologists are generally clause-level structures and their components, rather than larger units such as the structure of texts or extended chunks of discourse. The reason for this level of focus is that the clause is the linguistic unit that most closely corresponds to the human conceptualization of simple events, that is, particular conceptualizations of situations or occurrences that are formulated in language in the course of speaking and understanding.

There is, it must be emphasized, no uniformity among languages as to precisely how a non-linguistic, perceived situation will be broken down into clauses for linguistic expression; in fact, there is no such uniformity even among speakers of the same language, given that languages afford their speakers many choices. Nevertheless, there is a relation between perceived situations and their expression in clauses; this relation is mediated by the conceptualization of *events*, which fall into a relatively small number of types. An event type can be thought of as a unit of conceptual structure that allows human beings to quickly and conveniently structure complex, temporally extended experience for purposes of thought and communication.

There appears to be a common core of simple conceptual event types that can be expressed in single clauses across languages, and that reflect certain characteristics of the external world, our perceptual facilities and universal human experience.[5] These types can be fruitfully analyzed and compared; and one can generalize over them to arrive at a description of the basic structure of a simple event (as is done in the following paragraph). Against the backdrop of this common core, languages show considerable variation as to how much and what types of information they can put

---

[4]It must be mentioned that lexicon versus grammar is not a dichotomy, but a continuum. More general and schematic lexical items tend to be recruited for expressing grammatical concepts and functions and gradually become less lexical and more grammatical in form and content over time, a process called grammaticalization (see, e.g., Bybee, Pagliuca, & Perkins, 1994; Heine, 1997; Hopper & Traugott, 1993). The study of grammaticalization is part and parcel of the study of linguistic typology.

[5]This assumption, although not often stated, underlies much cognitive linguistic research; see, for example, the work collected in Talmy (2000). My particular formulation of the relation between the world, event conceptualizations, and clauses is taken essentially from Pawley (1987), who compared English and Kalam, languages of radically different structural type. He found that the two languages differ greatly in the set of conceptual situations that can be expressed as a single clause, but that there is a shared set of "more or less isomorphic" conceptual situations that can be so expressed in both languages. This finding accords with my own experience in typological research, and I take such overlaps to be indicative of common conceptual event structures in human language and their natural correlation with simple clause structure.

into a clause, which aspects of the information communicated by the clause are highlighted versus backgrounded, and even the extent to which a conceptualization is integrated into a single conceived event (single eventhood, like single-clause status, is a matter of degree). And, as we see in the course of this chapter, sometimes a single language will provide the resources for speakers to systematically vary the way a given situation is viewed, such that the internal structure of an event can be brought into greater or lesser focus. Thus, event structure is to a certain extent language-specific, even utterance-specific. Nevertheless, all such variation consists essentially of conventional modifications, along certain specifiable dimensions, of the same basic conceptual structures: the simple basic event types that can be expressed in simple clauses in the languages of the world.

Now we come to the basic semantic structure of a simple event. Events are composed of *participants* (the entities involved in situations) and the *relations* among those participants. For example, consider the meaning of a sentence in the form of a simple clause, like *Have some candy.* Here one participant (the unexpressed "you" in the situation) is in a particular relation, in this case a potential possession and consumption relation, with another participant, "some candy." Event structure refers to the overall configuration of participants in an event and their relations: how many participants are there, and what roles do they play in the event in terms of initiation (or lack thereof) of action, impingement on one another, other kinds of relations to one another (e.g., participant roles of various types), and the temporal properties of the predicate relations.

In the following section I introduce a grammatical distinction that is extremely well attested cross-linguistically, and which, I claim, corresponds to fundamental cognitive categories in the form of two basic event structure types that humans utilize in organizing and expressing thought.

TWO BASIC EVENT STRUCTURES

It is well known that languages of the world typically make a formal distinction between transitive and intransitive clauses. At a minimum, the distinction between the two clause types includes the fact that a transitive clause typically has two noun phrases (or other signals of referential participants, such as agreement markers), whereas an intransitive clause has one.

But in addition, many languages have ways of distinguishing the two clause types either distributionally and/or with distinctive overt marking. A common distributional distinction is one in which the verbs of a language divide into classes defined by their possibility of use in transitive or intransitive clauses. Such a division is made with varying degrees of sharpness in a great many languages. Further, there is a widespread occurrence in languages of overt markers that can be added to a verb of one class (i.e., a verb usually or always found in one of the two clause types) to make it usable in the other clause type. Such transitivizing and detransitivizing morphology is extremely common in languages, and exists even where the distinction between transitive and intransitive verbs is not a sharp one (i.e., even in languages where there are many verbs that can be used in clauses of either type).

We might at first take the widespread existence of a formal transitivity distinction to be a reflection of the structure of the world: Some events involve two entities, one acting on the other (as in *I ate some cake*), whereas others simply involve one (as in *She ran away*).

However, it soon becomes evident when examining languages that whether a given verb can appear in a transitive or intransitive clause is not strictly predictable from some language-independent notion of how many entities are involved in a particular kind of event. The inventories of intransitive versus transitive verbs found across languages are far from lining up neatly according to whether a given verb meaning intuitively has one or two participants associated with it. Sometimes a verb that is intransitive in one language most closely corresponds to a transitive verb in another, or vice versa. For example, the English verb *go*, an intransitive verb of motion, can occur with various prepositional elements (as in *go around, go across*, etc.) to describe motion with respect to some landmark. To describe essentially the same scenes in Luo, speakers must choose from a set of transitive verbs, including *yoro* "to go across," *luoro* "to go around," *donjo* "to go in," where the landmark is expressed as a direct object and there is no preposition. Even in the same language, we find different ways of expressing the same basic idea, one transitive, one intransitive: English, after all, does have transitive verbs like *cross* and *enter* alternating with the intransitive *go* + PREPOSITION structures.

Because every language, whether overtly or distributionally, shows some difference between transitive and intransitive structures, and because there are myriad and widespread formal manifestations of such a difference, we must conclude there is something cognitively significant about this difference. Despite the lack of a predictable correlation within or across languages between the idea of a particular action and a particular transitivity structure, there is nonetheless a set of strong regularities that lead us to an understanding of transitivity and its function in language.

For example, it is predictable that the transitive clause structure in any given language will be the structure most typically used with verbs of physical contact or force in which one entity volitionally acts on another, like English *hit, punch, beat,* and so forth. And it is also predictable that an intransitive structure will be used with verbs of animate entities moving through space, such as *go, run, swim* and similar. Many other types of verbs may fit into each of these structures; but cross-linguistically, these two classes of verbs show the most consistent association with simple transitive and intransitive structures respectively. Further, although some crossover use of each of these verb classes with the other structure is possible, it is precisely with such uses that one finds evidence of a less natural "fit." For example, the contact verbs in English resist placement in an intransitive structure (?*I hit*); such usage is restricted to particular kinds of participants and interpretations (as in *the bomb hit*) and hence, is far less frequent than the transitive use of such verbs. Similarly, although common English verbs of motion through space might be used in a transitive structure, the direct object is likely to be of a very restricted type, such as a unit of distance (*run a mile*), or else the interpretation is not simple motion, but caused motion and/or metaphorical motion (*run a business*).

Similar kinds of observations can be repeated across languages in various forms. In some languages, one can or must use special marking, that is, transitivizing or intransitivizing morphology on the verb, to use a verb of one of these classes in the noncorresponding clause structure. In others, the difference is just a matter of distributional frequency: A given motion verb simply occurs more often in an intransitive than a transitive structure; and/or, the most frequently used and semantically general motion verbs occur as intransitives rather than transitives. Taken as a whole, the relation of particular verb types and particular clause structures is not random, but patterned.

These facts support the idea that basic transitive and intransitive clause structures are grammatical manifestations of two important conceptual archetypes: two-participant and one-participant events. Languages differ as to precisely which verbal actions are typically expressed by means of one structure or the other, and moreover within individual languages it is often possible to describe the same occurrence in terms of one or the other structure. But this variation is constrained; certain kinds of actions have a natural affinity for one or the other construction.

Moreover, these two archetypes are experientially based: They correlate with major kinds of "scenes," or types of conceived situations basic to human experience (cf. Goldberg, 1998). The basic transitive structure lines up with humans' propensity to pay attention to actions involving an animate entity volitionally acting on a second entity, and exerting physical force on it that leads to contact. This type of event is what has been termed the *prototypical transitive event* (Givón, 1984) or prototypical two-participant event. The basic intransitive structure corresponds to our conception of situations of motion of animate entities, an event structure called the *prototypical intransitive event*[6] or prototypical one-participant event. Each of these prototype event structures represents what is called a cognitive model (Lakoff, 1987), a rich conceptual structuring of experience that allows us to

---

[6]There are actually four basic intransitive clause structures in human language, identified in an important cross-linguistic study by Stassen (1999). They include, in addition to the intransitive of action (prototypically animate motion) discussed here, clausal predications of location/existence, property/state, and class membership. Each corresponds to its own experiential conceptual scene. Only the intransitive of action is associated with lexical content verbs, rather than grammatical, relatively contentless verbs or with zero expression.

quickly and effortlessly categorize complex information and reason on the basis of such categorizations.

These two important conceptual archetypes, although corresponding broadly to linguistic units (transitive and intransitive clause structures), clearly go beyond language to deeper levels of conceptualization. Mandler (1992) found evidence of these basic event structures already in prelinguistic infants. Among other evidence, Slobin (1985) found that children acquiring different languages early on showed evidence of having developed a category used consistently in the expression of situations involving asymmetrical physical force—even where the categories of the adult languages differed from one another and from the categories the children created.

Thus, the linguistic structures are based on, or as we might put it, grounded in the conceptual archetypes. Both language and conceptualization are flexible enough to allow alternative conceptualizations and forms of expression, a property of the mind that will be of significance in the discussion of the reflexive and middle event types in the following section. But as we will see, conceptualizations that are in some sense less typical or less in line with our most entrenched experiences are given some kind of special marking, such as additional formal complexity; and moreover they evince greater cross-linguistic variability in form.

The transitivity prototypes in effect form the endpoints of a scale, rather than representing a bipolar opposition. Situations come in all degrees of similarity to the basic cognitive transitivity prototypes, and it has been well-documented that certain specific kinds of contextual and discourse properties affect the degree of formal assimilation of clauses to the two prototypical clausal structures (Hopper & Thompson, 1980; Rice, 1987). Deviations from the conceptual prototypes along certain parameters (e.g., coreference of two participants) lead to formal deviations of various sorts from the two basic clausal structures, another manifestation of the special marking referred to earlier. It is worth emphasizing that transitivity is not fundamentally a property of particular linguistic elements such as verbs or even clauses, but is rather an aspect of the cognitive models that structure conceptualizations.

GRAMMATICAL CONSTRUCTIONS
IN AN INTERMEDIATE SEMANTIC DOMAIN:
REFLEXIVE AND MIDDLE

Transitive constructions and intransitive constructions predicating actions are two of the most basic clause structures in human language. A third clause type that occurs in many languages is the reflexive construction, which describes an event in which one participant acts, not on another entity, but on itself. The following examples illustrate reflexive constructions from languages originating in four different continents (Europe, North America, Australia, and Asia, respectively):

(3) *Spanish*
Se   vio   en el espejo.
REFL see.PRET.3SG in the mirror
"S/he saw him/herself in the mirror."

(4) *Nahuatl*
Ti-to-caqui'.
1pl-REFL-hear
"We hear ourselves." (Sullivan & Styles, 1988, p. 34)

(5) *Ngandi*
ṇi-jawulpa-mak-i-č-mayʔ
3MASC.SG-old man-call-REFL-NEG-PRES
"He does not call himself an old man." (Heath, 1978, p. 286)

(6) *Turkish*
Orhan kendini aynada gördü.
Orhan self   mirror saw
"Orhan saw himself in the mirror." (Underhill, 1976, p. 356)

The reflexive is one of a number of what may be called marked clause types (cf. Langacker, 1991, ch. 8). Marked clause types are, intuitively, clause types that are in some sense less basic than unmarked clause types such as simple transitive and intransitive clauses. This non-basic status is indicated in a number of objectively observable ways, considering linguistic properties such as distribution, frequency, and complexity of form, as well as degree of variability. For example, marked types are relatively restricted as compared to more basic types. Unlike the basic types, they do not necessarily occur in all languages, and even within a language show more restrictions on their occurrence. Functionally, they have very specific semantic/pragmatic functions rather than having a very general or default use; and formally they display more structural restrictions. Hence, in terms of both form and function they are less general in occurrence and as a result are less frequent in discourse than corresponding basic types. In addition, they are structurally more variable across languages and are structurally more complex, or at least never less complex, than the unmarked types.[7]

---

[7]The identification of units and structures that are more versus less basic in language is the study of what is called markedness: unmarked categories are more basic, and marked ones are less basic. In a pioneering study of markedness in human language, Greenberg (1966) built on earlier classic work by Trubetskoy and by Jakobson on phonological markedness, extending the theory to morphosyntax. Croft (1991) has further extended the theory in the area of syntactic constructions.

Although most of these markedness criteria have not been investigated in detail for reflexive constructions, the reflexive is generally agreed to be a marked clause type. Considering at least structural complexity, in surveys of reflexive constructions such as Faltz (1977) and Kemmer (1993a), reflexive constructions are always as least as structurally complex as their simple transitive counterparts (and, a fortiori, more so than intransitive action clauses, which, lacking objects, are simpler than basic transitive clauses).

Although reflexive marking is not found in every language, Kemmer (1988, 1993a) found that of 31 languages in geographically and genetically diverse languages surveyed, all had a reflexive construction distinct from the simple transitive and intransitive clause structures. With further searching on a wider database of over 100 languages, only a few languages were identified that do not make a systematic distinction between situations in which the actor is the same as the acted-on entity, and situations in which the two are distinct (e.g., Tongan, Tuvaluan, and some other languages of the South Pacific). This near ubiquity shows that the reflexive is an important conceptual category in language; humans find it functionally useful to distinguish situations in which the two participants involved are distinct entities, from those in which they are the same entity.

We can think of the reflexive as a kind of in-between semantic category, falling between prototypical transitive events, on the one hand, and prototypical intransitive events, on the other. Reflexive constructions mark cases in which, like the typical transitive situation, there are two participant roles, but like the intransitive, there is only a single entity involved. In a sense, in a reflexive situation there are both *two* things involved (two participant roles) and at the same time only *one* thing (one participant playing both roles in the event).

Looking further at the distribution of reflexive marking on particular kinds of situations in languages allows us to refine this characterization further, and in fact to discover yet another closely related conceptual category in the conceptual realm intermediate to the two opposing poles of transitive and intransitive events.

Reflexive constructions are often used in languages to express situations of a person's acting on their own body, for example, shaving, washing, bathing, or grooming the hair; or changing their body position by moving the body into a sitting, standing, or lying position. We can refer to all such actions, for convenience, as body actions. Examples (7) through (10) show the use of the reflexive marker for body actions in languages native to Europe, North America, Africa, and Asia, respectively:[8]

---

[8]In Djola and Turkish, the verbal afffixes shown are not reflexive markers, because in each language they contrast with another form used productively to signal reflexive semantics. I have glossed these affixes MM for "middle marker," which will be explained later.

(7) *Spanish*
Maria se   pein-ó.
Maria 3.REFL comb-PRET
"Maria combed her hair." (lit. "combed herself")

(8) *Nahuatl*
mo-tema.
3SG.REFL-bathe
"S/he bathes him/herself." (Sullivan & Styles, 1988, p. 34)

(9) *Djola*
ni-pɔs-ɔ-pɔs-ɔ   i-ban.
1SG-wash-MM-REDUP 1SG-finish
"I have finished washing." (Sapir, 1965, p. 52)

(10) *Turkish*
çocuk giy-in-di.
child dress-MM-past
"The child got dressed." (Underhill, 1976, p. 359)

Because in such examples the person is acting on him or herself, just as in the cases exemplified in (3) through (6); and because the same marker is used in many languages (e.g., Spanish and Nahuatl) for both kinds of situations, the body action cases in (7) through (10) are often assumed to be semantically identical with reflexive situations. As a result, many grammar writers use body action verbs when giving examples of the reflexive construction in the language they are describing.

However, more in-depth cross-linguistic investigation shows that the two sets of cases are not identical, and considering body action verbs as typical examples of reflexive verbs is mistaken. Rather, body action verbs represent a distinct event type that is related to, yet describably different from, reflexive semantics. This semantic category is called the *middle voice*, and its grammatical expression is termed a *middle marker*.

First let us consider some formal evidence for distinguishing a separate grammatical category that body action verbs exemplify. There are a good many languages that formally distinguish body actions from reflexive constructions, that is, they use two different constructions for these types. In the following, the (a) examples represent body action cases, and the (b) examples reflexive constructions. (The gloss MM stands for middle marker.)

(11) *Luo*
a. Nyako ruak-ore.
   girl   dress-MM
   "The girl got dressed."

   b. Woi her-ore kend-e.
      boy love-MM self-3sg
      "The boy loves himself." (Field data[9])

(12) *Hungarian*
   a. Borotvál-koz-ott.
      shave-MM-PAST.3SG
      "He shaved." (Haiman, 1983, p. 805)
   b. Fel-emel-t-e   mag-á-t.
      up-lift-PAST-3SG self-his-ACC
      "He lifted himself up." (Haiman, 1983, p. 797)

In these languages, there are two constructions, one used productively with transitive verbs in general to form the reflexive construction, and the other, more restricted, used with body action verbs and a range of other situations that are clearly not reflexive in meaning (some of these will be described later). The difference in usage of these constructions goes along with a systematic difference in form: The productive reflexive marker is cross-linguistically almost always a more phonologically substantial form than the middle marker, and is certainly never less substantial, a fact to which I return later.

This systematic differentiation already suggests that there is something special about body actions that distinguish them from reflexives, despite their similar semantics. But the pattern goes further: In languages having such a formal contrast, there is also a systematic meaning distinction that appears when the two constructions are compared.

English is a language that illustrates the pattern very well. Consider the examples of bodily actions given in (13) and (14).

(13) a. He quickly shaved and got dressed.
     b. I don't need a barber to shave me—I shave *myself.*
     c. Tammy dressed herself today.

(14) a. I sat up, looked around, then got up and walked away.
     b. I pulled myself up, looked around, then dragged myself to my feet and staggered away.

The (a) examples illustrate normal uses of body action verbs. In English, these are expressed as intransitive constructions of various sorts; there is no pronominal or other object, so we can think of them as zero-marked. The

---

[9]The Luo data were collected in my Field Methods class at Rice University (1997–1998). It represents a dialect spoken near Lake Victoria in Kenya, which is in some respects different from the Luo represented in published sources available to me. (Tone is not shown here.)

(b) and (c) examples, on the other hand, contain the productive reflexive form PRONOUN+*self,* an overt, phonologically substantial form that designates the acted-on entity.

In addition to the extra reflexive marking found with these body action verbs, the (b) and (c) examples all express situations associated with special circumstances of some type. Example (13b) involves a contrast between two different potential actors, such that the reflexive pronoun points back to one of them, to the deliberate exclusion of the other. From Example (13c) we are likely to infer some out-of-the-ordinary circumstance or some specific kinds of participants, rather than just anyone: For example, we can readily believe that Tammy is a small child who has not hitherto been able to dress herself; or perhaps a woman who is handicapped and has trouble putting her clothes on each morning. In either case, the person described does not have full control of her limbs—it is as though there is some impediment between Tammy's intentionally acting mind, aiming to get dressed, and her relatively passive body. The limbs are not acting in the way normally expected by able-bodied adults, that is, as a direct extension of the will of the acting person.

A similar situation holds in Example (14b). Rather than the relatively effortless motions described in Example (14a), the motions here are effortful—as though the body is a dead weight, rather than a participatory medium for executing the actions directed by the intentional mind. The verbs used are not typical body action verbs this time, but ordinary transitive verbs usually used for designating force applied to inanimate objects (*pull, drag*).

Parallel distinctions are found in other languages with two contrasting constructions. In Russian, for example, we find the following pair, in which the middle marker *-sja* represents the normal way of expressing body actions in Example (15a), but the reflexive marker *sebja* is used in the special case of contrast with another potential participant in Example (15b).

(15) *Russian*
      a. Ja každyj den' moju-s'.[10]
         I every day wash-MM
         "I wash every day."
      b. Ja myl   sebja.
         I washed self
         "I washed *myself.*" (not someone else) (Haiman, 1983, p. 804)

In (15b), there is a contrast made between potential objects of the washing that the speaker has in mind—another person, versus the speaker him

---

[10]The Russian middle marker *-sja* is in standard transliteration orthography spelled *s'* after vowels.

or herself. The result is a special emphasis put on the direct object, expressed as extra stress.

In language after language in which such a pair of constructions is found, a similar semantic differentiation holds. The fuller reflexive construction, when used with body actions, is the unusual case: It denotes a contrast between two potential participants, as in Examples (13b) and (15b); or a separation between the acting and acted-on entities, as in (13c) and (14b), that is not the usual conceptualization for humans carrying out body actions.

These differences in the meaning of the reflexive and middle constructions in body actions lead us to conclude that the fuller, reflexive constructions have an essentially different function from the lighter constructions more usually used for body actions. Moreover, these cases provide us with a clue as to how to characterize the semantics of each of these constructions, in a way that not only captures the cross-linguistic generalizations regarding their contrasting use, but also more generally the distribution of reflexive and middle constructions in all languages.

Let us consider first the range of application of reflexive and middle constructions. Where there are two constructions in a given language, the fuller one is always the general reflexive form, and is thus used productively with transitive verbs to form marked, reflexive forms. This systematic alternation with simple transitive events suggests that the reflexive is considered a special case of such events—the case in which the two participant roles that are evoked in a transitive event happen to be filled by the same entity.

The other form, in contrast, cannot be used across the board with transitive verbs: It is restricted to particular semantic verb classes that include the body action classes exemplified earlier. All such "light" forms can be used with at least some verbs designating typical actions performed on the body. Moreover, they are typically also found with other, non-reflexive classes of verbs: verbs of cognition and emotion, for example, as well a particular kind of reciprocal action, verbs of spontaneous process, and a number of other recurrent categories described in Kemmer (1993a). The verb roots found with this construction have a number of things in common: for one thing, none are prototypically transitive verbs, that is, verbs whose meanings are across languages associated with transitive constructions. A number of these non-reflexive predicate types, for example, the verbs of cognition, are generally *intransitive* in their usual (non-reflexive-marked) use, rather than transitive. In fact, very often there is no corresponding non-marked form at all for verbs found with the lighter construction, whether body action verbs or not. Such non-alternating forms are called "deponents." Middle-marked deponents are typically found, and are perhaps universal, in languages with middle markers. Some examples of light-marked deponents include Turkish *Is-in* "become warm," Latin *vereo-r* "fear," and

Old Icelandic *grøna-st* "turn green." Full reflexive forms, in contrast, are never deponents.

These observations lead us to an explication of the semantics of the two types. Reflexive and body action verbs have in common the fact that they refer to situations in which there is an entity that is in some sense the source or origin of the event, as well as at the same time being an entity affected by the event. This entity plays in both cases what we might call an initiating and an endpoint role in the conception of the event.

Beyond this, the event structures of reflexive and body action verbs diverge. With reflexive semantics, the types of predicates that occur are those with an inherent conception of two roles and two participants in those roles—that is, prototypical transitive events. The reflexive marks the unexpected case that those two roles are filled by the same individual. The body action situations, on the other hand, are different—they are events in which the initiating and affected entity are *predictably* the same, that is, the sameness is inherent to the semantics of the predicates. There is no expectation that the two will be different entities; only one entity is thought to be involved in such actions in the first place. Thus, the two kinds of events differ in how conceptually distinguished the participants are from one another. In the reflexive, two roles are distinguished that are both played by one individual;[11] in the body action type, there is not even the conceptual differentiation of two participant roles. The body action types have, in effect, a partially fused participant conception: The participant is conceptually complex enough to have both an initiating and an endpoint aspect, but not so conceptually differentiated as to have two full-blown participant roles associated with it.

The cases of the body actions unusually expressed with reflexive markers illustrated in (13b), (13c), (14b), and (15b) support this analysis. In the case of contrast (13b and 15b), the linguistic context introduces an idea of two roles, potentially filled by separate participants. When a reflexive marker is used contrastively with a body action, it is consistent with the universal function of reflexive markers—to signal the unexpected identity of the actor and acted-on participant. The contrastive context, however, has effectively forced a differentiation between aspects of an entity that are not usually distinguished.

The analysis holds also for the case of reflexives used with participants lacking full control over the body, as in (13c) and (14b) (also 12b). An im-

---

[11]Talmy (2000, pp. 460–461) described the English reflexive construction in the realm of mental events (such as *control oneself, restrain oneself*) in terms of "the divided self": the controlling aspect of a person pitted against unconscious or involuntary desires. There are some fascinating complexities of mental predicates in interaction with both reflexive and middle marking that require deeper analysis than I am able to give them here; suffice it to say that mental events are quite intermediate semantically and are susceptible to either reflexive or middle construal (cf. Kemmer, 1993a, pp. 127–142).

pediment or other lack of full control is an indication of a separation between acting on and acted-on entities that is unusual with ordinary grooming or other body type actions. Such actions normally have a single participant that is not overtly distinguished into the two aspects of body and mind:
The two potentially distinguishable aspects are, except in these unusual
kinds of situations where there is a special reason to highlight this duality,
conceptually fused into a single, less differentiated entity.

    The partial conceptual fusion of participants characteristic of the middle
is mirrored by the more minimal, morphologically fused expression conventionally found with body action types, that is, the light forms. Reflexive
markers are very often full lexical forms, for example, nouns or pronouns
serving as direct objects, whereas the form used in the expression of body
actions is typically a bound morpheme, or else simply an intransitive construction of some sort (i.e., it has no overt marking separate from the verb
root). This situation is illustrated in Hungarian in (12), in which the middle
verbal affix -kod-/koz- is contrasted with the full, inflected noun object mag.
Sometimes, as in Luo (Example 11b), the reflexive form is efffectively composite, consisting of the middle marker with the addition of another element, often lexical. In still other cases, both forms are bound verbal affixes,
but the reflexive simply has more phonological material than the other
form (e.g., Djola -ɔrɔ "REFLEXIVE MARKER" vs. -ɔ "MIDDLE MARKER"). I am
not aware of any case in which the reverse relation in substance holds; the
reflexive form is always at least as substantial as the middle form, and in
most cases more substantial. The relation of the form and the meaning of
middle and reflexive markers is taken up in more detail in the following
section.

    Body actions, it turns out, represent only the most prototypical type of
situation among many that share the property of having lower conceptual
differentiation of participants vis-à-vis the reflexive. Other kinds of events
have this property, and are in fact expressed with the same light markers as
the body action types. This is further evidence that languages treat partial
conceptual fusion of participants as a significant property, susceptible to
conventionalization as a grammatical category distinct from the reflexive.
Light marking contrasting with heavy reflexive marking is found recurrently on, besides body actions, verbs of cognition ("think," "consider," "believe," etc.), emotion ("fear," "be happy"), spontaneous process ("break,"
"collapse," "melt," "rot"), and on naturally reciprocal actions ("kiss,"
"touch," "meet"; cf. the later section "Degree of Elaboration of Events"). All
of these cases of lower conceptual differentiation of participants can be referred to as middle categories.

    Each of these semantically middle types is related to the body action types
in specifiable ways, of which I give just one example here. Mental predicates,
which include the cognition and emotion type events, are like the body ac-

tions in that there is a participant that is seen as in some sense initiating the event. The participant called for in such events is a person whose mental action the predicate describes, that is, a conceptualizer. This conceptualizer has to provide some mental initiative for events of these types, if only to direct his or her attention to a perceptual stimulus that gives rise to the thought or emotion. At the same time, the conceptualizer is also an affected participant, who is aware of and indeed participating in the thought or emotion experienced. These types of events are more obviously different from reflexives than the body actions, because it is harder to think of the affected entity (the mental experiencer) as someone acted on. In the case of body actions we can think of the event as a person acting on their own body, and we can even contrast acting on one's own body with acting on someone else's (as in Examples 13b and 15b). Events of cognition, in contrast, are not so readily decomposable into two such aspects of an individual. This is why such events are cross-linguistically generally intransitive: They are intrinsically one-participant events whose single entity, a conceptualizer, resists conceptual decomposition. Mental events in which such a partial decomposition is in fact made are therefore a subtype of middle semantics, one that happens to evince minimal conceptual differentiation.

Reflexive markers, as we saw previously, primarily signal unexpected coreference between two participants. This is their basic function in all languages, including those that that do not differentiate between reflexive and middle constructions. In such languages, the reflexive form extends to cover the body action situations and often the other non-reflexive semantic classes typically found with light verbs as well. For example, the Spanish and Nahuatl constructions illustrated in (3) and (4) are used both as productive reflexives and also for body actions (e.g., 7 and 8) as well as for other middle verb types (cognition, emotion, naturally reciprocal action, spontaneous process, etc.). Yet despite this lack of formal differentiation, the difference between reflexive and the middle semantic types still emerges distributionally—only the middle verb types, including the body actions, exhibit deponent verbs, which, as mentioned earlier, are verbs that lack a transitive counterpart and have middle meaning. Deponents from languages with no formal distinction between reflexive and middle include German *sich nähern* "come close, approach," Spanish *encapuzarse* "cloak oneself or put one's hood on," Kanuri *har-t-in* "wash oneself (while partially dressed)" (Hutchison, 1981), and numerous Guugu Yimidhirr verbs including *daga-dhi* "sit down" and *miira-dhi* "show oneself" (Haviland, 1979, p. 126).

We can conclude from this discussion that the reflexive and the middle are two distinct semantic categories, whose distinctness is shown by the fact that many genetically and geographically diverse languages (Hungarian, Turkish, Djola, English, and Russian, among many others) distinguish them; and, at the same time, whose close semantic relation can be seen from the propensity of many other languages to subsume them under the same formal expression (these include Spanish, Nahuatl, Guaraní, Kanuri, and Guugu Yimidhirr, among a great many others). The closer a given middle use is to the reflexive, in fact, the more likely it is to be given the same formal marking as the reflexive. The body action types are the middle uses that are most similar semantically to the reflexive proper, and indeed they designate the kinds of situations that are most often subsumed under reflexive marking across languages.

A second conclusion we can draw is that the two categories established differ in regard to the degree to which the participants involved in the events are conceptually distinguished from one another. The reflexive distinguishes two participants to the extent that it evokes two distinct participant roles in its conception, which are then signaled as being the same entity. The middle, on the other hand, evokes no such role distinction. There is only one participant, but it is conceptually internally complex, given that reference is made to its inherent initiating and affected aspects.

We have thus identified a conceptual parameter that links and at the same time differentiates the reflexive from the middle. We can call this parameter the *relative distinguishability of participants*. We can also generalize further by noticing that this parameter actually relates all of the categories in the realm of transitivity that we have considered so far. The reflexive, as pointed out in the previous section, falls in between the prototypical transitive and intransitive event types. It is in between in the sense that the entity involved is partially distinguished into two: Unlike the transitive type, which has a full-blown differentiation of two participants and participant roles, the reflexive has one actual entity filling its two participant roles. The middle fuses the participants further, by having a single, internally complex participant. And the prototypical intransitive event type displays the opposite extreme from the transitive: It is characterized by a single and conceptually completely undifferentiated participant.

Figure 3.1 sums up the relation among the four transitivity categories. The categories at the opposite extremes of distinguishability are the transitive and intransitive prototypes; the intermediate ones are the reflexive and middle.

Figure 3.1 effectively represents a semantic map of the type described in the Cognitive-Typological Approach section. The particular set of semantic relations portrayed is based on just one dimension of relationship; it is somewhat analogous to a simple map of a road showing only the sequence of towns lying along it. It is useful in that it shows the relative semantic proximity of the categories along this dimension: the middle is semantically farther away from the transitive and closer to the intransitive prototype. This arrangement generates predictions about which categories are most likely to have similar marking in the languages of the world. Non-contiguous cate-

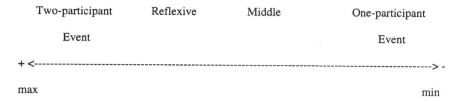

FIG. 3.1. Relation of transitivity categories by degree of participant distinguishability.

gories are predicted to have the same grammatical marking only when the immediately adjacent intermediate categories also share that marking.

A more complex semantic map of the middle and related semantic categories that makes explicit the relations of the various middle subcategories and that takes into account other dimensions of semantic relation is found in Kemmer (1993a, ch. 6).

DEGREE OF ELABORATION OF EVENTS

We can generalize still further when we observe that distinguishability of participants is just one aspect of a more general conceptual parameter. Just as one can distinguish participants to a greater or lesser degree, one can also do the same with the relations among participants, the kinds of events and subevents that, along with the participants, make up the overall event structure.

A good example of the way that languages can distinguish events to different degrees is found with reciprocal constructions, which express situations in which two participants act on each other. In the situation described by *Alice and Ted kissed each other*, Alice and Ted are performing similar actions, but in opposite role configurations: Alice kissing Ted, and Ted kissing Alice. English, like many languages, allows an alternative form of expression for such "mirror-image" actions. In English we can employ verbs with reciprocal semantics intransitively, as in *Alice and Ted kissed*. With the latter expression, it is clear that a single kissing action is portrayed in which both protagonists have engaged. In the alternative, overtly marked reciprocal construction with *each other*, however, we can easily obtain the interpretation that the two kissed each other sequentially, for example, each giving the other a peck on the cheek one after the other. In effect, the two forms of expression provide alternative ways of describing similar situations: one in which there are two separable subevents taking place (temporal separation being one aspect of event separability), and the other in which the event is a relatively undifferentiated whole.

A number of languages, including Russian, Turkish, Hungarian, and Icelandic, have similar differentiations between two reciprocal constructions. As in the case of the body action middle, specific predicates with special inherent semantics are involved; and as with the body actions, a lighter marking is found with these predicates than is found with ordinary reciprocal constructions. The predicates found with light reciprocal marking are those in which the action is very often or expected to be reciprocal between two participants: "argue," "fight," "meet," "wrestle," "embrace," and similar verb meanings, what can be termed naturally reciprocal actions.

Because the light reciprocal marker is in many languages the same as the middle marker, and even when it is not (e.g., in Turkish) it patterns with the middle marker in terms of relative formal substance, and because of the semantic relatability of the light-marked reciprocal category to the middle in terms of distinguishability, it makes sense to consider this special reciprocal a subcategory of middle semantics. The two types of distinguishability (of participants, and of events) can be generalized to an overarching semantic parameter that I call *degree of elaboration of events*: the degree to which the components of an event structure, whether participants or events/subevents, are conceptually distinguished into more fine-grained components.

The notion of degree of elaboration of events, it turns out, is applicable to a wide range of grammatical phenomena, including collective marking on both verbs and nouns (Kemmer, 1993b), and many other kinds of alternating structures involving the degree to which events are conceptually fused versus separated: causatives (Haiman, 1983); complement constructions (Givón, 1980); serial verbs; and noun incorporation constructions (Velazquez, 1996). In all of these cases, languages provide a conventional means for categorizing similar situations as involving, alternatively, elements with more conceptual separation, and those with more conceptual fusion.

This general phenomenon highlights the crucial role of language as a means of providing conventionalized construals, or shared ways of viewing and portraying the situations that are the subject matter of communication (Langacker, 1987). Human language, unlike other forms of animal communication we know about, has the flexibility to provide its users with multiple ways of conceiving and expressing a given situation, adapted to speakers' various discourse and other communicative purposes.

In the case of the degree of elaboration of events, it appears that we are dealing with a capacity that is fundamentally an attentional one. We can, as it were, turn up or turn down the "resolution" that we bring to bear on a given conceptual content, accordingly as our language makes available conventional categories to do so. In the specific case of the voice and transitivity categories we have been discussing, if a language provides the requisite communicative resources, speakers may place a greater focus of attention on an event's component parts, such as participants or component subevents, and the result is a relatively more elaborated event structure such as a reflexive or an ordinary reciprocal. If, on the other hand, it suits such a speaker's communicative purpose to leave these aspects of the situation relatively undifferentiated, then the situation is categorized as a middle. Languages that happen to lack the formal category of middle categorize such conceptually in-between situations as body actions as either reflexive, or as intransitive, one-participant events. In such cases basically middle semantics is assimilated to a certain degree to the semantics of similar constructions and hence given the form of these other constructions.[12]

It is an open question as to whether there are unambiguously identifiable factors that determine how many categories in this general domain a language will have available (within, of course, the constraints that appear to govern the number and types of categorizations made as identified previously). What makes one language, like Spanish, distinguish the reflexive as a distinct conventional category but not the middle, whereas another language, like Turkish or Russian, separately distinguishes all four of the possible categories of voice and transitivity identified here? It is unlikely, given the odd groupings of languages found with these various categories, that such differences correlate with cultural or social factors.

The best that can be said at this point is that what grammatical categories a language conventionalizes, within the available human linguistic possibilities, is a matter of historical contingency. Every language comprises a complex ecology of available and competing forms, a vast system of linguistic knowledge shared to a certain extent by speakers of the language, yet displaying patterns of heterogeneity across subgroups of those speakers. This complex system absorbs motivated innovations and accommodates itself to gradually changing patterns of linguistic usage, as innovations are adopted and spread through the community. A language will have a dedicated middle voice marker just in case at some point in its history some speakers begin to extend an appropriately similar category, such as the reflexive, to express situations that differ semantically from the reflexive, such as the body actions; and when that marker at some point loses its formal connection with the reflexive marker. Precisely this development has taken place in many languages in different parts of the world (see Kemmer, 1993a, ch. 5 for descriptions of these developments).

Whether there are any structural, ecological factors within a linguistic system that will influence if and when such an innovation occurs or begins

---

[12]That middle situations never quite lose their semantic identity as middles, even in languages that have no formal category for the expression of the middle, is seen in a number of ways. For example, there is evidence that middles do not quite behave entirely like reflexives syntactically in languages in which the two are putatively "the same" category (cf. Kemmer, 1993a, pp. 216–218). Further, languages lacking a formal distinction between reflexive and middle show deponents in the same verb categories as those that do have distinct reflexive and middle forms, as noted in the Grammatical Constructions in an Intermediate Domain section.

to spread is unknown. To investigate this, we need a typological database of correlations of grammatical properties in the languages of the world, a vast project that has hardly been attempted.

To summarize, the degree of elaboration of events is a broadly significant linguistic and conceptual parameter. It is a subcase of the general human capacity to construe situations in alternate ways, and of the propensity for the grammatical systems of languages to conventionalize specific construals and potentially contrast such construals. Elaboration of events is a specifically attentional phenomenon, relating to the possibility for viewing situations at different levels of detail, or granularity, dependent on relevant communicative and contextual factors. Although the possibilities for grammatical categories referring to elaboration of events in the domain of transitivity and voice are highly constrained, the existence of any structural factors influencing the precise division of such categories in specific languages is unknown.

ICONICITY

We saw in the section on Grammatical Constructions in an Intermediate Domain that in languages having both a reflexive and a middle marker, these two forms align in a predictable way with the two categories they express. The marking associated with the category of reflexive is recurrently associated with greater phonological substance, compared to the form used for the middle, which is phonologically lighter. Haiman (1983) pointed out this basic contrast, and explained it in terms of two functional motivations, iconic and economic motivation.

Economic motivation refers to the tendency, found in communication systems, to minimize formal signals for known or predictable information. An illustration is found in e-mail addresses, which in the United States do not have a country code suffixed to them. The Internet began as a mode of communication within the United States, so the country of destination was predictable and thus did not need to be overtly signaled. When computers outside the United States began to be linked to the Internet, non-U.S. addresses were the "unexpected" case, and country codes began to be added to clarify the destination.

According to Haiman (1983), the light marker is phonologically light because the identity of actor and acted-on participants is predictable, in fact inherent to body action and naturally reciprocal verbs. Thus such verbs do not require much, if any, extra marking to signal this function. On the other hand, full reflexive and reciprocal forms signal the case of unexpected reflexivity and reciprocality. As we know from the study of markedness, it is the unexpected cases that require extra marking, not only in this semantic domain, but in language and communicative systems more generally.

The other functional motivation described by Haiman (1983) is *iconic motivation*, the tendency to align properties of linguistic form with observably similar properties of linguistic function or meaning, such that form appears to mirror function. In the case of the reflexive/middle contrast, Haiman found that the tendency for reflexives to be free forms, rather than bound verbal affixes, as opposed to the almost inevitably bound middle markers, shows a remarkable iconic correlation with the function of the markers, in terms of the notion of distance: Reflexive forms show more formal distance from the verb root, and at the same time exemplify, in their semantic structure, a greater conceptual separation (and hence distance) between the actor and acted-on entity. The latter, as we saw in the Grammatical Constructions section, are conceptually differentiated into two different participant roles. The middle, the form that is more formally bound up with the verb root, likewise signals an acted-on "entity" that is less conceptually separable from the actor—indeed, from the event itself. A conceptually fused participant displays minimal conceptual distance between its initiating and affected aspects.

Both of these two independently attested motivations, the iconic and the economic, are operative in the case of the middle and reflexive and the two types of reciprocal, as Haiman showed. I would like to go further and say that conceptual distance is just one aspect of what we have identified as degree of elaboration of events; and secondly, that the correlation goes beyond the categories Haiman considered to the broader domain of transitivity introduced in the section on Two Basic Event Structures.

First, let us consider what conceptual dimension is at issue in these categories. Iconic motivation is operating not just in terms of distance, but also of what we might call "weight" or substance. Just as degree of formal distance mirrors conceptual distance, degree of formal weight or substance also corresponds to the degree of conceptual substance associated with the respective semantic categories expressed by the two forms. The more conceptual "material" there is in a given expression, the more formal substance there will be to signal it. Formal substance comprises segmental material and other phonological properties of a marker; morphological substance is measured in terms of degree of morphological/lexical autonomy (degree of boundness and invariability); and syntactic substance in terms of syntactic autonomy and degree of constituency. Conceptual substance corresponds to the degree of elaboration of an event: how distinct are the participants, from one another and from the event itself (this is degree of distinguishability of participants); to what extent are the events "pulled apart" into temporally separable subevents (degree of distinguishability of events); and most generally, what and how many things, roles, and relations are identified in the conceptualization the speaker wants to get across or to understand. It is this "pulling apart" of participants, elaborating them into conceptual units in their own right, that gives the effect of adding conceptual distance to an expression.

When we think about it, a general correlation between degree of elaboration of events, and the amount of formal substance used to talk about the events, makes functional sense. We can expect that speakers will reach for more linguistic material to express the events and participants they wish to place in the forefront of consciousness and attention, and will leave unexpressed or minimally expressed those aspects of the scene that are not, for whatever reason, placed in the communicative foreground. If the reason for this attentional backgrounding happens to be that such aspects are already known or predictable, then we have a convergence between iconic and economic motivations.

What is interesting about the particular correlations found in the reflexive and middle domain (and the reciprocal domain) is that they go beyond a general or rough correlation between amount of form and amount of content. In this case, we find that some significant subset of languages has developed a grammatical opposition between minimally contrasting pairs associated with rather fine distinctions in degree of elaboration and, moreover, these precise distinctions are cross-linguistically recurrent. These facts suggest that this particular correlation has a specific function. What this function is, is not obvious, but we can suggest as a first hypothesis that such a strong and precise iconic correlation in the realm of reflexive, reciprocal, and middle semantics perhaps makes the associated conceptual distinctions and their corresponding forms easier to learn and/or process. The correlation might have a partially redundant communicative function such that, in effect, the amount of formal substance of the linguistic form helps to actually signal the amount of conceptual substance comprising the event to be communicated.

The question of the function of iconicity and economy in the learning and processing of language has been barely recognized as an issue in linguistics, let alone explored in any detail. Yet such investigation promises to shed light on one of the most fascinating aspects of human cognition, and one which may link human communication functionally with the communicative systems of other organisms.

SOME RESULTS AND CONCLUSIONS

Having examined the range of possibilities in marking patterns in the semantic domain of reflexive and middle marking, we can draw some interesting conclusions about human conceptual organization.

First, it is significant that human language recurrently provides grammatical distinctions for a conceptual dimension like degree of participant distinguishability. Instead of having a simple one- versus two-participant distinction in clause structure, which would presumably be grounded in some human cognitive ability to perceive that either one or two things (or groups of things) are carrying out particular roles in an event, languages overwhelmingly tend to add a third category, the reflexive. The reflexive covers cases that are two-participant-like, yet also one-participant-like: A person acting on him or herself is clearly just one entity, but it is one that, by fulfilling two participant roles in the same event, effectively functions like two entities. Then, a smaller number of languages have a fourth grammatical category for an even more subtly "in-between" category, the middle, which is designed to express situations in which there is only one participant, but one that is conceived as in some measure internally complex.

A second noteworthy result is that the scale of transitivity, which had been found independently to be of importance in human language, correlates with the more general conceptual dimension of degree of elaboration of events. The categories of reflexive and middle exist in order to express divergences from canonical or archetypal event types falling at opposite extremes along the scale of semantic transitivity, which correlates directly with a scale of relative degree of elaboration of events. Marking systems in the reflexive/middle domain integrally involve alternative conceptualizations of participant structure and event structure as a whole. Languages may differ as to the morphosyntactic means they have conventionalized for coding such differences in conceptualization, but the variation is highly constrained by the underlying conceptual system.

Thus we have a situation in which (a) humans make a finer-grained set of conceptual distinctions than would be warranted by the sheer perceptual differentiation between one entity versus two; (b) the range of conceptual distinctions is potentially infinite, because once cut loose from perception, all degrees of variation in conceptual event structure along the relevant parameters are logically possible; yet (c) only a maximum of four distinct grammatical categories are found in the languages of the world to express differentiations in degree of participant distinguishability and more generally elaboration of events. The attested variation in languages as to precisely which types of situations are grammatically distinguished in the reflexive/middle realm is thus sharply limited, both by the semantic parameters defining the variation space, and also by the semantic relations between the various categories. Categories closest to one another semantically are the ones found to be grouped together in terms of grammatical expression.

The immediate significance of the analysis presented here is that it has allowed us some insight into the question of what is universal about certain known grammatical categories, and what aspects of such categories are language-specific. Moreover, these formal categories can now be linked with specific, describable categories of human thought.

In addition, the analysis raises some far broader questions, including the following: What is the role of iconicity and economy in grammatical structure, and to what extent do these and other functional motivations link language with other communication systems? (For some discussion of these motivations in biological systems, see Haiman, 1994). In regard to the degree of elaboration of events, is attunement to this conceptual dimension species-specific; and if so, where does it come from? Is it acquired experientially, and if so, how? Similarly for the apparent limit on the number of categorial distinctions in this conceptual realm: Why is there such a limitation, and in what way does it relate to our general conceptual make-up? Regarding the most general ability supporting these conceptual attunements and constraints, is human beings' capacity for alternate construal of situations shared to any degree by other species? Or is such conceptual flexibility a hallmark of humanity?

I have not answered these broader questions here, but I hope to have succeeded in the more immediate aim of demonstrating the potential for the study of cognitive language typology to shed light on human conceptual capacities and the categorization of experience.

ACKNOWLEDGMENTS

This chapter was prepared in part with the generous support of the Max Planck Institute for Evolutionary Anthropology in Leipzig where I was a visiting research scientist in 2000. I am grateful to Michael Tomasello for sponsoring my visit and to the colleagues at the Institute for a wonderfully stimulating research environment. Thanks also to Michael Barlow for comments on an earlier version of the manuscript and to Maura Velazquez for helpful discussion of Guaraní. All errors are my own responsibility.

REFERENCES

Bowerman, M. (1996). The origins of children's spatial semantic categories: Cognitive vs. linguistic determinants. In J. J. Gumperz & S. C. Levinson (Eds.), *Rethinking linguistic relativity* (pp. 145–176). Cambridge: Cambridge University Press.

Bybee, J., Pagliuca, W., & Perkins, R. (1994). *The evolution of grammar: Tense, aspect and modality in the languages of the world.* Chicago: University of Chicago Press.

Carlin, E. (1993). *The So language.* (Afrikanistische Monographien 2.) Cologne: Institut für Afrikanistik, Universität Köln.

Clark, E. V. (1978). Locationals: Existential, locative, and possessive constructions. In J. H. Greenberg (Ed.), *Universals of human language: Vol. 4. Syntax* (pp. 85–121). Stanford, CA: Stanford University Press.

Comrie, B. (1981). *Language universals and linguistic typology.* Chicago: University of Chicago Press.

Comrie, B. (1985). *Tense.* Cambridge: Cambridge University Press.

Croft, W. (1991). *Syntactic categories and grammatical relations: The cognitive organization of information.* Chicago: University of Chicago Press.

Faltz, L. (1977). *Reflexivization: A study in universal syntax.* Unpublished doctoral dissertation, University of California, Berkeley. (Reprinted 1985, New York: Garland)

Ferguson, C. (1970). Grammatical categories in data collection. *Working papers in language universals* 4, F1–F15. Stanford, CA: Project on Language Universals, Stanford University.

Givón, T. (1980). The binding hierarchy and the typology of complements. *Studies in Language, 4*(3).

Givón, T. (1984). *Syntax: A functional-typological introduction* (Vol. 1). Amsterdam: Benjamins.

Goldberg, A. E. (1998). Patterns of experience in patterns of language. In M. Tomasello (Ed.), *The new psychology of language: Cognitive and functional approaches to language structure* (pp. 203–219). Mahwah, NJ: Lawrence Erlbaum Associates.

Greenberg, J. H. (1966). *Language universals, with special reference to feature hierarchies.* (Janua Linguarum Series Minor, 59). The Hague, Netherlands: Mouton.

Greenberg, J. H. (1978). (Ed.). *Universals of human language.* Stanford, CA: Stanford University Press.

Haiman, J. (1983). Iconic and economic motivation. *Language, 59,* 781–819.

Haiman, J. (1994). Ritualization. In W. Pagliuca (Ed.), *Perspectives on grammaticalization* (pp. 3–28). Amsterdam: Benjamins.

Haviland, J. (1979). Guugu Yimidhirr. In R. M. W. Dixon & B. J. Blake (Eds.), *Handbook of Australian languages* (Vol. 1, pp. 24–183). Amsterdam: Benjamins.

Heath, J. (1978). *Ngandi grammar, texts, and dictionary.* Canberra: Australian Institute of Aboriginal Studies.

Heine, B. (1997). *Cognitive foundations of grammar.* Oxford: Oxford University Press.

Hopper, P. J., & Thompson, S. (1980). Transitivity in grammar and discourse. *Language, 56,* 251–99.

Hopper, P. J., & Traugott, E. (1993). *Grammaticalization.* Cambridge: Cambridge University Press.

Hutchison, J. P. (1981). *The Kanuri language: A reference grammar.* Madison: University of Wisconsin.

Kemmer, S. (1988). *The middle voice: A typological and diachronic study.* Unpublished doctoral dissertation, Stanford University, Stanford, CA.

Kemmer, S. (1993a). *The middle voice.* (Typological Studies in Language, 23.) Amsterdam: Benjamins.

Kemmer, S. (1993b). Marking oppositions in verbal and nominal collectives. *Faits de Langues, 2,* 85–95.

Lakoff, G. (1987). *Women, fire and dangerous things: What categories reveal about the mind.* Chicago: University of Chicago Press.

Langacker, R. W. (1987). *Foundations of cognitive grammar: Vol. 1. Theoretical prerequisites.* Stanford, CA: Stanford University Press.

Langacker, R. W. (1991). *Foundations of cognitive grammar: Vol. 2. Descriptive application.* Stanford, CA: Stanford University Press.

Mandler, J. M. (1992). How to build a baby II: Conceptual primitives. *Psychological Review, 99,* 587–604.

Mandler, J. M. (2000). Perceptual and conceptual processes in infancy. *Journal of Cognition and Development, 1,* 3–36.

Pawley, A. (1987). Encoding events in Kalam and English: Different logics for reporting experience. In R. S. Tomlin (Ed.), *Coherence and grounding in discourse* (pp. 329–360). Amsterdam: Benjamins.

Rice, S. (1987). *Towards a cognitive model of transitivity.* Unpublished doctoral dissertation, University of California, San Diego.

Savage-Rumbaugh, S., Shanker, S. G., & Taylor, T. J. (1998). *Apes, language, and the human mind.* New York: Oxford University Press.

Slobin, D. I. (1985). Cross-linguistic evidence for the language-making capacity. In D. I. Slobin (Ed.), *The cross-linguistic study of language acquisition: Vol. 2. Theoretical Issues* (pp. 1157–1256). Hillsdale, NJ: Lawrence Erlbaum Associates.

Slobin, D. I. (2000). Form/function relations: How do children find out what they are? In M. Bowerman & S. Levinson (Eds.), *Language acquisition and conceptual development* (pp. 406–449). Cambridge: Cambridge University Press.

Stassen, L. (1999). *Intransitive predication.* Oxford: Oxford University Press.

Sullivan, T. D., & Styles, N. (1988). *Thelma D. Sullivan's compendium of Nahuatl grammar.* (W. R. Miller & K. Dakin, Eds. and Trans.). Salt Lake City: University of Utah Press.

Talmy, L. (1988). The relation of grammar to cognition. In B. Rudzka-Ostyn (Ed.), *Topics in cognitive linguistics* (pp. 166–205). Amsterdam: Benjamins.

Talmy, L. (2000). *Toward a cognitive semantics: Vol. 1. Concept structuring systems. Vol. 2. Typology and process in concept structuring.* Cambridge, MA: MIT Press.

Tomasello, M. (1992). *First verbs: A case study of early grammatical development.* Cambridge: Cambridge University Press.

Tomasello, M. (2000). *The cultural origins of human cognition.* Cambridge, MA: Harvard University Press.

Tomasello, M., & Call, J. (1997). *Primate cognition.* New York: Oxford University Press.

Underhill, R. (1976). *Turkish grammar.* Cambridge, MA: MIT Press.

Velazquez, M. (1996). *The grammar of possession: Inalienability, incorporation, and possessor ascension in Guaraní.* (Studies in Language Companion Series, 33.) Amsterdam: Benjamins.

Wierzbicka, A. (1992). *Semantics, culture, and cognition: Universal human concepts in culture-specific configurations.* New York: Oxford University Press.

Chapter 4

Social Interaction and Grammar

Cecilia E. Ford
University of Wisconsin

Barbara A. Fox
University of Colorado

Sandra A. Thompson
University of California, Santa Barbara

In this chapter we share some of what we find valuable about the study of grammar as sets of practices adapted to social interaction. Clearly, we are not able to cover all the fascinating and fruitful research that has appeared in this area in recent years, but we hope, through several examples from our own work and through references to other research, to spark further interest in the reader. To begin with, let us consider how we conceive of grammar and then how that relates to the centrality of social interaction as a major habitat to which grammar is adapted.

In interactional settings, we can see grammar "at work." By studying people talking, we can gain a deeper appreciation of what grammar must be understood to be. Three major contributions to our understanding of grammar have arisen from this focus on grammar at work.

The first of these is, in our opinion, one of the most significant contributions to recent linguistic scholarship, a view of linguistic structure itself as rooted in, and shaped by, everyday language use (Bybee, 1995, 1998, 2001, in press; Hopper, 1987; Langacker, 1987). This process of "grammaticization" is an ongoing one. Thus grammar cannot be a fixed property of human brains, but is emergent, constantly undergoing revision as it is deployed and redesigned in everyday talk.

The second is a recognition that if linguistics is to include an accounting for language in everyday use, then its perspective on the nature of grammar must be both cognitively realistic as well as interactionally sensible. Conversational data support the position that grammar is a rather loosely organized set of sorted and categorized memories we have of how speakers have resolved recurrent communicative problems (Hopper, 1987, 1988; Weber, 1997). Edelman (1992) suggested that the human brain is exquisitely adapted to be very good at remembering, storing, categorizing, and using routines that have proven useful for solving everyday problems; with frequent repetition, as synapses become strengthened, these routines become crystallized as habits. Grammar can thus be seen as a collection of crystallizations of linguistic routines (Bybee, 1998, 2001, in press; Bybee, Perkins, & Pagliuca, 1994; Haiman, 1994, 1998; Langacker, 1987).

A third contribution to our understanding of grammar at work is the discovery that grammar is tightly intertwined with the interactional activities that people are engaged in (Auer, 1992, 1996; Clark, 1996a, 1996b; Goodwin & Goodwin, 1987, 1992a, 1992b; Schegloff, 1995, 1996a, 1996b). One way in which these activities implicate the nature of grammar is that certain kinds of activities precipitate certain recurrent kinds of grammar. For example, the activities motivating posing questions and giving answers have a number of grammatical consequences (Heritage & Roth, 1995; Schegloff, 1996b; Weber, 1993). But activities can be seen to implicate grammar at more subtle levels as well. There is evidence in favor of a view of the "clause" as being closely related with the way in which people manage the give-and-take of their linguistic interaction, in other words, with the way they negotiate turns, with the business of who will talk when in the service of larger activities. What activities they are engaged in has been shown to have much to do with the grammatical shape that turns take.

Among the far-reaching implications of this approach to grammar is a focus on local, often collocational, rather than global, patterns (Bybee, 1985, 1989, 1995, 2001, in press). To take just one example, let us consider what the data tell us about systematic local patterns in usage that suggest that speakers store and retrieve individual verbs as such rather than as members of "classes." The English verb *remember* is typically considered to be a member of the class of transitive verbs that can take two types of "direct object": it can take an ordinary noun phrase as a direct object, as in:

(1) *She remembered **her keys**[1]*

and it can occur as a "complement-taking predicate" (Noonan, 1985), meaning that it can occur with a "complement" clause as its direct object, such as *that I had locked the door* in a sentence like:

(2) *I remembered **that I had locked the door***

---

[1]Our examples have been taken from a number of sources. We have not attempted to retranscribe them, but have left them as the authors whose works we are citing have them. A transcription summary is provided in the Appendix. Examples in italics are constructed.

In particular *remember* is considered to be a complement-taking predicate in the class of "private verbs" (Biber, 1988; Quirk, Greenbaum, Leech, & Svartvik, 1985) or "verbs of cognition" (Givón, 1980; Noonan, 1985). The construction of such classes of verbs is based on sets of imagined sentences whereby *remember* can be viewed as behaving like other verbs that take similar complements and have similar meanings involving cognition, such as:

> (3) *I **thought** that I had locked the door*
> *I **said** that I had locked the door*
> *I **discovered** that I had locked the door*
> *I **hoped** that I had locked the door*
> *I **forgot** that I had locked the door*
> *I **realized** that I had locked the door*

Grounded in idealized data of this type, the class of transitive, complement-taking verbs of cognition, with *remember* as a prototypical exemplar, seems robust. However, Tao (2001), in an extensive corpus study of the actual everyday usage of the verb *remember*, drew some surprising conclusions, which seriously challenge this view of classes of verbs as falling into neat categories based on imagined similarities in syntactic behavior and meaning.

Among a number of valuable results, of particular relevance to our point here is Tao's (2001) finding that (a) *remember* rarely takes a complement clause, and (b) the environments in which *remember* occurs are unlike those in which other members of the illusory class of cognitive verbs occur. Here is a typical environment for *remember*, from a conversation between a pair of fiancés:

> (4) JEFF: **remember,**
> JILL: .. @@@
> JEFF: .. you're gonna spend the rest of your life with m=e.

Tao noted that in this example, the verb *remember* is used (in the present tense) without any subject, occurs as an imperative, forms an intonation phrase of its own, and is followed by a pause. Syntactically, it is possible to analyze this example as either a verb *remember* followed by a complement clause or as a discourse particle followed by a main clause. Tao suggested that the prosody, rhythm, and pausing all support the second analysis.

Here is another typical environment for *remember*:

> (5) LOIS: she probably **remem[bers]**.
> JANICE: [uh Ev] [elyn,
> EVELYN: [I don't **remember**.

In (5), the verb *remember* occurs twice. In the first instance, it also has no direct object (either a noun phrase or a complement clause), occurs in the present tense, and finishes a turn. In the second instance, it occurs with the pronoun *I*, again has no direct object (either a noun phrase or a complement clause), occurs in the negative in the present tense, and finishes a turn. Tao's quantitative analysis revealed that these are among the highly recurrent properties of instances of *remember* in the data.

Tao concluded that "the entire notion of *remember* as a complement-taking cognitive verb should be called into question," arguing that his findings strongly supported an analysis in which *remember* is seen as an interactional marker of epistemic stance, rather than as a member of a class of transitive cognitive verbs. That is, from an interactional point of view, *remember* is best understood as a marker that indexes the speaker's stance toward a state of affairs. In the case of an example like (4), it also invites the listener's affiliation with this stance, and in the case of an example like (5), it indexes the speaker's uncertainty toward the state of affairs as a response to a previous speaker's invitation to provide information.

We find Tao's study compellingly revealing in showing some of the ways in which an analysis of actual language use in ordinary interactional contexts suggests a very different picture of the storage and retrieval of grammatical patterns than what we would imagine from working with idealized data. In particular, we see patterns emerging at a very local collocational level (what some linguists have referred to as "syntagmatic") rather than at a more global level of stored classes of types of words and morphemes (what some linguists have referred to as "paradigmatic").

Such findings reinforce the view that grammar is a set of local regularities; they further show us that the discovery of these regularities depends on a study of interactional talk engaged in by people going about their everyday activities. Thus we understand grammar as a minimally sorted and organized set of memories of what people have heard and repeated over a lifetime of language use, a set of forms, patterns, and practices that have arisen to serve the most recurrent functions that speakers find need to fulfill.

Considering language from this perspective, conversational interaction is the ontogenetically and phylogenetically first habitat for language development and use, and that it is the arena of language use from which other uses derive (Chafe, 1994; Fillmore, 1981; Schegloff, 1993, 1996b, *inter alia*). Any adequate account of grammar, what has been taken to be linguistic **structure**, must, then, include attention to the functions of language in face-to-face interaction.

Much fruitful research in discourse linguistics over the past several decades has concentrated on cognitive processing and information packaging as the functional bases for linguistic structure, and work on grammar in interaction certainly maintains and builds on that understanding. However, in the "primordial" (Schegloff, 1993, 1996a, 1996b) site of language use, such processing and packaging functions are always intertwined with, and in simultaneous service of, social interactional functions.

In the following section, we present five examples, from our work and from that of colleagues, of the close fit between grammar and social interaction. We have chosen these examples because they display a wide range of ways in which grammar has been shown to be intimately related to the social actions that people are involved in when they talk. We start with showing how grammar is related to the way people construct turns, then move to a discussion of grammar and sequences of turns. Next we talk about the intimate ways in which grammar is involved in the way people repair utterances. We conclude with two specific and much-discussed areas of grammar that recent research has shown to also be intimately intertwined with, and ultimately explainable in terms of, social interaction.

THE SOCIAL RELEVANCE OF GRAMMAR: CASES IN POINT

Coparticipation and the Construction of Turns

The fact that talk in interaction is produced in the presence of active coparticipants brings into play the constant relevance of how and when addressees produce responsive behaviors. There are at least two far-reaching implications of the socially distributed nature of talk-in-interaction: The first has to do with the grammar of turn construction as a resource for the prediction of upcoming points for speaker change. The second involves the input of addressees and how a speaker can use that input as a source for revision and extension in the production of a single turn.

With respect to the units of turn building, it is clear that interactants both build their own turns and closely monitor their interlocutors' turns with special attention to recurrent grammatical and prosodic trajectories. If this were not true, pauses would not have the clear meanings that they evidently do have in interaction. A pause, from a cognitive perspective, is regularly taken to reflect processing time. However, in real time, on-line interaction, one's verbalizations and one's "lapse time" is always given a social meaning. Research on interaction demonstrates unequivocally that split seconds of silence in talk are points of heightened social significance, points where who will speak next and how they will speak are at issue. A pause, though having no verbal reality from a traditional linguistic point of view, can be interpreted in very precise ways by interlocutors. In an oft-cited case from a lecture by Harvey Sacks (1987), we find a speaker responding to a pause by revising a question to what is essentially its opposite:

(6) A: They have a good cook there?
      ((pause))

A: Nothing special?
B: No, everybody takes their turns.

As can be seen from this example, meaning is attached to emergent pauses after grammatically and prosodically complete turns. Thus, prosody and grammar facilitate a critical practice for meaning making in interaction, the practice of either initiating a next turn right at the predictable point of a previous turn's completion or, alternatively, allowing a pause or starting early, both options carrying social meaning. In real-time interaction, grammar and prosody are not only produced with reference to the encoding of information, they are also crucially deployed and monitored in order for speakers to achieve turn transfer. Analysts working closely with conversational data have termed this property of turn construction "projectability" (Sacks, Schegloff, & Jefferson, 1974), and grammar has been implicated as a central resource for the projection of turn trajectories.

The evident attention that speakers give to smooth turn transfer has significant consequences for the ways in which grammar has arisen within the massively recurrent functional environment of turn construction (Sacks et al., 1974, p. 721; Schegloff, 1993, 1996a, 1996b). The work of Lerner (1991, 1996) and of Jefferson (1973, 1983) has, in particular, demonstrated the social meanings that are produced through the close monitoring of a turn's trajectory. Lerner's work has concentrated on the collaborative production of grammatical units and Jefferson has shown how transition spaces are treated with heightened salience, with early starts of next turns being deployed as a means for emphasizing prior knowledge of what is encoded in the overlapped turn. Neither the collaborative production of turns nor the strategic deployment of uptake timing is possible in the absence of the projectability of the unit in progress. This constant need for managing turn projection has clear implications for an account of the psycholinguistic processes of language production in interaction. We see the exploration of projectability as an area in which much research is needed and to which the attention of psychologists could be of great value.

A second consequence of the dynamic social context of language use in interaction relates to the manner in which grammatical units can be revised and expanded during their production, allowing a speaker to be responsive to his or her interlocutor even if that addressee has not yet produced a verbal response. Although sentences have traditionally been analyzed as finished units and as products of single speakers, in language in interaction, empirical evidence implicates the moment-by-moment monitoring of addressee verbal and nonverbal responses in the production of what may appear to be a single authored turn (Goodwin, 1979; Schegloff, 1987).

The work of Charles Goodwin has been essential in demonstrating the interrelatedness of clause grammar and the real time construction of turns, especially as concerns the extension of clauses to meet interactional demands. Goodwin (1979, 1981, 1989) has argued that in building single clauses a speaker may change the course of, add to, or extend, a clause-in-progress in direct and documentable response to interactional considerations, considerations that emerge as the turn itself is being developed. One case that Goodwin has extensively examined involves a turn that is produced by a single speaker, but that in its incremental extensions is addressed to several different speakers until adequate uptake is offered. We reproduce this sentence here, with each extension past a point of possible grammatical completion given a separate line:

(7) 1 I gave, I gave up smoking cigarettes::.
    2 I-uh: one-one week ago
    3 today.
    4 actually.

What Goodwin showed is that each of these additions comes as a result of problems with the response of a potential addressee, as visible from the gaze of the speaker. Goodwin further accounted for the manner in which each added unit is built not only to extend the grammar of the previous one but to provide information that is of particular relevance for a new addressee. Note for example that the unit in lines 1 and 2 would not be "news" for the speaker's wife, but the units added at 3 and 4 would recontextualize the turn as being a realization that the speaker could be sharing with his wife, toward whom the speaker gazes during lines 2 and 3. What is striking about this case and Goodwin's analysis of it is that this utterance *could* be viewed as a single sentence, that is, as having been planned as such from the very beginning. This may, in fact, be just what the speaker tries to pull off by adding the specific increments he does. However, if we look at the utterance in real time, and in visual and embodied space, we can see the way it unfolds through an interactional give and take.

Building on research with turn projection and turn extension, Ford (1993) examined the particular work of adverbial clauses in interaction. Significantly, adverbial clauses may be placed either before or after the material they modify. In naturally occurring interaction, the use of such clauses in initial position can be a resource for constructing longer turns. This works because initial placement of the adverbial clause projects at least one more clause before a point of completion is reached. A speaker can exploit this projection and, after using the adverbial clause, he or she can parenthetically add more material before coming to the projected completion point; this strategy successfully manages the constantly present pressure of the turn-taking system, which encourages uptake at points of grammatical completion (recall that pauses when uptake is expected will have social interpretations).

In the following example, note the way that V interrupts the progress of her turn to introduce a conditional clause, at the arrow. In so doing, she is able to produce a rather long utterance before she comes to a point of possible turn completion.

(8) V: So the doctors said, that they would- (0.3)
→   IF he: (0.5) didn't wanna keep being active,
        an' do sports n' things, right now, at his age,
        an' with the bad condition of his knee,
        they normally put in a plastic knee.

Had V completed the turn as she began it, that is, with the main clause first, she would have reached a possible point of grammatical completion before she had added the crucial conditions on this case, as illustrated in (9):

(9) Constructed alternative
    V: *So the doctors said that they would normally put in a plastic knee.*

From a purely cognitive processing perspective, this choice of presentation format could be explained in terms of information structuring of a different sort (see Chafe, 1984; Ford & Thompson, 1986), but given what we know about the contingencies of turn projection and turn transfer, it would make the most sense to consider *both* information flow and social interactional exigencies in accounting for the ways that speakers deploy such grammatical options in conversation.

In line with Goodwin's observations regarding turn extension in the face of problems with addressee uptake, Ford (1993) also found recurrent patterns in the use of added adverbial clauses after possibly complete turns. In the following example, an adverbial clause is added after no immediate uptake from an addressee.

(10) Discussing R's back pain
     A: .hhh Well do you think it's: umm (0.2) ahm (0.2)
         stress?
         (.)
→   'Cause a lot of back- I know back pain, (0.2)
         comes with stress.
     R: .hhh we:ll I'm thinking it might be uh (0.2) I um:
         (0.5) I haven't ever had- ahh directly related
         physical symptoms of stress before, and it could
         easily be that,

The addressee finally does provide some form of uptake after the added clause, but it is worth noting that the uptake is not demonstrative of a strong agreement. The format of R's response shows many of the proto-typical signs of what might best be termed weak agreement. In fact, the par-ticle *Well* is a regular preface to fully disagreeing turns; R's agreement is far from a wholehearted one.

The English adverbial clause represents a traditional grammatical cate-gory, one that has a long history in the sentence-level description of clause combining and also has a history of semantic analysis in terms of such cate-gories of conditionality and causality. Recent discourse analytic research has shown the significance of adverbial clause placement in relation to in-formation structuring (Chafe, 1984; Thompson, 1987), and pragmatic analysis has led to our understanding of the different levels at which such clause connections can be operating (Sweetser, 1990). What we would sub-mit, however, is that in addition to these information and semantic proc-esses that a speaker must attend to, in naturally occurring conversation, a speaker must crucially and continuously attend to the contingencies of turn construction and turn transfer. In real interaction, individual speakers are always accountable to these interactional exigencies, and there is never a lapse in which they are off the hook, so to speak. For a complete functional account of traditional grammatical categories, we need to look beyond iso-lated sentences, and we also need to look beyond monologic conceptions of the natural conditions of language production and processing demands. In the case of adverbial clauses, usage is responsive to moment-to-moment interactional contingencies, whether the need to project further talk be-yond a single clause, or the interactional problem of lack of immediate up-take from the addressee. Thus, in order for psychological accounts of lan-guage to come to terms with the ubiquitous use of language in interaction, pause time, for example, needs to be considered as an interactional re-source rather than only a reflection of lapsed time with respect to cognitive processing.

Grammar and Interactional Sequences

The production of a turn involves an ordered progression through a ver-bally structured action, and the operation of turn taking depends on an ordering of speaking opportunities. Looking at yet another kind of conver-sational structure, we observe that interactants organize their talk into un-folding activities—predictable, yet collaboratively and contingently con-structed, sequences. Sequences, thus, involve the temporal and progressive ordering of actions in interaction. Certain actions are expectable or rele-vant after certain other actions. This observation has led to documentation of specific sequence types. Sequence structure has been demonstrated by research on paired utterances ("adjacency pairs"), preferred response types and shapes (Pomerantz, 1984; Sacks, 1987), and the interactional emergence of special speaking roles such as those manifested in story sequences (Jefferson, 1978; Sacks, 1972, 1974).

Grammar, viewed as an interactional resource, is also adapted to structured sequences of turns that form bounded activities within conversations. This can be seen in another traditional area of grammar that has been described at both sentence and discourse levels, but that has been further shown to be tightly intertwined with interactional practices as well. The study of alternations between full nouns and pronouns comes under the linguistic heading of anaphora. In a variety of ways, the work of Fox (1986, 1987) has shown that the choice of a full Noun Phrase (NP) or a pronoun in English conversation is bound up with the display of the structure of conversational sequences.

Through attention to the structure of conversational sequences, Fox's research provided a more complex picture than one that attends mainly to issues of continuity of reference, as put forth by Givón (1983). Givón held that the choice of anaphoric device was correlated with the distance to the last mention of that referent, with consideration of intervening referents as well. In conversational sequences, Fox (1987) found that in choosing a full NP or a pronoun, a speaker can also be proposing that a sequence has either ended or is continuing. Thus, in the following example, although a common information management-based explanation would predict that the referent first indexed as "Hillary" would, in this continuous environment, be referred to with pronouns, note the reference at line 11:

```
(11)   1  M:     Well  (anyway listen) I gotta (go), I gotta(-) do
       2                a lotta studying
       3                (0.3)
       4  M:           Oh and Hillary said she'd call me if- she was
       5                gonna go to the library with me
       6                (0.9)
       7  M:           But- (0.1) I don't think she will
       8  M:           So anyway (0.2) tch. I'm gonna go have these
                       xeroxed
       9                and I'll come back in a little bit.
      10  (M):         (hhhh[hh)
      11  R:           (Oka[y. Say]) hi to Hillary for me.
      12  S:                [Okay ]
      13  M:           Okay I will.
```

Lines 1 to 7 involve a sequence that is treated as closed by M's *So anyway* at line 8, which moves into a new sequence, the closing of the conversation (Schegloff & Sacks, 1973). Thus when the person referred to in lines 1 to 7 is again referred to at line 11, the reference is part of a new sequence, a closing sequence, and is done with a full NP. It is the interactional structuring that produces an environment in which the re-referencing would be done in this uneconomical form, a discovery that follows only from a close interactional analysis.

In what might be considered as an opposite strategy to that in (11), in the telephone conversation in (12), a sequence that has been closed is subsequently reopened with the help of a pronoun:

```
(12)  1  A:  Hello
      2  B:  Is Jessie there?
      3  A:  (No) Jessie's over at her gramma's for a couple da:ys.
      4  B:  Alright thank you,
      5  A:  You're wel:come?
      6  B:  Bye,
      7  A:  Dianne?
      8  B:  Yeah,
      9  A:  OH I THOUGHT that was you,
→    10  A:  Uh-she's over at Gramma Lizie's for a couple of days.
     11  B:  Oh okay,
```

Note that "gramma" is referred to in line 3, after which prototypical conversational closing turns follow (lines 4–6) (Schegloff & Sacks, 1973, p. 317). It takes special work by A, at line 7, for the conversation to reopen. A, apparently having just now recognized to whom she is speaking, uses a summons, *Dianne?* What follows, in line 10, is a re-referencing of *Jessie* through the use of a pronoun, even though the last mention of *Jessie* is many lines earlier and in what was then treated as a closed sequence. Speaker A effectively accomplishes a continuation of that earlier sequence with the aid of this artful choice of NP form.

Although there is much to say about the complexities of interactional sequences, for now, let us observe that speakers work on a turn-by-turn basis to show each other what sort of sequence they are co-constructing, where it begins, how it continues, and how they might close it and move to another sequence or end the interaction. Grammatical structures are prime resources for working out where one is sequentially, as illustrated in Fox's work with reference formulation.

Grammar and Repair

Fox, Hayashi, and Jasperson (1996) explored the ways in which same-turn self-repair, whose operation is rooted in various interactional pressures, is managed in languages with vastly different syntactic practices to meet these pressures. To this end, they discussed ways in which the organization of re-

pair differs across two languages, English and Japanese, and argued that
these differences in repair organization—and possibly even differences in
the mechanisms of turn-taking—correlate, at least in part, with larger differences in the syntactic practices employed by speakers of these two languages. Here we present two of their findings regarding the differences between repair organization and syntactic organization between Japanese and
English. Before turning to the differences in repair between Japanese and
English, a brief sketch of the grammatical organization of each language is
in order.

Syntax in Conversational Japanese

Japanese is often described as an SOV, or verb-final, language (where S
stands for subject, O for direct object, and V for verb). In conversational
data, many utterances are verb-final:

> (13) H: de: tashoo   maketoku.
>   and more.or.less discount
>   "and (we) discount more or less."

However, certain elements can occur after the predicate (e.g., so-called final particles). Moreover, it is commonly known that S and O are often not
expressed in conversational Japanese (Hinds, 1982; Kuno, 1973; Maynard,
1989; Ono & Thompson, 1997; Tanaka, 1999). Consider the following examples (nouns that are not expressed in Japanese are given in parentheses
in the English translations):

> (14) H: hajimete   mita kedo.
>   for.the.first time saw but
>   "(I) saw (her) for the first time."

In (14) neither the subject nor the object is expressed. Even verbs can remain unexpressed.

The result of these patterns is that clauses in conversational Japanese often show one or more overt nouns that are not S or O but are rather nouns
describing locations, times, and other settings; these are then followed by a
verb in some utterances, though not in all; final particles often follow the
verb. The order of nouns that do occur in an utterance is flexible, responding to the interactional needs of the moment of utterance.

Referring nouns in Japanese conversation can be followed by case particles, or postpositions, which indicate the role of the noun in the clause
(e.g., subject, direct object, locative). These particles function somewhat
like case marking systems in languages like German and Russian (but see
Shibatani, 1990, ch. 11, for a discussion of the complexity of Japanese case

particles, and Fujii & Ono, 2000; Matsuda, 1996; Ono, Thompson, & Suzuki, 2000; and Tanaka, 1999, for discussions of the use of case particles in Japanese conversation).

Syntax in Conversational English

English is usually described as a rigid SVO language. Although there is some word order variation in our conversational data, in fact most utterances do tend to be SV(O), with prepositional phrases coming after the direct object, if one is present. Subjects in English conversation are overwhelmingly human and pronominal (Dahl, 1997; Scheibman, 2001, in press).

It is important to point out here that English is somewhat odd cross-linguistically in requiring the presence of a subject in nearly all utterances; it is rare, even in fast conversation, for speakers to produce a main clause without explicit mention of the subject.

Organization of Repair

What Fox, Hayashi, and Jasperson (1996) found is a number of ways in which repair is organized differently across the two languages in question. We discuss two of these first, and then present their argument that these differences in repair organization arise, at least in part, from more general syntactic differences exhibited across the two languages (the findings reported here were first noted in Hayashi, 1994).

Procedures for Delaying Next Noun Due. The first type of difference in repair has to do with the general function of delaying the production of a next item due. Fox, Hayashi, and Jasperson (1996) focused on delays involved in the production of lexical parts of noun phrases—in particular, nouns. Syntactic differences between the two languages may be implicated in a different set of repair procedures for delaying the production of a noun. Consider first the following examples from English (in this discussion of repair, an asterisk indicates the site at which repair is initiated, and brackets indicate the "repairable" material):

(15) M: on the back of his pickup truck [with a,*] (0.4) with a jack.
(16) B: We're gonna take it [through the*] through the mill so to
        speak.

In these examples, the speakers have begun a prepositional phrase, initiated repair, and then recycled the preposition and a possible article before progressing with the rest of the phrase. In each of these cases, recycling constitutes a procedure for delaying the production of a next item due.

This procedure could, for example, be part of a word search, a request for recipient-gaze, management of overlapping talk, and/or production of a dispreferred.

Japanese speakers, it turns out, do not use recycling to delay the production of nouns. The reason for this seems to be that whereas prepositions and articles in English precede their nouns, postpositions, such as case particles, in Japanese follow their nouns. It is clear that English speakers make use of the fact that prepositions and articles precede their nouns; prepositions and articles provide material to be recycled before the speaker must produce a noun. Japanese speakers, on the other hand, do not have available to them non-lexical material to recycle before a noun, as case particles follow their nouns (and Japanese has no articles).

Because of the syntactic organizations of the two languages, then, English speakers can make use of preposition and article recycling as part of a delay strategy, whereas Japanese speakers cannot. The data indicate that Japanese speakers make use of other practices for delaying the production of a next item due.

From these facts we can see how it is possible that the syntactic practices employed by speakers shape the organization of the repair strategies that are used.

The Scope of Recycling.   The second type of difference in repair also involves recycling. In this case the difference suggests the possibility of very basic differences in the turn-taking mechanisms of the two languages. Consider the following examples from our English data:

(17) B: in this building- we finally got [a-*] .hhh a roo:m today in- in
           the leh- a lecture hall,

(18) K: Plus once [he got- (0.8) some*] um (1.3) he got some battery
           acid on: (0.2) on his trunk or something.

In (17), repair is initiated after a noun phrase (defined as a noun plus any modifier that might occur) has been started. In recycling, the speaker only repeats the part of the noun phrase that has been produced so far—the indefinite article. The speaker does not recycle "back to" anything earlier in the utterance. In Example (18), the speaker also initiates repair after starting a noun phrase; in this case, however, the speaker repeats the whole clause (excluding *plus once*) rather than just the part of the noun phrase produced so far.

One way of stating the pattern in English is to say that the domain of recycling can either be the local constituent under construction at the time repair is initiated (e.g., noun phrase), or it can be the clause. This pattern holds for all constituents, including verbs and prepositional phrases.

In comparison to this pattern, the Japanese data show only constituent-internal recycling; that is, at least in these data, Japanese speakers do not make use of clausal recycling. This means that if a speaker initiates repair after starting a noun phrase, he or she will recycle back to the beginning of that noun phrase but not further back; repair initiated during the construction of the verb usually is handled by recycling just the verb, not other elements that might have preceded the verb (except in one case the direct object of the verb, which makes a local constituent—a verb phrase). So one does not find counterparts in the Japanese data to Example (18). Here we give examples of recycling in Japanese:

(19) M: tteyuuka koko denwa   [kaket-*] kakete kite   sa,
         I.mean   here telephone ca-   call   come FP
         "I mean, (they) ca- called us here,"

(20) T: . . . mukoo   no [sutahhu-*] sutahhu mo sa: yuushuu.
         the.other.party GEN staff   staff   also FP excellent
         ". . . their staff- staff is also excellent."

We thus seem to have a systematic difference in the possible domains of recycling between the two languages. The reason for this difference, it seems, lies in the different syntactic practices employed in managing local interactional needs.

The syntactic practices that seem to be at the heart of this difference in repair are the following. As mentioned earlier, all referring nouns in Japanese can be marked for case, and the order of nouns before the verb is flexible. In addition, subjects and objects in Japanese, particularly subjects, are often not explicitly realized (as seen in (14)). The verb in Japanese comes at or near the end of the clause.

The kind of turn structure these facts lead to typically, although of course not always, starts with some kind of discourse marker (e.g., *ano, nanka*), followed by adverbials, or nouns either not marked to show any relationship with other parts of the clause or indicating setting of some kind, followed by the verb, and possibly followed by so-called final particles. So what occurs early in the turn-constructional unit (or "TCU"; see Sacks, Schegloff, & Jefferson, 1974) is often only loosely associated structurally with what is to follow. Conversational utterances in Japanese thus seem not to show tight syntactic organization (for similar findings and further discussion of their implications, see Hayashi, 2000; Iwasaki, 1993; Iwasaki & Tao, 1993; Tanaka, 1999).

English, on the other hand, requires the presence of an overt subject and is fairly rigidly SV(O). This leads to turns that may begin with a discourse marker (e.g., *well, so*) and then continue with a subject, then a verb, and then a direct object, or prepositional phrase, or adverbial, if these are

appropriate. Conversational utterances in English thus could be said to exhibit a higher degree of syntactic coherence.

From a syntactic perspective, then, we can say that in English the subject
begins a tightly knit clause structure and hence syntactically is the "beginning" of the clause, whereas in Japanese there is no consistent element that
serves as the beginning of a tightly knit syntactic unit—in fact, there is no
such tightly knit unit. In Japanese, elements in an utterance seem to be
more independent from one another than are elements in an English utterance; we believe that the difference in the organization of recycling across
the two languages reflects this difference.

Fox, Hayashi, and Jasperson (1996) suggested that these syntactic facts
affect repair because they affect a crucial aspect of the turn-taking mechanisms of these two languages, namely projection. That is, they argued that
the beginnings of TCUs in Japanese do not tend to have elements that syntactically project the possible organization of what is to follow. For example,
from the presence of an adverbial or a location-indicating noun, a recipient
cannot necessarily predict what kind of syntactic element will come next. It
seems, however, that the beginnings of TCUs in English do project possible
organizations for what is to follow; for example, often in English as soon as
one hears the subject, one knows (in a practical sense) that a verb is coming; and as soon as one hears the verb, one knows what is likely to come after the verb. That is, the beginning of the clause in English is rich with information about how the clause is likely to continue. The beginning of the
clause in English projects its likely continuation.

So Fox, Hayashi, and Jasperson (1996) argued that English speakers and
recipients are able to use an "early projection" strategy because of the syntactic practices they employ. Japanese speakers and recipients, on the other
hand, engage in syntactic practices that do not make easy "early projection"
strategies; from their data, they suggested that it is possible that Japanese
speakers make use of "wait and see" strategies that are enabled by the syntactic practices available to them. At any rate, they suggested that syntactic
projection can take place earlier in an utterance in English than in Japanese. Obviously, neither set of strategies is in any way better than the other;
they simply provide different resources for accomplishing transition to a
next speaker.

We have seen so far that the beginning of a TCU carries with it different
interactional possibilities in English than in Japanese. In fact, it is possible
that TCU beginning, or "turn beginning," is not an interactional object in
Japanese the way it is in English. This fact suggests a possible motivation for
English speakers' return to the subject in some cases of recycling, whereas
Japanese speakers stay within local constituents for recycling: In English,
the beginning of the clause is a coherent syntactic and interactional object
from which a re-projection for the entire clause can be made, whereas in

Japanese the beginning of the clause may not be syntactically knit to what follows in the clause, and would not be the site of re-projection. In Japanese, projection may be done much more bit-by-bit than it typically is in English, and the organization of recycling reflects this fact. These hypotheses have been supported by further research (see, e.g., Hayashi, 2000; Tanaka, 1999).

So far we have considered some of the activities speakers engage in, and the bearing they have on the timing and grammatical shape of the turns they take. In addition to the implications of turn-organization for the shape of grammar, we can point to other areas of grammar where the activities in which coparticipants are engaged play a role in the way grammatical regularities emerge. In the following sections we examine some of these, and conclude with suggestions of further areas in which similar discoveries might be made.

Grammar and Assessments

Research has revealed a major activity that adjectives are used for in informal conversation, namely offering *assessments*, whereby coparticipants interactively evaluate persons and situations (Goodwin, 1980; Goodwin & Goodwin, 1987, 1992a, 1992b; Pomerantz, 1984; Strauss & Kawanishi, 1996; Uhmann, 1996).

Grammatically, it turns out that the primary way assessments are done is with adjectives.[2] Here is an example from our conversational data (adjectives bolded):

(21) K: it's **incredible** how they live.
　　　C: it IS **incredible**.

Linguists generally accept the idea that many languages can be shown to have a category of "adjective." English is one such language, where we can find distributional evidence of an "adjective" category that is distinct from other lexical categories such as "noun," "verb," and "adverb" (Ferris, 1993; Quirk et al., 1985).[3] Most linguists agree with Quirk et al., who argued that

---

[2]As the examples discussed in this research make clear, using predicative adjectives is not the only way in which assessments are done; other grammatical forms, such as the use of expressions like *I like*, intensifiers such as *really*, and prosody can also be used to convey evaluations. A valuable study would consider the activity-coordinating role of various recurrent grammatical schemas; in the absence of such a study we content ourselves here with the observation that a high proportion of the assessment sequences in our data and described in the literature involve predicative adjectives.

[3]However, many languages cannot be so easily argued to have a class of adjectives; for relevant discussion, see Croft, 1991; Dixon, 1977; Schacter, 1985; Thompson, 1988; and Wetzer, 1996.

membership in the category "adjective" should be considered to be gradient.

The use of adjectives has traditionally been described for English in terms of a broad distinction between "predicative" and "attributive" uses. A "predicative" use is an adjective in the role of the predicate of a clause, as in (21) and (22), all taken from our database:

> (22) they weren't that **good**
> they're really **expensive**
> it's **wrenching**

An "attributive" use is an adjective in the role of a modifier of a noun within the same Noun Phrase (NP), as in:

> (23) I would go to an **Italian** opera
> it's a **nice** place to doze
> it's a very **bleak** story
> that's a **big** hunk of fish

These traditional distinctions come alive when we consider how adjectives are manifested in everyday English conversation. Two interesting recent discoveries are relevant.

First, Englebretson (1997) has shown that the distinction between predicative and attributive adjectives is strikingly related to the type of interaction that participants are engaged in. For informal conversational English, where much background, and especially knowledge of the referents, is shared, the predicative use of adjectives is much more frequent than the attributive use. For more formal situations and for telling stories, where less background and less knowledge of referents is shared, attributive adjectives tend to be more frequent.

We can relate this finding to the argument that these two uses of adjectives, and their concomitant structural schemas, serve the participants in very different ways. Thompson (1988) argued that attributive adjectives play a major role in the way speakers introduce new referents into the conversation, whereas predicative adjectives evaluate or comment on a referent that is already shared knowledge between the participants. To illustrate, consider Example (24), as analyzed in Englebretson (1997):

> (24) (h)h h he had on a **white** suit, Liza had on a um, (.)
> a **black** suit, and then he stand there and tells her how it's
> not - (.) it needs to be **baggier** here, and they're analyz- -
> they are so **superficial,**

Ford, C. E. (1993). *Grammar in interaction: Adverbial clauses in American English conversations.* Cambridge: Cambridge University Press.

Ford, C. E., & Thompson, S. A. (1986). Conditionals in discourse: A text-based study from English. In E. C. Traugott, A. ter Meulen, J. S. Reilly, & C. A. Ferguson (Eds.), *On conditionals* (pp. 353–372). Cambridge: Cambridge University Press.

Fox, B. A. (1986). Local patterns and general principles in cognitive processes: Anaphora in written and conversational English. *Text, 6,* 25–51.

Fox, B. A. (1987). *Anaphora and the structure of discourse.* Cambridge: Cambridge University Press.

Fox, B. A., Hayashi, M., & Jasperson, R. (1996). A cross-linguistic study of syntax and repair. In E. Ochs, E. Schegloff, & S. A. Thompson (Eds.), *Interaction and grammar* (pp. 185–237). Cambridge: Cambridge University Press.

Fujii, N., & Ono, T. (2000). The occurrence and non-occurrence of the Japanese direct object marker *o* in conversation. *Studies in Language, 24*(1), 1–39.

Geluykens, R. (1992). *From discourse process to grammatical construction: On left-dislocation in English.* Amsterdam: John Benjamins.

Givón, T. (1980). The binding hierarchy and the typology of complements. *Studies in Language, 4*(3), 333–377.

Givón, T. (1983). *Topic continuity.* New York: Academic Press.

Goodwin, C. (1979). The interactive construction of a sentence in natural conversation. In G. Psathas (Ed.), *Everyday language: Studies in ethnomethodology* (pp. 97–121). New York: Irvington.

Goodwin, C. (1981). *Conversational organization: Interaction between speakers and hearers.* New York: Academic Press.

Goodwin, C. (1989). Turn construction and conversational organization. In B. Dervin, L. Grossberg, B. J. O'Keefe, & E. Wartella (Eds.), *Rethinking communication: Vol. 2. Paradigm exemplars* (pp. 88–101). Newbury Park, CA: Sage.

Goodwin, C., & Goodwin, M. H. (1987). Concurrent operations on talk: Notes on the interactive organization of assessments. *IPRA Papers in Pragmatics, 1*(1), 1–54.

Goodwin, C., & Goodwin, M. H. (1992a). Assessments and the construction of context. In C. Goodwin & A. Duranti (Eds.), *Rethinking context* (pp. 147–189). Cambridge: Cambridge University Press.

Goodwin, C., & Goodwin, M. H. (1992b). Context, activity and participation. In P. Auer & A. di Luzio (Eds.), *The contextualization of language* (pp. 77–99). Amsterdam: John Benjamins.

Goodwin, M. H. (1980). Processes of mutual monitoring implicated in the production of description sequences. *Sociological Inquiry, 50,* 303–317.

Haiman, J. (1994). Ritualization and the development of language. In W. Pagliuca (Ed.), *Perspectives on grammaticalization* (pp. 3–28). Amsterdam: John Benjamins.

Haiman, J. (1998). *Talk is cheap.* Oxford: Oxford University Press.

Hayashi, M. (1994). A comparative study of self-repair in English and Japanese conversation. In N. Akatsuka (Ed.), *Japanese/Korean linguistics* (Vol. IV, pp. 77–93). Stanford, CA: CSLI.

Hayashi, M. (2000). *Practices in joint utterance construction in Japanese conversation.* Doctoral dissertation, University of Colorado.

Heritage, J. C., & Roth, A. L. (1995). Grammar and institution: Questions and questioning in the broadcast news interview. *Research on Language and Social Interaction, 28*(1), 1–60.

Hinds, J. (1982). *Ellipsis in Japanese.* Carbondale, IL, and Edmonton, Alberta: Linguistic Research, Inc.

Hopper, P. J. (1987). Emergent grammar. *Berkeley Linguistics Society, 13,* 139–157.

Hopper, P. J. (1988). Emergent grammar and the A Priori Grammar constraint. In D. Tannen (Ed.), *Linguistics in context: Connecting observation and understanding* (pp. 117–134). Norwood, NJ: Ablex.

Iwasaki, S. (1993). *Subjectivity in grammar and discourse.* Amsterdam: John Benjamins.

Iwasaki, S., & Tao, H. (1993, January). *A comparative study of the structure of the intonation unit in English, Japanese, and Mandarin Chinese.* Paper presented at the annual meeting of the Linguistic Society of America, Los Angeles, CA.

Jefferson, G. (1973). A case of precision timing in ordinary conversation: Overlapped tag-positioned address terms in closing sequences. *Semiotica, 9,* 47–96.

Jefferson, G. (1978). Sequential aspects of storytelling in conversation. In J. Schenkein (Ed.), *Studies in the organization of conversational interaction* (pp. 219–248). New York: Academic Press.

Jefferson, G. (1983). Notes on some orderliness of overlap onset. In V. d'Urso & P. Leonardi (Eds.), *Discourse analysis and natural rhetoric* (pp. 11–38). Padua: Cleup.

Kuno, S. (1973). *The structure of the Japanese language.* Cambridge, MA: MIT Press.

Langacker, R. W. (1987). *Foundations of cognitive grammar: Vol. 1. Theoretical prerequisites.* Stanford, CA: Stanford University Press.

Lerner, G. H. (1991). On the syntax of sentences-in-progress. *Language in Society, 20*(3), 441–458.

Lerner, G. H. (1996). On the "semi-permeable" character of grammatical units in conversation: Conditional entry into the turn space of another speaker. In E. Ochs, E. Schegloff, & S. A. Thompson (Eds.), *Interaction and grammar* (pp. 238–276). Cambridge: Cambridge University Press.

Matsuda, K. (1996). *Variable case-marking of (o) in Tokyo Japanese.* Philadelphia: Institute for Research in Cognitive Science, University of Pennsylvania.

Maynard, S. (1989). *Japanese conversation: Self-contextualization through structure and interactional management.* Norwood, NJ: Ablex.

Noonan, M. (1985). Complementation. In T. Shopen (Ed.), *Language typology and syntactic description* (Vol. II, pp. 42–139). Cambridge: Cambridge University Press.

Ochs, E. (1983). Planned and unplanned discourse. In E. Ochs & B. Schieffelin (Eds.), *Acquiring conversational competence* (pp. 129–157). London: Routledge.

Ochs, E., & Schieffelin, B. (1983). Topic as a discourse notion. In E. Ochs & B. Schieffelin (Eds.), *Acquiring conversational competence* (pp. 158–174). London: Routledge.

Ono, T., & Thompson, S. A. (1997). On deconstructing "zero anaphora." *Berkeley Linguistics Society, 23,* 481–491.

Ono, T., Thompson, S. A., & Suzuki, R. (2000). The pragmatic nature of the so-called subject marker *ga* in Japanese: Evidence from conversation. *Discourse Studies, 2*(1), 55–84.

Pomerantz, A. (1984). Agreeing and disagreeing with assessments: Some features of preferred/dispreferred turn shapes. In J. M. Atkinson & J. Heritage (Eds.), *Structures of social action* (pp. 57–101). Cambridge: Cambridge University Press.

Quirk, R., Greenbaum, S., Leech, G., & Svartvik, J. (1985). *A comprehensive grammar of the English language.* London: Longman.

Sacks, H. (1972). On the analyzability of stories by children. In J. J. Gumperz & D. Hymes (Eds.), *Directions in sociolinguistics* (pp. 245–325). New York: Holt, Rinehart & Winston.

Sacks, H. (1974). An analysis of the course of a joke's telling in conversation. In R. Bauman & J. Sherzer (Eds.), *Explorations in the ethnography of speaking* (pp. 337–353). Cambridge: Cambridge University Press.

Sacks, H. (1987). On the preference for agreement and contiguity in sequences in conversation. In G. Button & J. R. E. Lee (Eds.), *Talk and social organization* (pp. 54–69). Philadelphia: Multilingual Matters.

Sacks, H., Schegloff, E., & Jefferson, G. (1974). A simplest systematics for the organization of turn-taking for conversation. *Language, 50*(4), 696–735.

Schachter, P. (1985). Parts-of-speech systems. In T. Shopen (Ed.), *Language typology and syntactic description* (Vol. 1, pp. 3–61). Cambridge: Cambridge University Press.

Schegloff, E. (1987). Recycled turn beginnings: A precise repair mechanism in conversation's turn taking organisation. In G. Button & J. R. Lee (Eds.), *Talk and social organisation* (pp. 70–85). Clevedon: Multilingual Matters.

Schegloff, E. (1993). Reflections on language, development, and the interactional character of talk-in-interaction. *Research on Language and Social Interaction, 26*(1), 139–153.

Schegloff, E. (1995). Discourse as an interactional achievement III: The omnirelevance of action. *Research on Language and Social Interaction, 28*(3), 185–211.

Schegloff, E. (1996a). Issues of relevance for discourse analysis: Contingency in action, interaction, and co-participant context. In E. H. Hovy & D. R. Scott (Eds.), *Computational and conversational discourse* (pp. 3–35). New York: Springer.

Schegloff, E. (1996b). Turn organization: One direction for inquiry into grammar and interaction. In E. Ochs, E. Schegloff, & S. A. Thompson (Eds.), *Interaction and grammar* (pp. 52–133). Cambridge: Cambridge University Press.

Schegloff, E., & Sacks, H. (1973). Opening up closings. *Semiotica, 8,* 289–327. (Reprinted in Baugh & Sherzer, Eds., 1984, Englewood Cliffs, NJ: Prentice-Hall)

Scheibman, J. (2000). *I dunno . . .* a usage-based account of the phonological reduction of *don't* in American English conversation. *Journal of Pragmatics, 32,* 105–124.

Scheibman, J. (2001). Local patterns of subjectivity in person and verb type in American English conversation. In J. Bybee & P. Hopper (Eds.), *Frequency and the emergence of linguistic structure* (pp. 61–89). Amsterdam: John Benjamins.

Scheibman, J. (in press). *Structural patterns of subjectivity in American English conversation.* Amsterdam: John Benjamins.

Shibatani, M. (1990). *The languages of Japan.* Cambridge: Cambridge University Press.

Strauss, S., & Kawanishi, Y. (1996). Assessment strategies in Japanese, Korean, and American. In N. Akatsuka, S. Iwasaki, & S. Strauss (Eds.), *Japanese-Korean linguistics* (pp. 149–165). Stanford, CA: Center for the Study of Language and Information.

Sweetser, E. (1990). *From etymology to pragmatics: Metaphorical and cultural aspects of semantics.* Cambridge: Cambridge University Press.

Tanaka, H. (1999). *Turn-taking in Japanese conversation: A study in grammar and interaction.* Amsterdam: John Benjamins.

Tao, H. (1992). NP intonation units and referent identification. *Berkeley Linguistics Society, 18,* 237–247.

Tao, H. (1996). *Units in Mandarin conversation: Prosody, discourse and grammar.* Amsterdam: John Benjamins.

Tao, H. (2001). Discovering the usual with corpora: The case of *remember.* In R. C. Simpson & J. M. Swales (Eds.), *Corpus linguistics in North America* (pp. 116–144). Ann Arbor: University of Michigan Press.

Thompson, S. A. (1987). "Subordination" and narrative event structure. In R. Tomlin (Ed.), *Coherence and grounding in discourse* (pp. 435–454). Amsterdam: John Benjamins.

Thompson, S. A. (1988). A discourse approach to the cross-linguistic category "adjective." In J. A. Hawkins (Ed.), *Explaining language universals* (pp. 167–185). Oxford: Basil Blackwell.

Uhmann, S. (1996). On rhythm in everyday German conversation: Beat clashes in assessment utterances. In E. Couper-Kuhlen & M. Selting (Eds.), *Prosody in conversation* (pp. 303–365). Cambridge: Cambridge University Press.

Weber, E. (1993). *Varieties of questions in English conversation.* Amsterdam: John Benjamins.

Weber, T. (1997). The emergence of linguistic structure: Paul Hopper's emergent grammar hypothesis revisited. *Language Sciences, 19*(2), 177–196.

Wetzer, H. (1996). *The typology of adjectival predication.* New York: Mouton de Gruyter.

Chapter 5

Cognitive Processes in Grammaticalization

Joan Bybee
University of New Mexico

All of linguistic theory is concerned with the enterprise of elucidating the nature of the grammar of human languages. But along with asking the question "What is the nature of grammar?," we can also ask "How do languages acquire grammar?." In the last 20 years, researchers interested in the latter question have elaborated a theory of grammaticalization, the process by which grammar is created, and in doing so have also come up with some interesting new perspectives on the former question.[1] Four main findings of this research are listed here:

Grammar is not a static, closed, or self-contained system, but is highly susceptible to change and highly affected by language use. The loss of grammar is generally acknowledged and often lamented by prescriptive grammarians, who mourn the loss of the distinction between *who* and *whom* but fail to rejoice in the creation of new grammar, such as the new future tense signaled by *gonna*. In fact, the creation of new grammatical morphemes and structures is as common as the loss of old ones.

Once underway, the course of grammaticalization is unidirectional and thus, in principle, predictable. Nouns and verbs lose their categorical status and become prepositions, auxiliaries, and other grammatical forms. Free elements become more restricted and fuse with other elements. Loosely conjoined main clauses fuse to become a main plus subordinate clause. The reverse directions are rarely attested.

---

[1]The terms *grammaticalization* and *grammaticization* are used interchangeably.

Both the general trends in grammaticalization and many of the very specific developments are not restricted to individual languages, but are common across genetically and geographically unrelated languages. This widespread distribution, which is illustrated later, provides a new view of language universals. Because patterns of change cannot in themselves exist in speakers' minds, the more basic universals must be the mechanisms that create the changes that are so similar across languages.

Many of the very basic mechanisms that constitute the process of grammaticalization are cognitive processes that are not necessarily restricted to language. By better understanding these cognitive processes and how they function in communicative situations, we will eventually learn the answers to the most fundamental questions that linguists ask.

GRAMMATICALIZATION

Grammaticalization is usually defined as the process by which a lexical item or a sequence of items becomes a grammatical morpheme, changing its distribution and function in the process (Heine, Claudi, & Hünnemeyer, 1991a, 1991b; Heine & Reh, 1984; Hopper & Traugott, 1993; Lehmann, 1982; Meillet, 1912). Thus English *going to* (with a finite form of *be*) becomes the intention/future marker *gonna*. However, more recently it has been observed that it is important to add that grammaticalization of lexical items takes place within *particular constructions* and further that grammaticalization is the creation of new constructions (Bybee, in press; Traugott, in press). Thus *going to* does not grammaticalize in the construction exemplified by *I'm going to the store* but only in the construction in which a verb follows *to*, as in *I'm going to help you.* If grammaticalization is the creation of new constructions (and their further development), then it also can include cases of change that do not involve specific morphemes, such as the creation of word order patterns.

For illustration let us consider the canonical type of grammaticalization, that in which a lexical item becomes a grammatical morpheme within a particular construction. Examining the details will help us understand what cognitive mechanisms are involved in the process. Some characteristics of the grammaticalization process are the following:

1. Words and phrases undergoing grammaticalization are phonetically reduced, with reductions, assimilations, and deletions of consonants and vowels producing sequences that require less muscular effort (Browman & Goldstein, 1992; Mowrey & Pagliuca, 1995). For example, *going to* [goɪŋtʰuw] becomes *gonna* [gənə] and even reduces further in some contexts to [ənə] as in *I'm (g)onna* [aimənə].

2. Specific, concrete meanings entering into the process become generalized and more abstract, and as a result, become appropriate in a growing range of contexts, as, for example, the uses of *be going to* in sentences (1) through (3). The literal meaning in (1) was the only possible interpretation in Shakespeare's English, but now uses such as those shown in (2) and (3) are common.

(1) movement: *We are going to Windsor to see the King.*

(2) intention: *We are going to get married in June.*

(3) future: *These trees are going to lose their leaves.*

3. A grammaticalizing construction's frequency of use increases dramatically as it develops. One source of the increased frequency is an increase in the types of contexts in which the new construction is possible. Thus when *be going to* had only its literal meaning, as in (1), it could only be used in contexts where movement was to take place, with subjects that were volitional and mobile. Now it can be used even in (3), where no movement in space on the part of the subject is implied, or indeed possible. As the *gonna* construction becomes appropriate with more types of subjects and verbs, it occurs more frequently in texts.

4. Changes in grammaticalization take place very gradually and are accompanied by much variation in both form and function. I have already illustrated the variation in form with *be going to* and *gonna*. Variation in function can be seen in the three examples above, of "movement," "intention" and "future," all of which are still possible uses in Modern English.

The mechanisms underlying these changes is the main focus of this chapter, but before examining them in greater detail, it is important to document the fact that grammaticalization occurs spontaneously and in the same form at all documented time periods and in all languages.

GENERAL PATTERNS OF GRAMMATICALIZATION

Let us first list some changes that have occurred in the English language over the last millenium. Since English began to appear in writing some 1,200 years ago, we can document the development of the definite article, *the*, out of the demonstrative, *that*, and the development of the indefinite article *a/an* out of the numeral *one*. The function of articles such as *the* and *a* is to distinguish between nouns that the hearer can identify as already known in the discourse or conversational context and those that are being introduced for the first time. (For example, *I met a man at the bank* . . . where this is the first mention of *a man* vs. *The man I met at the bank* . . . which refers back to some previous mention.) Old English (as documented in manuscripts from about A.D. 800–1100) did not use articles, but rather could change the position of nouns to show which were new and which were previously mentioned.

Similarly, the English modal auxiliaries, which express grammatical distinctions within the categories of tense (future *will*) and modalities such as possibility (*can* and *may*), all developed from verbs. *Will*, which now indicates future tense, developed from a verb, *willan*, which meant "to want"; *can* came from a verb, *cunnan*, meaning "to be acquainted with or to know how to"; *may* came from a verb, *magan*, meaning "to be able to, to have the power." *Could* and *might* developed from the past tense forms of *cunnan* and *magan* respectively. We have already mentioned the more complex phrase *be going to*, which in Shakespeare's English still described actual movement in space, fuses into *gonna* and comes to be used for future time reference.

Even affixes derive from full words. For instance, the English suffix *-ly* derived from a noun, which in Old English was *liç*, meaning "body." The compound *mann-liç* originally meant "having the body or appearance of a man" whence it generalized to "having the characteristics of a man," the modern sense of *manly*.

These facts of English are interesting enough as isolated facts about one language, but they develop a profound importance with the discovery that all around the world, in languages that are not related genetically or geographically, we find analogous examples: definite articles developing from demonstratives, indefinite articles from the numeral "one," future tenses from verbs meaning "want" or "go to," and auxiliaries indicating possibility and permission from verbs meaning "know" and "be able."

For instance, in many European languages, an indefinite article has developed out of the numeral "one": English *a/an*, German *ein*, French *un/une*, Spanish *un/una*, and Modern Greek *ena*. Whereas these are all Indo-European languages, in each case this development occurred after these languages had differentiated from one another and speakers were no longer in contact. Furthermore, the numeral "one" is used as an indefinite article in Moré, a Gur language of the Burkina Faso (Heine et al., 1993), in colloquial Hebrew (Semitic) and in the Dravidian languages Tamil and Kannada (Heine, 1997). Examples of demonstratives becoming definite articles are also common: Latin *ille, illa* "that" became French definite articles *le, la* and Spanish *el, la*; in Vai (a Mande language of Liberia and Sierra Leone) the demonstrative *mɛ* "this" becomes a suffixed definite article (Heine et al., 1993).

Parallel to English *will*, a verb meaning "want" becomes a future marker in Bulgarian, Rumanian, and Serbo-Croatian, as well as in the Bantu languages of Africa—Mabiha, Omyene, and Swahili (Bybee & Pagliuca, 1987; Heine et al., 1993). Parallel to English *can* from "to know," Baluchi (Indo-Iranian), Danish (Germanic), Motu (Papua Austronesian), Mwera (Bantu), and Nung (Tibeto-Burman) use a verb meaning "know" for the expression of ability (Bybee, Perkins, & Pagliuca, 1994). Tok Pisin, a creole language of New Guinea, uses *kæn* (from English *can*) for ability and also *savi* from the Portuguese *save* "he knows" for ability. Latin **potere* or *possum* "to be able" gives French *pouvoir* and Spanish *poder*, both meaning "can" as auxiliaries and "power" as nouns. These words parallel English *may* (and past tense *might*), which earlier meant "have the physical power to do something." Verbs or phrases indicating movement toward a goal (comparable to English *be going to*) frequently become future markers around the world, as found in languages such as French and Spanish but also in languages spoken in Africa, the Americas, Asia, and the Pacific (Bybee & Pagliuca, 1987; Bybee et al., 1994).

Of course, not all grammaticalization paths can be illustrated with English examples. There are also common developments that do not happen to occur in English. For instance, a completive or perfect marker (meaning "have [just] done") develops from a verb meaning "finish" in Bantu languages, as well as in languages as diverse as Cocama and Tucano (both Andean-Equatorial), Koho (Mon-Khmer), Buli (Malayo-Polynesian), Tem and Engenni (both Niger-Congo), Lao (Kam-Tai), Haka and Lahu (Tibeto-Burman), and Cantonese and Tok Pisin (Bybee et al., 1994; Heine & Reh, 1984). In addition, the same development from the verb "finish" has been recorded for American Sign Language, showing that grammaticalization takes place in signed languages the same way as it does in spoken languages (Janzen, 1995).

For several of these developments I have cited the creole language, Tok Pisin, a variety of Melanesian Pidgin English, which is now the official language of Papua New Guinea. Pidgin languages are originally trade or plantation languages that develop in situations where speakers of several different languages must interact, though they share no common language. At first, pidgins have no grammatical constructions or categories, but as they are used in wider contexts and by more people more often, they begin to develop grammar. Once such languages come to be used by children as their first language, and thus are designated as creole languages, the development of grammar flowers even more. The fact that the grammars of pidgin and creole languages are very similar in form, even among pidgins that developed in geographically distant places by speakers of diverse languages, has been taken by Bickerton (1981) to be strong evidence for innate language universals. However, studies of the way in which grammar develops in such languages reveals that the process is the same as the grammaticalization process in more established languages (Romaine, 1995; Sankoff, 1990).

150	BYBEE

PATHS OF CHANGE AND SYNCHRONIC PATTERNS

The picture that emerges from the examination of these and the numerous other documented cases of grammaticalization is that there are several highly constrained and specifiable *grammaticalization paths* that lead to the development of new grammatical constructions. Such paths are universal in the sense that development along them occurs independently in unrelated languages. For instance, the two most common paths for the development of future tense morphemes in the languages of the world are the following:

(4) The Movement Path
    movement toward a goal → intention → future

(5) The Volition Path
    volition or desire   → intention → future

The first path is exemplified by the development of *be going to* and the second by *will.*

New developments along such paths may begin at any time in a language's history. In any language we look at, we find old constructions that are near the end of such a path, as well as new constructions that are just beginning their evolution and constructions midway along. Grammar is constantly being created and lost along such specifiable and universal trajectories.

Development along the Movement Path begins when a verb or phrase meaning "movement toward a goal" comes to be used with a verb, as in *They are going to Windsor to see the King.* At first, the meaning is primarily spatial, but a strong inference of intention is also present. (*Why are they going to Windsor? To see the King.*) The intention meaning can become primary, and from that, one can infer future actions: *He's going to (gonna) buy a house* can state an intention or make a prediction about future actions.

Such developments are slow and gradual, and a grammaticizing construction on such a path will span a portion of it at any given time. Thus, English *be going to* in Shakespeare's time could express both the "change of location" sense and the "intention" sense. In Modern English, the intention sense is still present, but the future sense is also possible, with no intention or movement implied (*That tree is going to lose its leaves*). As a result of the gradualness of change, and the fact that in any particular language a future morpheme might be anywhere on one of these paths, there is considerable cross-linguistic variation in the meaning and range of use of a future morpheme at any particular synchronic period.

Considering just synchronic states, then, it is extremely difficult to formulate universals of tense, or even to give a universal meaning to "future" that would be valid across all languages. Indeed in the 1950s and 1960s it was common for linguists to exclaim that any attempt to find universals of grammatical meaning would be futile and ethnocentric (Chomsky, 1957; Weinreich, 1963). Now there are attempts to formulate the innate universals of tense and aspect (Smith, 1991), but it is very difficult to find a small set of features that accommodate all the cross-linguistic variation in the area of tense and aspect.

Comparing grammatical categories across languages from only a synchronic perspective is something like comparing an acorn to an oak tree: They appear to have distinct and unrelated properties. Only when we observe these entities across the temporal dimension do we see the relationship between them. Similarly with grammatical categories and constructions: New relationships are observable when we take into account where particular grammatical constructions and categories come from and where they are going.

The examination of the grammaticalization process across many grammatical domains and many different languages makes it clear that the true language universals are universals of change. At one level, these universals can be stated as paths of change, such as those in (4) and (5). To understand grammar more fully, however, we must look behind these paths of change to the actual mechanisms that cause change and then seek to understand these mechanisms in terms of more basic cognitive and interactive processes. If we are successful, we will begin to understand how human language acquires grammar.

CONCEPTUAL SOURCES FOR GRAMMATICAL MATERIAL

The examples discussed in the preceding sections showed lexical items entering into the grammaticalization process. One of the major cross-linguistic similarities noted in the previous section is that the same or very similar lexical meanings tend to grammaticalize in unrelated languages. Of all the tens of thousands of words in a language, only a small set are candidates for participation in the grammaticalization process. Are there any generalizations that could be made concerning the members of this set?

Researchers in this area have made some interesting observations about the lexical items that are candidates for grammaticalization. Heine et al. (1991b) have observed that the terms in this set are largely culturally independent, that is, universal to human experience. Furthermore, they represent concrete and basic aspects of human relations with the environment, with a strong emphasis on the spatial environment, including parts of the human body. Thus we find terms for movement in space, such as "come" and "go" in future constructions, postures such as "sit," "stand" and "lie" in progressive constructions. The relationship in space between one object and another is frequently expressed in terms of a human body part's relation to the rest of the body. Thus the noun for "head" evolves into a preposition meaning "on top of," "top," or "on." "Back" is used for "in back of" (English provides an example of this derivation), "face" for "in front of," "buttock" or "anus" for "under," and "belly" or "stomach" for "in" (Heine et al., 1991b, pp. 126–131). In a survey of such relational terms in 125 African languages, Heine et al. found that more than three quarters of the terms whose etymology was known were derived from human body parts. Svorou (1993), using a sample representative of all the language families of the world, also found human body parts to be the most frequent sources of relational terms.[2] Less concrete, but nonetheless basic and culturally independent notions such as volition, obligation, and having knowledge or power also enter into the grammaticalization process.

The relation between locational terms and abstract grammatical concepts has been recognized for several decades. Anderson (1971) proposed a theory of grammatical cases (nominative, accusative, dative, etc.) based on spatial relations. Thus a relational term meaning "toward" further develops to mean "to" whence it can become a dative marker (*I gave the book to John*) or can even further develop into an accusative (as in Spanish: *Vi a Juan* "I saw John"). Or, with a verb, "to" can signal purpose and eventually generalize to an infinitive marker (Haspelmath, 1989; see the section entitled "The Grammaticalization of Subordinate Clauses"). Thus even the most abstract of grammatical notions can be traced back to a very concrete, often physical or locational concept involving the movement and orientation of the human body in space.

Another important observation about the lexical items found in grammaticalizing constructions is that they are themselves already highly generalized in meaning. Thus among motion verbs, "go" and "come" are the most general in meaning, incorporating only movement and directionality and not manner (i.e., the more specific "saunter," "waddle" or "run" do not grammaticalize, though in some cases the most basic form of human locomotion "walk" does grammaticalize). Among stative verbs, it is "be" and "have" that grammaticalize, and for active verbs, the most generalized, "do" (Bybee et al., 1994).

The claim here is not that the abstract concepts are forever linked to the more concrete, only that they have their diachronic source in the very concrete physical experience. Grammatical constructions and the concepts they represent become emancipated from the concrete (see section titled

---

[2]The other frequent sources for relational terms are the body parts of livestock and landmarks.

"Emancipation") and come to express purely abstract notions, such as tense, case relations, definiteness, and so on. It is important to note, however, that the sources for grammar are concepts and words drawn from the most concrete and basic aspects of human experience.

GRAMMATICALIZATION AS AUTOMATIZATION

Some recent studies of grammaticalization have emphasized the point that grammaticalization is the process of automatization of frequently occurring sequences of linguistic elements (Boyland, 1996; Bybee, in press; Haiman, 1994). Boyland (1996) pointed out that the changes in form that occur in the grammaticalization process closely resemble changes that occur as non-linguistic skills are practiced and become automatized. With repetition, sequences of units that were previously independent come to be processed as a single unit or chunk. This repackaging has two consequences: The identity of the component units is gradually lost, and the whole chunk begins to reduce in form. These basic principles of automatization apply to all kinds of motor activities: playing a musical instrument, playing a sport, stirring pancake batter. They also apply to grammaticalization. A phrase such as *(I'm) going to (VERB)*, which has been frequently used over the last couple of centuries, has been repackaged as a single processing unit. The identity of the component parts is lost (children are often surprised to see that *gonna* is actually spelled *going to*), and the form is substantially reduced. The same applies to all cases of grammaticalization.[3]

It follows then that grammatical constructions of all types are automatized motor routines and subroutines that can be strung together or embedded in one another to produce fluent speech. This conclusion, arrived at from the study of linguistic data, is similar to the proposal of Kimura (1979, 1993), who argued on the basis of neuropsychological data for a strong association between grammar and motor skill (see also Lieberman, 1984). However, grammar is not just motor activity, but motor activity appropriate to, and meaningful in, specific contexts. Thus it is important to pursue the question of how motor activities and meaning associate to make grammar.

Haiman (1994, 1998) noted that the chunking and reduction features of the grammaticalization process bear a resemblance to non-linguistic ritualized behavior, citing rituals in both human and non-human species that show chunking and reduction in form. In addition, Haiman cited two

---

[3]Bybee, Pagliuca, and Perkins (1991) and Bybee et al. (1994) demonstrated for a large cross-linguistic sample that a significant relationship between degree of grammaticalization in semantic terms and formal reduction obtains.

other characteristics of ritualized behavior that apply to grammaticalization. First, repeated practices lead to *habituation*, the process by which an organism ceases to respond at the same level to a repeated stimulus. A repeated word or phrase tends to lose much of its semantic force (consider the loss of the power of the *f*-word when it is used very frequently). Thus habituation helps to bring about the generalization or bleaching of semantic content that occurs in grammaticalization. Second, repeated practices can also change their function, through the process of *emancipation*, by which the original instrumental function of the practice takes on a symbolic function inferred from the context in which it occurs. These two processes and other related processes are crucial to the understanding of how grammatical meaning develops.

EMANCIPATION AND HABITUATION
IN THE CREATION OF GRAMMATICAL MEANING

The phrase "grammatical meaning" refers to the type of meaning conveyed by grammatical morphemes and grammatical constructions. This type of meaning is often contrasted with "lexical meaning," which is the meaning of nouns, verbs, and adjectives. The study of grammaticalization makes it clear that there is no discrete cut-off point between the two types of meaning, but rather a continuum from one to the other. However, we can still note the properties of the polar types. Lexical meaning is specific and concrete, with nouns referring to physical entities and their parts, and abstract notions of cultural import. The lexical meaning of verbs describes perceived events and relations among entities, events that often have concrete physical results. The specificity of lexical meaning is shown by the large number of contrasts that can be made, that is, in the number of names for species of trees (*oak, elm, fir, pine, willow,* etc.) or the number of designations for ways to move through space (*walk, swim, climb, run, hop, trot,* etc.). The more specific the meaning of a lexical item, the more stable it remains across differing contexts.

Grammatical meaning, on the other hand, is typically abstract, referring to large, abstract domains such as time or modality, or referring to abstract grammatical relations such as "subject of the verb," or abstract relations among clauses, such as "although." It is also highly general, being applicable to a large number of contexts. For instance, every English sentence has a grammatical designation of tense, showing that tense is general enough to apply to any verb in the language. It is this type of meaning, so typical of human language, that is responsible for the great versatility of language, making it applicable to any human communicative context. It is also this type of meaning that is the most difficult to describe or explain.

Another important difference between lexical and grammatical meaning concerns the extent to which language users have conscious access to the meaning of units. Speakers can often report directly and accurately on the meanings of nouns, verbs, and adjectives, much as they can report pieces of propositional or declarative knowledge (such as "Washington, DC is the capital of the United States"). However, grammatical meaning is much less accessible, and if speakers can report on uses of grammatical constructions, they often seem aware only of the most concrete of these uses. In this way, grammatical knowledge resembles procedural knowledge or skilled ability (Boyland, 1996), providing further evidence that grammatical constructions are automated procedures.

The approach that studies the way grammatical meaning evolves out of lexical meaning has a great deal to contribute to the general understanding of grammar and its meaning. Some of the mechanisms for semantic change in grammaticalization have been identified and are discussed briefly here.

Emancipation

Emancipation in ritualistic language is extremely common. Polite expressions of concern about a person's well-being in mutual greetings, such as *how are you*, reduce to simple greetings that require no substantive response, such as *hi*. In some varieties of Black English *hi* is still answered with *fine*, reflecting its source in a question, but in most dialects it is answered with *hi*. A string of words that originally had literal meaning or instrumental function has lost its instrumental function and become a symbol for the situation itself due to repetition in a particular context—in this case the greeting situation.

The change from a lexical to a grammatical function in grammaticalization involves a process that is quite parallel and could also be considered emancipation. As I mentioned earlier, in Shakespeare's English *be going to* had its literal meaning of movement in space toward some goal. However, given an apparent interest by human beings in goals and purposes, even in Shakespeare's English, the information value of *be going to* was less about movement in space and more about purpose. Consider Example (6):

(6) *Duke:* Sir Valentine, whither away so fast?
    Val.: Please it your grace, there is a messenger
           That stays in to bear my letters to my friends,
           And <u>I am going to deliver them</u>.
(Shakespeare, *Two Gentlemen of Verona*, III.i.51, from Hopper & Traugott, 1993)

Note that even though the Duke asks about movement ("Where are you going so fast?"), what he really wants to know is Valentine's intention or purpose. Note also that although Valentine answers in terms of movement, he
also includes the appropriate information about his intention.

The frequent association of *be going to* with contexts in which the intentions of the subject are also being revealed leads to its gradual emancipation from the earlier meaning of movement in space. The new function of
expressing a goal or intention also gradually becomes the main function of
the construction.

Pragmatic Inference

In the grammaticalization literature, the mechanism of change in this example has been called *pragmatic inference* (Hopper & Traugott, 1993;
Traugott, 1989). It is widely accepted that an important feature of the communication process is the ability to make inferences: The speaker must be
able to judge which details the hearer can supply and formulate his or her
utterances accordingly, and the hearer must fill in details not supplied by
the speaker. Thus, the hearer is constantly asking "why is he or she asking
me or telling me this?" In the example, Valentine knew that the Duke's
question was not just about movement in space but also about intention
and he answered appropriately. When the same pattern of inferences occurs frequently with a particular grammatical construction, those inferences can become part of the meaning of the construction. If *be going to* is
frequently used to talk about intentions, it begins to have intention as part
of its meaning. The literature on grammaticalization is full of such instances (Bybee et al., 1994; Traugott, 1989).

Traugott (1989, 1995) has identified several important patterns of inferencing that create semantic change in grammaticalization and lead to
the expression of more abstract grammatical meaning. She argued that
more concrete propositional (lexical) meaning, describing external situations, such as spatial movement or location, is regularly inferred to have
meanings that describe internal (evaluative, perceptual, or cognitive) situations, such as intention. A second trend that she posited is that both external and internal meanings can be reinterpreted as having meanings based
in the textual situation, such as meanings that place the described situation
in time before or after the moment of speech, that is, tense. A third trend
infers the speaker's subjective beliefs or attitudes from the other two types
of meaning. The claim is that the abstract meanings of grammatical constructions arise from common patterns of inference. The types of meanings
that arise in this way suggest that hearers are commonly working to infer as
much as possible about the relations of narrated descriptions to the current

speech situation and to the speaker's subjective evaluation of it. The content of grammar, then, is directly related to, and arises from, the very act of communication. It is not autonomous from the meanings it conveys or the purposes it serves.

Note further that common paths of change, such as those shown in (4) and (5), would not be attested across languages unless users of these languages made very similar inferences under similar conditions. That is, the repetition across languages of the change in meaning from "movement toward a goal" to "intention" is evidence that speakers in different cultures tend to infer intentions; similarly, changes from temporal sequence (as English *since*, originally meaning "after the time that") to causation indicate that language users are prone to infer causation.

Generalization or Bleaching as Habituation

Another important mechanism of change in grammaticalization is related to habituation. The earliest discussion of grammaticalization recognized that grammatical morphemes lose components of their original lexical meaning and become much more general and abstract. For instance, *will* loses the volitional aspect of its meaning and *be going to* loses the spatial movement components. This process has been called *bleaching* or *generalization of meaning*. The latter term is especially appropriate because the loss of specificities of meaning makes a morpheme applicable in a more general range of contexts. For example, if *will* does not signal volition, it can be used with a wider range of subjects, including inanimate objects.

Repetition itself diminishes the force of a word, phrase or construction. Examples are legion. *Iterate* doesn't seem to mean "repeat" quite strongly enough, so we tend to add *re-*; with repetition the strength of that fades and we have to say *reiterate again*. *You guys* generalizes to include females and the word *guy* now can be used in colloquial speech even for inanimate objects. In grammaticalization, the generalization or bleaching of the meaning of a construction is caused by frequency, but it also contributes to additional frequency, as a generalized construction can be used in more contexts, leading to an almost inexorable movement along a grammaticalization path.

Constructions that have been bleached of their more specific lexical meaning are more likely to pick up inferential meaning from the context, that is, grammatical meaning (Bybee et al., 1994). The French negative phrase *ne (VERB) pas* originally contained both a negative element *ne* and the noun *pas* meaning "step" and was used only with motion verbs, with the sense "not (go) a step." Now *pas* has lost all of its independent meaning in the construction and has absorbed the negative meaning from the construction. As *ne* is gradually being deleted, *pas* becomes the sole negative marker.

Categorization

An important feature of generalization is the expansion of contexts in which a construction can occur. For instance, the French construction *ne (VERB) pas* was originally restricted to use with motion verbs. The verb slot in this construction gradually expanded to include all verbs. The *be going to* construction in English originally required human subjects and active, agentive verbs, but now its use has expanded to all types of subjects and verbs.

Constructions always contain a variable slot (otherwise we consider them set phrases), and the variable slot is restricted to items of a certain category. These categories are usually defined semantically, with terms such as "human," "volitional," "change of state," and so on. Some constructions require quite specific categories. For instance, the construction typified by the phrase *to wend one's way* allows a verb of motion, or a verb construable as describing movement or the creation of a path (*swiggled his way, made our way, cut their way*). The position after the verb requires a pronoun that is coreferential with the subject.

The various positions in a construction, then, require categorization. These categories are based on the experience one has with the construction, just as the categories we create for classifying cultural and natural objects are based on our experience with the world (Lakoff, 1987; Rosch, 1978). Linguistic categories, both those based on form and those based on meaning, have a prototype structure. They cannot be defined adequately as a series of necessary and sufficient conditions, but rather must be characterized in terms of more central and more peripheral members (see Taylor, 1998). The possibility of adding new peripheral members to a category allows productivity and change. New items can be used in a construction if they are perceived as similar in some way to existing members. Accumulated change in membership will lead to change in what is considered central and what is considered peripheral.

The productive use of constructions, or automated subroutines, is what allows speakers to generate new utterances, as speech consists of these routines concatenated and embedded in one another. Through practice one's fluency in manipulating and stringing together constructions increases. Linguistic categorization determines the appropriateness of particular combinations of constructions and takes the same form as categorization for non-linguistic percepts. Note that all the component processes that lead to the development of new grammatical constructions come out of language use in context and they involve cognitive skills and strategies that are also used in non-linguistic tasks.

THE GRAMMATICALIZATION OF SUBORDINATE CLAUSES

Grammatical markers that are highly associated with the syntax also develop in the same way as other grammatical morphemes. For instance, English *to* that marks an infinitive has developed within the documented period between Old English and the present. The resemblance between the preposition *to* and the infinitive marker is no accident. Haspelmath (1989) demonstrated that it is extremely frequent cross-linguistically for a preposition meaning "to, toward" to develop into an infinitive marker. In Old and Middle English *to* could be used with an infinitive (marked with a suffix) to indicate purpose, and optionally after verbs such as "begin," "cease" or "teach" but was otherwise not used with verbs (Sweet, 1882). In Middle English *to* was used in purpose clauses but it had also expanded to clauses with main verbs of desiring or ordering (Mossé, 1952). Note that the infinitive suffix *-en* still appeared on the verb:

(7) *thanne wolde he maken hem to drynken*
    "then he wanted to make them drink"

The use of *to* before an infinitive continued to expand to a variety of contexts as the infinitive suffix was lost. The result is the loss of much of the prepositional meaning of *to* in this context and the development of a new form of the verb for use in a variety of subordinate clauses. (See Haspelmath, 1989, for more details about this development in German and other languages.)

Certain constructions in English use the infinitive without *to*, in particular the modal auxiliaries (*will, shall, may, can, would, could,* etc.). The difference between constructions such as *will go* without *to* before the infinitive and *want to go* with the *to* infinitive can be partly explained in terms of the period in which the constructions developed and began grammaticalizing. Already in Old English, the modern modal auxiliaries were used with infinitives, which at that time were marked with a suffix. During the Middle English period such constructions increased in frequency and became entrenched. The new infinitive marker *to* was also gradually expanding during the same period, but because the [MODAL AUXILIARY + VERB] construction was already formed and entrenched without *to*, the new marker has not affected these constructions. In contrast, the construction of [*want*

+ INFINITIVE] developed much later and so uses the infinitive marker that was current when it developed. Other conservative features of the modal auxiliary construction are discussed in Bybee (in press).

Other types of subordinate clauses develop out of main clauses. Givón (1979) noted that over time loosely joined structures or clauses tend to become more tightly fused, resulting at times in new subordinate clauses. This can be seen in the development of the English complementizer *that*, which derives from the demonstrative pronoun *that*. Hopper and Traugott (1993, pp. 185–189) presented examples from Old English where the complementizer *that* still shows some characteristics of being a pronoun and the structures it occurs in are more loosely connected (more hypotactic) than today. Consider the use in (8) where a fronted demonstrative pronoun corresponds to the complementizer later in the sentence:

(8) *Thæt gefremede Diulius hiora consul, thæt thæt angin*
DEM arranged Diulius their consul, COMP DEM beginning
wearth tidlice thurhtogen.
was in-time achieved

The loose or hypotactic structure of this sentence is reflected in my translation in (9). Today, a subordinate structure, such as (10), would be used.

(9) "That, their consul Diulius arranged, that the beginning was on time."

(10) "Their consul Diulius arranged (it) that it was started on time."

Another example of a loose, hypotactic structure becoming a tighter subordinate structure is the development of a complementizer and complement clauses in some related West African languages, as studied by Lord (1976) (see also Heine et al., 1991a, Hopper & Traugott, 1993).

In Ewe, with the main verb *bé* "to say," two clauses can be loosely joined as in (11):

(11) *me-bé me-wɔ-e*
I-say I-do-it
"I said, 'I did it'/I said that I did it"

With other verbs of saying, however, *bé* occurs without the pronominal prefix and functions more like a complementizer:

(12) *me-gblɔ bé me-wɔ-e*
I-say say I-do-it
"I said that I did it"

From uses such as (12), *bé* has been extended, and it can be used as a complementizer with many different main verbs, including verbs of cognition (*nyá* "know"), perception (*kpɔ* "see") and verbs of desire, as in (13):

(13) *me-dí   bé   máple*   *awua dewoi*
      I-want say I-SUBJUNCT-buy dress some
      "I want to buy some dresses"

Not only has *bé* lost its original meaning of "say" and taken on an abstract grammatical function, it has also produced a tighter syntactic structure, as it introduces a subordinate clause.

GRAMMATICAL CHANGE IN GRAMMATICALIZATION

The recent surge in research on grammaticalization has made it clear that the same set of processes and mechanisms are responsible for all aspects of grammar. All grammatical morphemes have developed out of lexical morphemes, principally nouns and verbs, and all grammatical structures have developed out of more loosely organized constituents. In this section, the processes of decategorialization and reduction of constituent structure is illustrated.

Decategorialization

Decategorialization is the term applied to the set of processes by which a noun or verb loses its morphosyntactic properties in the process of becoming a grammatical element (Heine et al., 1991a; Hopper, 1991). In some cases, the lexical item from which a grammatical morpheme arose will remain in the language (*go* retains many lexical uses, despite the grammaticalization of *be going to*), and in other cases, the lexical item disappears and only the grammatical element remains (*can* is grammaticalized, and the main verb from which it developed, *cunnan* "to know," has disappeared). In both cases the grammaticalizing element ceases to behave like a regular noun or verb.

    Verbs lose canonical verbal properties when they become auxiliaries. Consider the auxiliary *can*, which derives from the Old English main verb *cunnan* "to know." In Old English, *cunnan* could be used with a noun phrase object, but today *can* occurs only with a verb complement: **I can that* and **I can her* are ungrammatical. The English modal auxiliaries have lost all their inflected or derived forms and are invariable. There is no infinitive **to can*, no progressive or gerund form **canning*, and the past form of *can*, which is *could*, is developing non-past uses (*I could do it tomorrow*) and will perhaps lose its function as the past of *can*, just as *should* no longer expresses the past of *shall*. The auxiliaries rarely modify one another. Whereas the use of *shall can* was possible in Middle English, such constructions have disappeared from Modern English. In other words, *can* has no main verb uses.

An example of a noun that has lost much of its categoriality is the conjunction *while*, which was previously a noun meaning a length of time. Today it is very limited in its use as a noun. When it is clause-initial and functioning as a conjunction, it has no noun properties. Thus it does not take articles nor can it be modified as in (14).

(14) *I was there the same while you were.

In other contexts, its use as a noun is restricted to set phrases such as *all the while, a long while*. It cannot be freely used as a noun; thus (15) through (17) are unacceptable:

(15) *I've been there many whiles.

(16) *I waited a boring while.

(17) *The while was very long.

Loss of Constituent Structure

The elements in constructions that are grammaticalizing become more tightly fused together and the internal constituent structure of the construction tends to reduce. Thus two clauses become one, two verb phrases become one, and so on. A few illustrative examples follow.

Heine et al. (1991a) reported that in Teso (a Nilo-Saharan language of western Kenya and eastern Uganda) the negative construction (18) derived from a construction with a main clause and subordinate clause, as in (19):

(18) *mam petero e-koto   ekiŋok*
     not Peter 3SG-want dog
     "Peter does not want a dog"

(19) *e-mam   petero   e-koto   ekiŋok*
     3SG is not Peter (who) 3SG-want dog
     "It is not Peter who wants a dog"

The sentence in (19) consists of the main verb *-mam*, which originally meant "not to be," with Peter as its object, and a relative clause modifying Peter. In the current construction as in (18), the verb is grammaticalized to a negative particle and negative sentence consisting of one clause rather than two.

The English main plus complement clause construction exemplified in (20) is undergoing grammaticalization, which results in the loss of the main clause status for the phrase *I think* (Thompson & Mulac, 1991).

(20) I think that we're definitely moving towards being more technological.

Common uses of *I think (that)* and *I guess (that)* show that the actual assertion in utterances like (20) is contained in the complement clause and the introductory "main clause" just gives an epistemic evaluation of how much confidence the speaker has in the truth of the assertion. It is with these two erstwhile main verbs that the omission of *that* occurs most frequently, as in (21). Also these phrases can be used parenthetically, in which case the former complement clause is the main clause in every respect, as in (22). (Examples from Thompson & Mulac, 1991).

(21) I think exercise is really beneficial, to anybody.

(22) It's just your point of view, you know, what you like to do in your spare time, I think.

Thus a complex clause consisting of a main verb and a complement clause has become a single main clause modified by an epistemic expression.

In other cases in which verbs grammaticalize the result is the reduction of two verb phrases to one. Consider the case of a verb becoming an auxiliary. As illustrated in (23), as the original main verb becomes an auxiliary, the embedded verb takes on main verb status. The result is a single VP where formerly there were two.

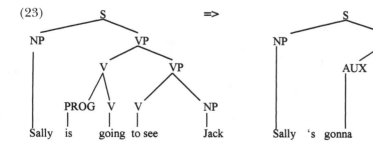

Another interesting case of the reduction of two VPs to one occurs in languages that allow serial verb constructions. The following example from Yoruba illustrates this nicely (Givón, 1975; Heine & Reh, 1984; Stahlke, 1970). In (24) there are two verbs that each have direct objects and approximately equal status:

(24) *mo fi   àdé   gé igi*
      I   took machete cut tree*o*

This can either be interpreted as "I took the machete and cut the tree" or, because *fi* is grammaticalizing as an instrumental preposition, it is more likely to be intrepreted as "I cut the tree with the machete." The fact that the serial verb construction has become a single VP with the grammaticalization of *fi* is underscored by examples such as (25):

(25) *mo fi   ǫgbǫ   gé igi*
      I   took/with cleverness cut tree
      "I cut the tree cleverly"

Almost every case of grammaticalization involves such a change in constituent structure. When viewed in terms of a structural analysis of the successive synchronic states, it is tempting to say that a reanalysis has taken place. For example, in the two cases just examined, what was a verb is reanalyzed as an auxiliary in one case and a preposition in the other. But it is important to note that even these reanalyses take place gradually, which means that when grammaticalization is occurring, it may not be possible to uniquely assign elements to particular grammatical categories or structures. Heine (1993) argued that the reason there is so much controversy surrounding the category of auxiliary verb, in that some linguists argue that they are verbs and others argue that they are a separate category, is that auxiliaries derive gradually from verbs and have not always lost all their verbal properties even though they have become grammaticalized.

IMPLICATIONS OF GRAMMATICALIZATION

Now that the researchers mentioned in this chapter (and others working on this topic) have studied the grammaticalization process and its outcome from a cross-linguistic perspective as well as in language-specific detail, we have a much clearer picture of the nature of grammar. We have seen that grammatical constructions arise through frequent repetition and their meanings change through processes of generalization and pragmatic inferencing. Grammatical constructions are automated, conventionalized units, which I claim are also processing units. The meanings and functions of constructions are not fixed and categorical, but allow variation that leads to gradual change over time. An essential factor in the development of grammatical constructions is language use.

Because all grammatical categories and constructions are derivable from experience with language, there is no reason to suppose that they are innate. In fact, the notion of innate grammatical rules is incompatible with the gradual, usage-driven nature of grammatical change. Innate rules and categories would be unchangeable over time and over generations, or if change occurred, an abrupt shift from one discrete category to another would be required.[4]

Strong universals of grammaticalization give rise to similarities among languages. Underlying these universals of change are cognitive and communicative universals. The cognitive processes in grammaticalization discussed in this chapter are:

1. the ability to automate neuromotor sequences through repetition
2. the ability to categorize recurrent linguistic elements
3. the tendency to infer more than is actually said
4. the tendency to habituate to repeated stimuli

Other mechanisms operative in the process of the creation of grammar may be identified by further research, perhaps by experimental means, or by the further examination of grammatical change in progress.

REFERENCES

Anderson, J. M. (1971). *The grammar of case: Towards a localist theory.* London: Cambridge University Press.

Bickerton, D. (1981). *Roots of language.* Ann Arbor, MI: Karoma.

Boyland, J. T. (1996). *Morphosyntactic change in progress: A psycholinguistic approach.* Unpublished doctoral dissertation, University of California, Berkeley.

Browman, C. P., & Goldstein, L. M. (1992). Articulatory phonology: An overview. *Phonetica, 49,* 155–180.

Bybee, J. L. (in press). Mechanisms of change in grammaticization: The role of repetition. In R. Janda & B. Joseph (Eds.), *Handbook of historical linguistics.* Oxford: Blackwell.

Bybee, J. L., & Pagliuca, W. (1987). The evolution of future meaning. In A. G. Ramat, O. Carruba, & G. Bernini (Eds.), *Papers from the VIIth International Conference on Historical Linguistics* (pp. 109–22). Amsterdam: John Benjamins.

Bybee, J., Pagliuca, W., & Perkins, R. (1991). Back to the future. In E. C. Traugott & B. Heine (Eds.), *Approaches to grammaticalization* (pp. 17–58). Amsterdam: John Benjamins.

Bybee, J., Perkins, R., & Pagliuca, W. (1994). *The evolution of grammar: Tense, aspect and modality in the languages of the world.* Chicago: University of Chicago Press.

Chomsky, N. (1957). *Syntactic structures.* The Hague, Netherlands: Mouton.

Givón, T. (1975). Serial verbs and syntactic change: Niger-Congo. In C. N. Li (Ed.), *Word order and word order change* (pp. 47–112). Austin, TX: University of Texas Press.

Givón, T. (1979). *On understanding grammar.* San Diego: Academic Press.

Haiman, J. (1994). Ritualization and the development of language. In W. Pagliuca (Ed.), *Perspectives on grammaticalization* (pp. 3–28). Amsterdam: John Benjamins.

---

[4]See Lightfoot's (1979) account of the development of the English modal auxialiaries, and Plank's (1984) response.

Haiman, J. (1998). *Talk is cheap: Sarcasm, alienation, and the evolution of language.* New York: Oxford University Press.

Haspelmath, M. (1989). From purposive to infinitive: A universal path of grammaticization. *Folia Linguistica Historica, 10,* 287–310.

Heine, B. (1993). *Auxiliaries.* New York: Oxford University Press.

Heine, B. (1997). *Cognitive foundations of grammar.* New York: Oxford University Press.

Heine, B., Claudi, U., & Hünnemeyer, F. (1991a). From cognition to grammar: Evidence from African languages. In E. Traugott & B. Heine (Eds.), *Approaches to grammaticalization* (Vol. 1, pp. 149–187). Amsterdam: John Benjamins.

Heine, B., Claudi, U., & Hünnemeyer, F. (1991b). *Grammaticalization: A conceptual framework.* Chicago: University of Chicago Press.

Heine, B., Güldemann, T., Kilian-Hatz, C., Lessau, D. A., Roberg, H., Schladt, M., & Stolz, T. (1993). *Conceptual shift: A lexicon of grammaticalization processes in African languages.* Afrikanistische Arbetispapier, 34/35. University of Cologne, Germany.

Heine, B., & Reh, M. (1984). *Grammaticalization and reanalysis in African languages.* Hamburg: Helmut Buske Verlag.

Hopper, P. J. (1991). On some principles of grammaticization. In E. Traugott & B. Heine (Eds.), *Approaches to grammaticalization* (Vol. 1, pp. 17–35). Amsterdam: John Benjamins.

Hopper, P., & Traugott, E. (1993). *Grammaticalization.* Cambridge: Cambridge University Press.

Janzen, T. (1995). *The polygrammaticalization of FINISH in ASL.* Master's thesis, University of Manitoba.

Kimura, D. (1979). Neuromotor mechanisms in the evolution of human communication. In H. D. Steklis & M. J. Raleigh (Eds.), *Neurobiology of social communication in primates* (pp. 197–219). San Diego: Academic Press.

Kimura, D. (1993). *Neuromotor mechanisms in human communication.* Oxford: Oxford University Press.

Lakoff, G. (1987). *Women, fire and dangerous things.* Chicago: University of Chicago Press.

Lehmann, C. (1982). *Thoughts on grammaticalization. A programmatic sketch.* Vol. I (Arbeiten des Kölner Universalien-Projekts 48). Köln: Universität zu Köln. Institut für Sprachwissenschaft. Also 1995, *LINCOM Studies in Theoretical Linguistics 01.* München and Newcastle: LINCOM Europa.

Lieberman, P. (1984). *Biology and the evolution of language.* Cambridge, MA: Harvard University Press.

Lightfoot, D. (1979). *Principles of diachronic syntax.* Cambridge: Cambridge University Press.

Lord, C. (1976). Evidence for syntactic reanalysis: From verb to complementizer in Kwa. In S. B. Steever, C. A. Walker, & S. S. Mufwene (Eds.), *Papers from the Parasession on Diachronic Syntax.* Chicago: Chicago Linguistic Society.

Meillet, A. (1912). L'évolution des formes grammaticales [The evolution of grammatical forms]. *Scientia* 12. (Reprinted from *Linguistique Historique et Linguistique Générale,* pp. 130–148, by A. Meillet, 1948, Paris: Edouard Champion.)

Mossé, F. (1952). *A handbook of Middle English.* Baltimore: Johns Hopkins University Press.

Mowrey, R., & Pagliuca, W. (1995). The reductive character of articulatory evolution. *Rivista di Linguistica, 7*(1), 37–124.

Plank, F. (1984). The modals story retold. *Studies in Language, 8,* 305–364.

Romaine, S. (1995). The grammaticalization of irrealis in Tok Pisin. In J. Bybee & S. Fleischman (Eds.), *Modality in grammar and discourse* (pp. 389–427). Amsterdam: John Benjamins.

Rosch, E. (1978). Principles of categorization. In E. Rosch & B. B. Lloyd (Eds.), *Cognition and categorization* (pp. 27–48). Hillsdale, NJ: Lawrence Erlbaum Associates.

Sankoff, G. (1990). The grammaticalization of tense and aspect in Tok Pisin and Sranan. *Language Variation and Change, 2,* 295–312.

Smith, C. S. (1991). *The parameter of aspect.* Dordrecht, Netherlands & Boston: Kluwer.

Stahlke, H. (1970). Serial verbs. *Studies in African Linguistics, 1*(1), 60–99.

Svorou, S. (1993). *The grammar of space.* Amsterdam: John Benjamins.

Sweet, H. (1882). *Anglo-Saxon primer.* Oxford: Clarendon Press.

Taylor, J. R. (1998). Syntactic constructions as prototype categories. In M. Tomasello (Ed.), *The new psychology of language* (pp. 177–202). Mahwah, NJ: Lawrence Erlbaum Associates.

Thompson, S., & Mulac, A. (1991). In E. Traugott & B. Heine (Eds.), *Approaches to grammaticalization* (Vol. 1, pp. 149–187). Amsterdam: John Benjamins.

Traugott, E. C. (1989). On the rise of epistemic meanings in English: An example of subjectification in semantic change. *Language, 65,* 31–55.

Traugott, E. C. (1995). Subjectification in grammaticalisation. In D. Stein & S. Wright (Eds.), *Subjectivity and subjectivisation: Linguistic perspectives* (pp. 31–54). Cambridge: Cambridge University Press.

Traugott, E. C. (in press). Unidirectionality in grammaticalization. In R. Janda & B. Joseph (Eds.), *Handbook of historical linguistics.* Oxford: Blackwell.

Weinreich, U. (1963). On the semantic structure of language. In J. Greenberg (Ed.), *Universals of language* (pp. 114–171). Cambridge, MA: MIT Press.

Chapter 6

Pronouns and Point of View: Cognitive Principles of Coreference

Karen van Hoek
Oakland University, Michigan

Language may be described as a medium by which one person can direct another person's attention through a series of conceptualizations, imagined scenes, and mental worlds. Using words, a speaker can give a hearer directions for constructing an imagined scene and mentally placing his or herself as viewer within it. Slight changes in wording may signal that one must mentally "zoom in" or "zoom out," see a scene through the eyes of a character, or imagine that the character is some distance away. Most of these effects are accomplished with little, if any, conscious preplanning on the part of the speaker; aside from trained fiction writers, the majority of speakers seem to use the tools of language without conscious awareness of the effects they are creating or the means by which they are doing it.[1]

One of the means by which these subtle nuances may be conveyed is the system of nominal reference and coreference, also known as *pronominal anaphora*. This is a term that describes a phenomenon such as in (1), in which the reference of a pronoun can be understood only via its relationship with another noun.

---

[1] The fiction writers' manual *Characters and Viewpoint* by Orson Scott Card (Writer's Digest Books, 1988) describes some of the linguistic devices a writer may use to signal different degrees of empathy with a character. The author observes correctly that although readers will notice the effects, they will not consciously recognize what the writer is doing linguistically to create them.

(1) <u>John</u> lost <u>his</u> briefcase.

The pronoun *his* may be understood to mean John (underlining is used to indicate that two nominals are intended to corefer, i.e., to refer to the same person or thing). Although this interpretation comes easily to a fluent English speaker, the conceptual system that produces the interpretation is remarkably complex and subtle. For example, in (2a) the pronoun *him* may refer to Ralph (or to someone else), but in (2b), *he* cannot refer to Ralph, it can only refer to someone else. The asterisk is used to indicate that (2b) is unacceptable (if the pronoun is read as referring to Ralph; under a different reading of the pronoun, the sentence is perfectly fine).

(2) a. Near <u>him</u>, <u>Ralph</u> saw a skunk.
    b. *Near <u>Ralph</u>, <u>he</u> saw a skunk.

Hundreds of different sentence pairs could be constructed showing similar contrasts across a wide range of grammatical constructions. In each case, a seemingly trivial change in the placement of the pronoun vis-à-vis the name utterly changes the range of possibilities for interpreting the pronoun.

Since contrasts of this type were first noticed, just over three decades ago, linguists have attempted to determine the unconscious rules that govern speakers' interpretation of pronouns, names, and other noun phrases. The problem is particularly intriguing because the rules are not explicitly taught by parents or English teachers (they themselves do not consciously know what the rules are), and yet there is remarkably widespread agreement across speakers.

Desiderata for a Theory of Pronominal Anaphora

Previous analyses of the anaphora problem have primarily been couched in the generative syntactic framework of Noam Chomsky (see Reinhart, 1983, and references there). They have accordingly assumed that there are special grammatical principles involved, principles that must be stated in terms of purely syntactic constructs (rather than general cognitive principles or even linguistic principles that pertain to other facets of language, such as meaning).

The most widely accepted analysis within the generative paradigm is the *c-command* analysis proposed by Reinhart (1983). C-command is a geometric relationship between elements in syntactic tree structures. Under this analysis, to determine whether a name and a pronoun within a given sentence can refer to the same person, one must first draw a tree diagram representing the abstract syntactic structure of the sentence (the structure does not represent the meaning of the sentence, nor its pronunciation—it is a purely abstract, syntactic construct). Within this tree structure, one then looks at the placements of the nodes that mark the locations of the name and the pronoun. One traces a path from the pronoun upward in the tree, to the first node above the pronoun that branches (i.e., that has multiple nodes beneath it), and then downward in the tree, through all the nodes that lie beneath that first branching node. If the path drawn in this way leads to the name, then the pronoun is said to "c-command" the name, and coreference is ruled out. In Fig. 6.1, which presents a very simplified representation of a syntactic tree structure, the first branching node above the pronoun *he* is the very topmost node in the tree; one can trace a path from the pronoun to that top node and then down again to reach the name *John*. Coreference is therefore ruled out.

This analysis successfully predicts many of the judgments that speakers make concerning the possibility for coreference, but it has several drawbacks. First, there is no explanation whatsoever of the reason or reasons that this particular geometric relationship between points on a tree should be so significant. The analysis is defined in terms of purely syntactic constructs, abstract tree structures that represent neither meaning nor pronunciation and that are therefore highly suspect from a cognitive linguistic standpoint. Entire classes of data are routinely excluded from consideration in the c-command literature; in particular, phenomena involving point-of-view effects are generally not discussed, ostensibly because they often involve slippery and variable speaker judgments, but perhaps also because c-command fails to predict point-of-view effects. By its nature, the c-command analysis is limited to phenomena in which the name and pronoun are located within a single sentence; it cannot account for cross-sentential phenomena of any kind (generative syntax explicitly claims that the rules of syntax are part of an autonomous "syntactic module" that is fully distinct from any modules or principles governing discourse). The key generative analysis thus claims, implicitly or explicitly (see Reinhart, 1983), that nominal coreference cannot be treated as a unified system with a single coherent set of principles; instead, any evidence of parallelism or unity between the rules governing coreference within sentences and across discourse is to be viewed as nothing more than a coincidence.

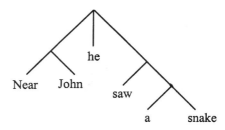

FIG. 6.1.   Tree structure for
"Near John, he saw a snake."

A very different approach is suggested by the cognitive linguistic paradigm and particularly by the theory of Cognitive Grammar (Langacker, 1987, 1991, 1998). Cognitive Grammar (CG) treats language as just one facet of human cognition, and requires that all linguistic constructs used within the theory have non-linguistic analogues elsewhere in cognition. Basic abilities, such as the ability to make comparisons or the ability to perceive figure/ground distinctions, are the building blocks from which the theory is constructed. CG does not posit the existence of an independent "syntactic module" or "autonomous syntax" with special theoretical primitives and constructs. Instead, CG defines grammar as *conventional symbolization*: recurrent patterns of association between forms and meanings.

CG defines meaning conceptually: The meaning of an expression is the concepts that it activates in a speaker's mind. Thus it may include activation of networks of associated concepts, knowledge structures, mental images (including, but not limited to, visual images), and so forth. Sentence-level grammar is part of the means by which speakers direct attention through these networks of interconnected concepts.

In accordance with the fundamental orientation of CG theory, I argue that a satisfactory account of pronominal anaphora should have the following characteristics:

- It should be based on an insightful characterization of the semantics of different nominal forms, on the assumption that different forms correspond to different meanings.
- It should be stated in terms of general principles and properties of language and, if possible, human cognition more generally.
- On the reasonable assumption that (pro)nominal usage reflects a coherent and unitary set of principles, the account should give a unified explanation of usage within sentences and across discourse, instead of accounting only for the within-sentence ("syntactic") usage and relegating the cross-sentential, discourse usage to another domain of study.

THE MEANINGS OF NOUNS AND PRONOUNS

To begin, we must recognize that different nominal forms invoke subtly different conceptions of the entities they refer to. Calling someone *he* is not the same as calling him *Ronald Reagan* or *Ronnie* or *the former president of the United States*, even if all of these expressions are understood to point to the same individual. The differences between these expressions, though subtle, are highly significant. The differences can be expressed in two ways, in terms of the concepts of *accessibility* and *conceptual distance*.

Accessibility Theory (Ariel, 1990; Givón, 1989, 1998) claims that nominal forms are chosen to signal differing degrees of accessibility of the conceptions that they reference, where accessibility refers to the amount of effort that one must expend to retrieve the conception of the referent.[2] Use of a full name, such as *James Duderstadt*, signals that the referent is relatively less accessible for the addressee, requiring more information and more effort to access a conception of the individual. A first name signals somewhat greater accessibility; one uses *Bill, Sally, Tom*, and so on, to refer to those whom the addressee is expected to be able to identify relatively easily due to their familiarity.

Pronouns signal much greater accessibility. A pronoun is used only when the speaker believes the addressee already has the conception of the individual in his or her current awareness—either because the person is physically present, or because she or he has recently been mentioned. (These comments apply most directly to English, but other languages seem to have a similar accessibility scale, with variations in the extent to which specific forms [pronouns, full names, etc.] are considered appropriate for different contexts. See Ariel [1990].)

The existence of these accessibility distinctions suggests that we can characterize the principles governing (pro)nominal reference fairly straightforwardly:

Speakers use full noun phrases (including names) to refer to entities that are not believed to be active in the addressee's immediate awareness. Speakers use pronouns to refer to entities that are believed to be active in the addressee's immediate awareness (Givón, 1998; Kibrik, 1999; van Hoek, 1995, 1997; *inter alia*). Immediate awareness can be defined in terms of the immediate context. A speaker uses a pronoun if a person who was attending to the immediate context would reasonably be expected to have the referent in immediate awareness (Kibrik, 1999, defined the relevant degree of accessibility in terms of presence within working memory). All that is needed to explain the usage of different nominal forms, then, is a sufficiently nuanced theory of context.

A different but complementary way of framing the issue comes from the notion of conceptual distance. Pronouns signal a subtle sense of closeness between the speaker and the person being referred to. We can see this most clearly if we consider the pronouns *I* and *you*, and how they differ from referring to the speaker or addressee by name. A useful metaphor for understanding the special role of the speaker and addressee in a conversation is the "stage model" (Langacker, 1985). The speaker and the addressee func-

---

[2]I use the term "reference" to describe the relationship between a nominal expression and the conception that it activates in a speaker's or addressee's mind; this is different than the formal semantic usage of the term.

tion in many ways like an audience watching a play. The conceptions that the speaker brings into the center of attention are like actors and events placed on a stage, and so the center of attention is termed the "on-stage region." This is illustrated in Fig. 6.2a, where the circles labeled *S* and *A* represent the speaker and addressee, the dotted arrows represent their focus of attention, and the on-stage region is shown as a box containing small interconnected circles, representing things in interaction.

There is an important conceptual distinction between the on-stage region and the off-stage region (where the speaker and addressee are). A concept that is placed on stage is fully in the center of attention, and so it is construed *objectively*, as the object of perception. The speaker and addressee, being the perceivers rather than that-which-is-perceived, are construed *subjectively*. The subjective/objective distinction is important because it distinguishes between the viewer (subjective) and that which is viewed (objective).

The pronouns *I* and *you* partially blur the distinction between the on-stage and off-stage regions, however. When a speaker says "I," she places on stage a conception that can be understood only by its relationship to part of the off-stage region, the speaker. The speaker cannot go fully on stage—that is, she cannot fully give up her role as "viewer" and view herself completely objectively (so long as she has any view of herself, she is obviously still playing the role of viewer, and so is construed semi-subjectively). But she can place herself partially on stage, and experience herself simultaneously as the speaker and as the one spoken about, as viewer and viewed. This is the meaning of the pronoun *I*, which signals that the person on whom the speaker and addressee are now focusing their attention is the same as the speaker. This is indicated in Fig. 6.2b by the dashed line representing the correspondence between the on-stage participant and the speaker. The pronoun *you* has much the same meaning, that is, a semi-subjective, semi-objective construal of one of the off-stage participants, except that it references the addressee.

Even a third-person pronoun (e.g., *he* or *she*) signals the same kind of split view of the referent, the same kind of blurring of the distinction be-

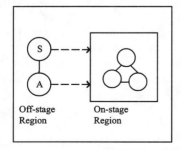 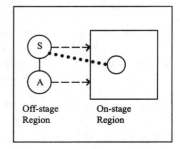

FIG. 6.2.   (a) Two conceptual regions. (b) The pronoun "I."

tween on-stage and off-stage participants. By saying "he," the speaker places on stage the conception of a person who is identified as someone who is already in the immediate awareness of the speaker and addressee (either because he is present in the room or because they have already been talking about him). That person is therefore part of the off-stage region, just as are the speaker and addressee themselves.

Because a third-person pronoun indicates that the person is part of the off-stage region, part of the intimate conceptual world shared between the speaker and addressee, it indicates a subtle sense of closeness or intimacy. In contrast, a name signals greater conceptual distance, "holding the person at arm's length," so to speak. This explains the finding by other researchers that speakers tend to refer to people by name if they wish to ridicule or criticize them. Parents who are critizing their children often call them by full name. Writers often use full names to refer to the butt of humor, as in (3). Note that the second appearance of the full names *Woody Allen* and *Mia Farrow* is not needed for clarity—the writer could have used pronouns—but rather seems to be motivated by the fact that they are being ridiculed.

(3) Also we have Woody Allen, whose humor has become so sophisticated that nobody gets it anymore except Mia Farrow. All those who think Mia Farrow should go back to making movies where the devil makes her pregnant and Woody Allen should go back to dressing up as a human sperm, please raise your hands. (Dave Barry, 1988, *Dave Barry's Greatest Hits*, p. 2)

Speakers also use names in contexts of negation, as when they are disagreeing with the previous speaker. Example (4) is from Fox (1987, p. 62), who observed this pattern but did not offer an explanation for it. If the choice of names or pronouns were determined simply by considerations of clarity, the second speaker could have used the pronoun *he* instead of *Alex*. The use of the name implies that the speaker is distancing himself from the conception proffered by the first speaker, instead of allowing it to become part of a shared conception in the discourse.

(4) R. Those are Alex's tanks, aren't they?
    V. Pardon me?
    R. Weren't—didn't they belong to Alex?
    V. No—Alex has no tanks, Alex is trying to buy my tank.

To summarize, a name (or descriptive noun phrase) portrays its referent as distant, fully on-stage and therefore fully distinct from the discourse participants in the off-stage region. A pronoun portrays its referent as relatively close and included in the off-stage conceptual world of the speaker and addressee. This is why it is bizarre, in most cases, for a speaker to refer to himself or herself by name, as when someone named Lisa announces, "Lisa loves to paint." By selecting a name instead of the pronoun *I*, she implicitly states that she is viewing herself at some distance away, the way that she would see another person. Conversely, overuse of pronouns and failure to use names may, depending on context, indicate excessive familiarity or psychological enmeshment with the person in question.

Given these observations, we can describe the constraints on coreference in these terms: The different nominal forms in a sentence or discourse have to contribute to a coherent conception, which means that the person(s) referred to have to be conceptually "viewed" in a consistent way. In (5), for example, (5a) would be acceptable because at one's first encounter with the conception of *Ralph*, he is referred to by name, which is appropriate inasmuch as he is not yet part of the discourse space shared by speaker and addressee; subsequently, he is referred to by a pronoun, which reflects the fact that, now that the speaker and addressee have incorporated him into their mental world, he is conceived as "closer."

(5) a. *Ralph* saw a skunk near *him*.
    b. **He* saw a skunk near *Ralph*.

In (5b), the reverse is true: The initial pronominal reference implies conceptual closeness, but the subsequent appearance of the name signals that he is farther away. If we think of language as a way to give another person instructions for constructing an imagined scene, (5b) is roughly equivalent to telling the addressee, "Imagine there is a man in the foreground, so close to you that you're looking over his shoulder, and as you look over his shoulder you see a skunk, and then you see the same man about 10 feet away." The sentence is rejected because it produces an incoherent conception of the scene, in much the same way that Lisa's reference to herself as "Lisa" implies that she has an anomalous view of herself.

These two ways of thinking about coreference—accessibility and conceptual closeness—are two sides of the same coin. A conception that is more accessible is one that is in, or close to, immediate awareness, and therefore is construed as part of the intimate world of speaker and addressee. A less-accessible conception is one that is outside of that immediate world, therefore farther away.

Both ways of framing the issue present the same challenge: To explain why a name or a pronoun will appear in a particular position, and when they are allowed to corefer, we have to determine what the starting points are—which elements in a sentence or discourse are construed as setting up the contexts within which other elements are interpreted. Another way of putting it is that we must know which things are viewed from which positions: which ways the "lines of sight" go within a sentence.

POINT-OF-VIEW EFFECTS

We can begin by looking at examples of what are called point-of-view (POV) effects in the anaphora literature. Traditionally, point-of-view effects have been considered peripheral to the main problem of pronominal anaphora. I argue, however, that they illustrate the same kinds of phenomena as the more "central," typical examples, and that starting with them will enable us to understand the issues more clearly.

To describe POV effects precisely, we can draw on the terminology of mental spaces theory (Fauconnier, 1985). A mental space is a kind of conceived context, such as the conception of the past, the future, the imaginary world of a story, or the contents of someone's thoughts and perceptions. Nominals access conceptions within different mental spaces. Even when the speaker is describing a thing that he or she thinks of as merely part of "reality," without any special context, it is located in a mental space: the conception of reality as viewed by the speaker. Describing something as viewed from another's POV means imagining a mental space that represents their perceptions, and locating the conception within it.

Consider the pair of sentences in (6). Example (6a) is acceptable even if *John* and *he* refer to the same person, but in (6b), *his* must refer to someone other than John.

> (6) a. John's worst fear is that he might have AIDS.
>   b. His worst fear is that John might have AIDS.

The reason for the contrast is fairly simple; intuitively speaking, it comes down to the fact that John would not think of himself as "John." In (6a), the phrase *John's worst fear* sets up a mental space, and the clause after the copula describes its contents, so it is interpreted as a description of John's thoughts. John would view himself semi-subjectively, meaning that he would think of himself as "I," not as "John." The use of the pronoun *he* in (6a) captures that semi-subjective view of himself.[3] In (6b), the implication is that "he" thinks of himself as "John," viewing himself objectively, from a distance; as this seems highly unlikely, the reader concludes that "his worst fear" must refer to the fear of someone other than John.

Now we can consider an example for which the judgments are less clear-cut. About half of the native speakers I have consulted judge (7) acceptable

---

[3]Although the pronoun is third person, and John would think of himself in the first person, it appears that that adjustment is not problematic. It is interesting to note that the pronoun may be third person and still be understood to describe John as viewed by John; however, for our purposes here what is important is simply that the nominal chosen must be congruent with the conceived viewer's perspective in terms of conceptual distance or subjectivity.

even if *him* refers to John, but half report that *him* must refer to someone else (this is my own judgment as well).

(7) That John might have AIDS worried him.

This sentence gets different judgments because there are (at least) two different interpretations. The embedded clause *that John might have AIDS* describes a conception that impacts on, and worries, someone described as *him*. But is the embedded conception being described from the perspective of the speaker—an external, objective view—or from the perspective of "him"? Under either interpretation, there are two mental spaces: the speaker's conception of reality, and the space representing the thoughts of "him" (which might be John or someone else). The question is which mental space the name *John* points to. Under one reading, illustrated in Fig. 6.3a, the name *John* points directly to the speaker's conception of John. That conception *corresponds to* someone located in the mental space that represents John's thoughts (the correspondence is indicated by the dotted line connecting the two), but there is no implication that the name "John" is actually how John would think of himself—the name is only a description of how the *speaker* sees him, as it only points directly to the speaker's conception of reality. The entire sentence is thus understood from the speaker's POV. This is the interpretation favored by those who believe the sentence is perfectly acceptable with coreference. Those who believe that the sentence is unacceptable (with coreference) assign it the interpretation shown in Fig. 6.3b. Here the name *John* is understood to point directly to the mental space representing his thoughts, and so "John" is a description of how he would actually think of himself. The speaker has his or her own view of reality, including John, of course, but the embedded clause *John might have AIDS* is viewed as a direct description of the contents of John's POV, not the speaker's. The sentence is therefore judged anomalous.

But why are there two different interpretations and two sets of judgments, when (6) gets unanimous, unequivocal judgments? In intuitive terms, (6) explicitly sets up the idea of "John's worst fear" (or "his worst

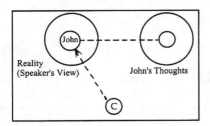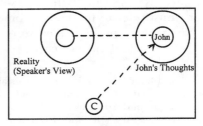

FIG. 6.3.   (a) John as seen by speaker. (b) John from John's point of view.

fear") as the mental space currently in focus, so that the material following it is unequivocally understood as a description of the contents of that space. In (7), there is more room for interpretation—some speakers take the mental space of John's thoughts to be the space currently in focus, so that the embedded clause *John might have AIDS* is interpreted as an exact description of the contents of that space. These speakers are probably guided by the verb *worry*, which suggests that the person who is worried must be "viewing" the contents of the embedded clause, so that their POV is the focus. Other speakers do not interpret it that way, possibly because the clause *John might have AIDS* comes earlier in the sentence than the phrase *worried him*; intuitively speaking, someone reading the sentence may just automatically understand the first phrase from their own POV, and not bother to go back and re-contextualize it within the conception of John's POV once they get to the end of the sentence.

Many of the classic examples from the pronominal anaphora literature involve very clear judgments rather than this kind of variability. This need not mean that fundamentally different principles are at work, however. Rather it may be simply that some sentences are constructed in such a way that the intended perspective is made very clear, and so all speakers "view" the conception from the same point of view; other sentences allow for a range of different perspectives. The interesting question is the factors that impel speakers to view a sentence from one perspective or another. How is it that for many different kinds of constructions, speakers overwhelmingly agree on something as subtle and seemingly ephemeral as the choice of perspective? Far from being a peripheral question, a small matter applying to only a few unusual sentences, this is a fundamental question that goes to the heart of our ability to construct and comprehend complex expressions.

The effects of point-of-view have traditionally been considered too ephemeral, too variable and untrustworthy, to be considered in the same category as the robust and reliable judgments that are attributed to the workings of genuine syntactic rules. An insightful account can be developed, however, starting from the assumption that all of these phenomena reflect one unified system, and that even examples that have traditionally been considered "purely syntactic" illustrate the same principles of conceptual organization as the most subtle POV examples.

Even as we look for unifying principles, we must acknowledge that in many cases, there is no vivid sense of adopting a referent's POV. In an example such as (2b) (*Near Ralph, he saw a skunk*), almost all speakers agree that *he* does not refer to *Ralph*, and yet not all speakers imagine themselves to be looking through "his" eyes as they understand the sentence. These kinds of examples must be explicable in terms of some more abstract notion, very similar to POV but without the vivid sense of identification with another person.

CONCEPTUAL REFERENCE POINTS

In place of the specific notion of POV, I want to suggest the slightly more abstract notion of a *conceptual reference point*. A reference point is a conception that is prominent and therefore is used as a starting point from which to apprehend a larger conception of which it is a part, such as the meaning of an entire sentence. Within a sentence, reference points function as "local topics," with other parts of the sentence functioning, in a sense, as comments on it. A POV of the kind already discussed is simply a more specific kind of reference point, the only difference being that non-POV reference points do not involve "seeing through the eyes" of the imagined individual.

Reference points provide a dynamic aspect to a conception, which may be described intuitively as a sense of moving through the sentence. Something is selected as a reference point because it is prominent (the definition of prominence is discussed later). Something that is prominent is construed highly objectively: It is in the center of attention. A reference point has a dual nature, however: Relative to material "viewed" from the reference point, it is construed *subjectively*, as part of the background. The impression of dynamism arises from the sense that one first encounters the reference point fully objectively, and then adopts the reference point as a subjectively construed position from which to view the rest of the conception. Regardless of whether a literal temporal sequence is involved at the level of processing, the effect is as if there were a temporal order, with each successive reference point serving as the point of entry to the conceptions associated with it.[4]

The material that is "viewed" from the position of the reference point, and interpreted in relationship to it, is termed the reference point's *dominion*. The mental space representing John's thoughts in (6) is a dominion. Within a sentence, there may be a sequence of reference points, each within the dominion of preceding reference points. The sequence of reference points and dominions defines a "line of sight" (in Langacker's 1995 term) extending into the sentence. Along this line of sight, nominals must be arranged in such a way as to provide coherent conceptions of their referents. This notion of "coherence" can be summed up as follows:

• A pronoun must appear within the dominion of a corresponding reference point (that is, a reference point that is understood to be the same

---

[4]This is very similar—or possibly identical—to MacWhinney's (1977) notion of a "starting point," which he described as a means by which the conceptualizer can "get inside the clause." MacWhinney did not attempt to use starting points as an explanation for pronominal anaphora facts. My model differs from his in other ways as well, primarily in that the choice of reference points is motivated by general principles of Cognitive Grammar, and my model is developed in more detail than his notion of a starting point. Nevertheless, I believe that MacWhinney's starting point is essentially the same thing as my reference point.

person or thing as the one the pronoun refers to). Because a pronoun such as *she* or *he* means very little by itself, it can only be used in a context in which its meaning can be supplemented by association with some prominent entity already included in the context.[5] And because a pronoun portrays its referent as conceptually close to the speaker and addressee, it must refer to someone or something that is conceived as a reference point, as part of the "position" from which the speaker and addressee are looking.

- A full noun phrase, such as a name or a descriptive phrase ("that man with the funny hat"), *cannot* appear in the dominion of a corresponding reference point. If the speaker and addressee are already viewing the sentence from a conceptual position that includes that person, then it is inappropriate to use a nominal form that implies that the person is conceptually distant.

Selection of Reference Points: How We Know Where to Start

How do we know which elements will stand out as reference points? In (7), speakers' judgments are almost evenly split. But in many cases, such as (2), speakers show approximately 95% agreement. If the name comes after the pronoun in the linear string (e.g., *He saw a skunk near Ralph*), the rate of agreement is essentially 100% (i.e., *he* cannot refer to Ralph). It is clear that there must be factors that reliably lead speakers to construe a sentence in a particular way.

The relevant factors turn out to make a great deal of intuitive sense. A nominal conception tends to be construed as a reference point if it is prominent (in a sense to be defined later) and if it comes earlier in the temporal sequence of words. This seems intuitively reasonable: Speakers tend to start with the most prominent elements in the sentence and/or those that they encounter first in the string, and construe other elements as belonging to the contexts (dominions) set up by those prominent and/or prior elements. When a nominal conception has been accorded reference point status, its dominion does not extend forever, but it does include all the elements that are conceptually connected with it (this is also made clearer later). Thus there are three general notions that we need to explore in more detail:

---

[5]This applies as well to the first- and second-person pronouns, such as *I*, *we*, and *you*. Though at first glance they may seem fairly informative by themselves, they in fact cannot pick out specific people unless they are interpreted within a particular discourse context—one must know who is the speaker, who is the addressee, and so on, to interpret them fully. The conceptions of the physically present speaker and addressee within a conversation function as reference points, as their very role within the discourse grants them considerable prominence.

• Prominence: A nominal tends to be construed as a reference point to the extent that it stands out as more prominent than its surroundings. Cognitive Grammar posits that certain elements within a sentence are more prominent than others, and that there is even a kind of figure/ground asymmetry between parts of the conception expressed by a sentence. Later we see that these prominence distinctions directly explain which nominals are selected as reference points.

• Connectivity: A prominent nominal tends to be construed as a reference point in relationship to elements with which it is directly interconnected (e.g., by a verb describing an interaction between them). Where elements are more loosely interrelated (as when they are both contained within the same paragraph but have no overt linkage between them), the speaker may conceive them as being relatively independent, and therefore not infer that either one must be a reference point in relationship to the other.

• Linear order: A nominal that is encountered earlier in the sentence tends to be construed as a reference point relative to nominals encountered later. This is a somewhat weaker factor than the combination of prominence and connectivity, however, and its effects can be seen most clearly when the other two factors do not strongly promote a particular construal.

Prominence

To be more specific about the notion of *prominence*, we can draw on basic notions of Cognitive Grammar (CG) as developed in Langacker (1987, 1991, 1998). My goal here is to give an introduction to the issues of pronominal anaphora, therefore I do not provide a thorough introduction to CG. It should be emphasized, however, that the theoretical notions used here are long-established, core elements in CG theory, not constructs that were developed specially to account for the pronominal anaphora data.

Figure and Ground: Why Subjects Are Special.   One of the central constructs of CG is *figure/ground asymmetry.* Within any relational conception—such as the conception described by a verb, adjective, or preposition—one element stands out as figure, whereas the rest of the relation functions as the ground. Within a sentence, the figure is the subject (Langacker, 1987). The subject of a sentence, being the most prominent element within the sentence, therefore functions as a reference point, with the rest of the sentential conception in its dominion. With a class of exceptions to be explained later, it does not matter whether other elements come before or after the subject in the linear string: They are invariably construed as belonging to its dominion. This explains the data in (8), of which the first two sentences repeat (2).

(8) a. Near <u>him</u>, <u>Ralph</u> saw a skunk.
    b. *Near <u>Ralph</u>, <u>he</u> saw a skunk.
    c. <u>Sam</u> keeps a frog in <u>his</u> pocket.
    d. *<u>He</u> keeps a frog in <u>Sam</u>'s pocket.
    e. <u>Sally</u> likes everyone <u>she</u> has ever worked with.
    f. *<u>She</u> likes everyone <u>Sally</u> has ever worked with.

The direct object of a verb is characterized as a secondary figure: less prominent than the subject, but still more prominent than other nominals within the sentence (Langacker, 1991). It accordingly functions as a secondary reference point, with all nominals other than the subject contained in its dominion. This explains the contrast in (9).

(9) a. I gave <u>John</u> a picture of <u>his</u> cat.
    b. *I gave <u>him</u> a picture of <u>John</u>'s cat.

In short, this analysis claims that these data reflect the workings of a psychological function that is not at all special to language. CG theory claims that the linguistic notion of "subject" is simply one manifestation of the much more general cognitive function of figure/ground perception. It is reasonable to suppose that the element that stands out as figure will function as a kind of foreground, the entry point for proceeding further into the sentence. Here we see that, combined with our assumptions about the different meanings of pronouns and names, it also explains certain pronominal anaphora facts.

Profile and Base: Why Some Nouns Don't Seem to Count

Thus far we have talked about the subject and object, the two nominals that may be considered most central to the clause. There are frequently other nominals within a sentence, serving more peripheral functions: functioning as part of a descriptive phrase attached to the subject, or describing the background setting, for example. Interestingly, it is possible for a pronoun to appear in one of these capacities and yet refer to someone who is mentioned by name later in the sentence, as in the following examples (underlining has been added to those that were drawn from actual texts):

(10) a. The people who have met <u>him</u> say that <u>Al Gore</u> is much more charming than one would expect.

b. Even <u>his</u> admirers admit <u>Mandela</u> is no miracle worker.[6]

c. In this temple, as in the hearts of the people for whom <u>he</u> saved the Union, the memory of <u>Abraham Lincoln</u> is enshrined forever.[7]

d. Even with a hatchet in <u>his</u> head, <u>the patient</u> wasn't docile.[8]

e. Less than a week before <u>he</u> was to face trial on felony charges relating to <u>his</u> activities in the Iran-Contra scandal, <u>Richard Secord</u> copped a plea. (*Time*, 11/20/89, p. 69)

Even though the pronoun in each case comes earlier in the sentence than the name, speakers do not seem to interpret the pronoun as a reference point with the name in its dominion. On the contrary, they correctly take the name to be the reference point, with the pronoun in *its* dominion. The first question is why speakers seem to be able to "skip past" the pronoun, rather than imagining that it sets up the context that the name must be fitted into.

Intuitively speaking, it is because the pronoun is not very prominent in the sentence—it is not one of the central elements, but is instead fairly peripheral. To be more specific, we need to draw on one more theoretical notion of Cognitive Grammar. CG posits that every linguistic expression activates a conception that has two parts: a **base**, which is the sum total of the knowledge networks that are activated by the conception, and a **profile**, which is the most prominent part, the part that stands out as that which the expression actually designates. A few examples should make this notion clear. The noun *Friday* invokes as its base the conception of the cycle of the week, and profiles one day within it (in Fig. 6.4, profiling is indicated by bold lines). The noun *roof* has as its base the conception of a house, and profiles just one portion of that structure. The noun *parent* profiles a person who occupies a particular role in a kinship relationship; the notion of the kinship structure is the base.

CG further posits that even at the level of complex expressions, such as whole sentences, there is a profile/base distinction: Some elements combine to form the core of the sentence, its profile, whereas other elements serve a more peripheral function as descriptors and background.[9] Within a sentence, the main verb, combined with its subject and object(s), forms the prominent core of the sentence, its profile. Other phrases are background,

---

[6]This sentence appeared as the title of a newspaper article.

[7]This is the inscription behind the statue of Abraham Lincoln at the Lincoln Memorial in Washington, DC.

[8]This sentence appeared as the title of a newspaper article.

[9]For those familiar with linguistic terminology, the profiled portion of the sentence consists of the head and its complements, and the unprofiled base is made up of modifiers. These technical labels are not strictly necessary in order to get an intuitive sense of the distinction.

FIG. 6.4.   Profile and base.

part of the unprofiled base. To use another metaphor, the verb and its subject and object(s) together form a peak of prominence, with everything else in its shadow. (Due to space limitations, I am not fully spelling out the principles that determine which elements are included in the composite profile of an entire sentence; for more detailed discussion, see van Hoek, 1997, pp. 69–73). Even when the less prominent elements come earlier in the sequence of words, speakers can "ignore" them in the sense that they need not construe them as reference points.

In a sentence such as (2b), repeated here, we can indicate which elements are included in the composite profile by putting the corresponding words in boldface capital letters; words that correspond to elements excluded from that profile are in lowercase plain type. Profiling is a matter of degree, as prominence is a gradient notion; elements that are partially included in the profile are indicated in boldface, lowercase type.

(2b′) near him, **RALPH SAW** a **SKUNK**

The sentences in (10) are repeated here, with profiling indicated by boldface, uppercase type, and partial inclusion in the profile indicated by boldface, lowercase type.

(10′) a. the **PEOPLE** who have met him **SAY** that **al gore is** much more **charming** than one would expect
  b. even his **ADMIRERS ADMIT mandela is** no **miracle worker**
  c. In this temple, as in the hearts of the people for whom he saved the Union, the **MEMORY of abraham lincoln IS ENSHRINED** forever.
  d. Even with a hatchet in his head, the **PATIENT WAS**n't **DOCILE**
  e. Less than a week before he was to face trial on felony charges relating to his activities in the Iran-Contra scandal, **RICHARD SECORD COPPED** a **PLEA**.

At this point in the development of CG theory, the profile/base distinction and figure/ground asymmetry are treated as two distinct kinds of prominence. It is possible that eventually they will be reduced to a single cognitive function, but for now they are treated as separate, orthogonal factors. Each of them plays a role in determining which nominals will be construed as reference points. There remains only the question of how far a reference point's dominion will extend.

Conceptual Connectivity: The Extent of the Line of Sight

Even once a particular nominal has been selected as a reference point, it does not stay in that role indefinitely. At some point, the prominence of a reference point fades and its dominion comes to an end. The fact that someone was mentioned 15 minutes earlier in a conversation, for example, does not mean that it will be anomalous to refer to them now by name. Even within smaller stretches of discourse—say, a single sentence, or a short sequence of sentences—one may find that the dominion of a reference point seems to end, and a person previously referenced by a pronoun may now be mentioned by name (in some cases, it will even be anomalous to attempt to continue using pronouns).

The extent of a reference point's dominion is determined by its conceptual connections with other elements. Intuitively speaking, a nominal that is explicitly connected with a reference point (e.g., by a verb of which both are complements) will be construed within its dominion. As the interconnections between elements become more tenuous, it becomes increasingly possible to construe a given nominal as independent of the dominion in question. A nominal might thus "escape" the dominion of a preceding reference point—in which case it would not sound strange to refer to the person by name, even though he or she had previously been referenced with a pronoun.

Conceptual connectivity is a continuum, but it can be roughly broken up into three categories or degrees, listed here with brief examples. The differences between them are discussed in more detail later.

Tight Connectivity: Elements so tightly bound together that there is no flexibility in construal:

(11) a. John loves his mother.
     b. *He loves John's mother.

Loose Connectivity: Elements a bit more loosely interconnected, so that some speakers will construe the name as being outside the dominion of the pronoun (and therefore acceptable), though other speakers will not (the question mark indicates that the sentence is questionable but not outright unacceptable):

(12) a. He lied to me—something that John was rather fond of doing![10]
     b. ?Mary hit him before John had a chance to get up.[11]
     c. ?People still regard him highly in Carter's home town.[12]

Non-Connectivity: Elements so loosely interrelated that many speakers prefer that the referent be re-established with a name, as the original reference point seems a bit too distant to continue reference via a pronoun (underlining has been added):

(13) Marina lay in bed, starving and staring at the ceiling. She didn't know what she was supposed to do. So she just stayed there, under the covers, waiting for Roger to make a sound.
      After what seemed a very long time, the doorbell rang and a moment later there was a lot of sharp, happy noise coming from the kitchen. Marina jumped into her jeans and tee shirt.... (Ann Druyan, 1977, *A Famous Broken Heart*, p. 40)

Tight Connectivity: Elements Within a Single Window of Attention. The first degree—expressions in which two elements are most closely interconnected—is defined by configurations in which two nominals are explicitly interconnected by virtue of their both participating in the same relation, such as the relation profiled by a verb.[13] In such cases, linear word order has very little effect: Regardless of which element comes first, speakers impose the same reference point/dominion relationship on the sentence.

This explains why speakers generally do not allow coreference in (2b) (*Near Ralph, he saw a skunk*): The phrase *near Ralph* describes an internal part of the relation profiled by the verb—that is, the location of the visual field that Ralph saw, and of the skunk—and so is inextricably included in the dominion of the subject. A mere change of word order is insufficient to enable it to "escape" the dominion of the subject (though it seems to slow down speakers' reactions—speakers are observably faster in judging *He saw a skunk near Ralph* to be impossible with coreference).

To be a bit more specific about this notion of tight connectivity, we need to think about the relationship between a verb and the noun phrases that describe its participants. We can use a simple example, *The cat entered the*

---

[10]Example from Bolinger (1979).

[11]Example from Brugman and Lakoff (1987).

[12]Example from Reinhart (1983).

[13]In the case of *John loves his mother*, the pronoun *his* does not describe a direct participant in the relation *loves*—that is, the sentence states that John loves his mother, not himself—but it is an integral part of the complete nominal *his mother*, which serves as the direct object of the verb. The pronoun is therefore interpreted within the context of the reference point *John*, simply because the larger nominal of which it is a part is interpreted within that context. See van Hoek (1997, p. 74) for discussion of this point.

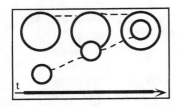

FIG. 6.5.   The verb *enter.*

house. The verb *enter* profiles two participants and the relationship between them. The relationship changes over time, as one participant starts out outside of the other and moves to the inside. Figure 6.5 shows three representative samples of the changing relationship; the arrow labeled *t* represents the flow of time. The dotted lines linking the circles together indicate that the participants are the same from one moment to the next (i.e., there are two participants shown in three configurations, not six different participants).

The verb *enter* says very little about the precise nature of its participants; to express a complete conception of the event, noun phrases are needed to fill in that information. The conceptions of a cat and a house correspond to the schematic participants in the event, as indicated in Fig. 6.6.

We do not simply understand a sentence as a collection of unassembled parts, however. At a higher level of organization, illustrated in Fig. 6.7, all of these components are integrated so that the complete expression is understood as a seamless, unified conception. (This description of the assembly of complex expressions is of course extremely abbreviated; see Langacker [1998] for a more thorough exposition.)

For our purposes here, there is an important observation to make about the relationship between the conception of the verb *enter* and the nominal conceptions that fill in its participants. The verb defines the profile for the entire expression: that is, the sentence *The cat entered the house* profiles the event of a cat entering a house, not just the cat or the house. The verb thus sets up a kind of "window of prominence," focusing attention on this imagined scene, within which the cat and the house figure as prominent participants. This means that the cat and the house—or any participants in a single relation of this kind—are caught in the same window of prominence. The flow of attention will lead immediately from the conception of the verb to the conceptions of the participants, and so they will be "viewed" together, or in other words, tightly interconnected.[14]

The things that are "viewed" in the window of attention set up by the verb are those things that describe central participants in the event and other internal elements of the scene: the setting, peripheral participants,

---

[14]For those familiar with linguistic terminology, what I am describing here in intuitive terms is the relationship between a head and its complements.

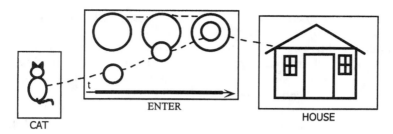

FIG. 6.6.   Noun phrases filling in participants.

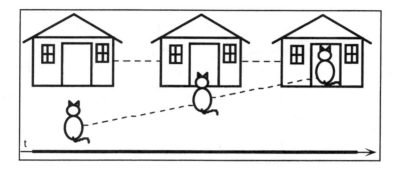

FIG. 6.7.   *The cat entered the house* as an integrated conception.

and so forth. Something that is tightly interconnected in this way with a reference point will not be able to escape its dominion—regardless of whether it comes before or after it in the sequence of words. It will inevitably be "viewed" from the location of the subject, which is the primary reference point for the entire sentence (some speakers will actually imagine the scene through the eyes of the subject, interpreting the reference point as a POV). This explains data such as (14).

(14) a. *He keeps a frog in Billy's desk.
     b. *In Billy's desk, he keeps a frog.
     c. *Near Ralph, he saw a skunk.
     d. *He said John needed a new job.
     e. *John needed a new job, he said.

Non-Connectivity: Elements Separated by Shifts of Attention.   Quite the opposite situation holds in the examples of loosest connectivity (essentially non-connectivity), in which there is some kind of a conceptual discontinuity or shift of attention in between the reference point and the nominal in question. Factors such as a change of setting or topic can bring about "closure" of a previous dominion, so that speakers or authors feel it necessary to

reintroduce characters by name. The example in (13) illustrates a phenomenon identified by Fox (1987): When a character in a narrative takes action,
the author will frequently reidentify the character by name. It appears that
the character's shift from passive to active mode is seen as initiating a new
narrative unit, so that simple continuation of the pronoun from the preceding paragraph(s) seems inappropriate.

Fox (1987) pointed out that other kinds of conceptual shifts between
textual units will prompt the re-use of a name, and suggests that in different
genres, there are slightly different conventions concerning the unit boundaries that will trigger re-use of a name (though she did not couch this within
a larger model of pronominal anaphora).

In an experimental study, Tomlin (1987) found that speakers narrating a
series of cartoon images tend to reidentify characters with noun phrases at
the beginning of each attentional unit. When frames were presented in
clumps of two or three frames at a time, speakers tended to reidentify the
characters with full noun phrases as they began to narrate each group of
frames. By breaking up the sequence of cartoon images into units of different sizes, so that the images would be clumped together in various groupings,
he could induce speakers to reidentify the characters with full noun phrases
at different points in the narrative. All of these findings support the claim
that a conceptual discontinuity of some kind, such as a shift in attention, will
bring about "closure" of a prior dominion. This is only to be expected, if a
dominion is a kind of "viewing frame" created by adopting a particular starting point from which to look into a complex conception; a break in the flow
of attention would mean starting over with a new viewing frame.

Thus we see that on the one hand, when elements are explicitly linked
together, a reference point's dominion will inevitably include the less-
prominent elements that are so clearly connected with it. On the other
hand, when there is a shift in attention, such as a textual unit boundary or a
change of narrative setting, a reference point's dominion will often come to
an end. This leaves only loose connectivity, which describes the situation
where two elements are not strongly interconnected, nor are they separated
by an obvious conceptual break. Here we find that speakers rely on additional cues, such as intonation breaks and word order, to decide whether
something is or is not included in the viewing window that is seen from a
particular reference point.

Loose Connectivity.   When we look at elements that are loosely interconnected, we can finally see the importance of linear word order. It is intuitively reasonable to expect that speakers will be sensitive to word order,
and that they will tend to construe a nominal as a reference point if it is the
first they encounter in the linear string. Yet in many of the examples we
have seen so far, prominence seemed to be by far the more important fac-

tor, and changing the order of words had little effect. The effect of word order becomes most visible when elements are more loosely interconnected.

What I mean by "loose interconnection" is that two nominals are included within the same larger linguistic unit, such as a sentence or a paragraph in written text, but they are not explicitly interconnected by a verb or a preposition. The first nominal is a reference point—in the following examples, it is the subject of the sentence—and the question is whether the second nominal is inevitably understood to belong to its dominion, or whether it may be taken as independent (in which case it would be all right to use a full noun phrase for the second nominal, just as in the earlier example of a narrative unit break). The examples in (15) (of which the first three repeat [12]) illustrate this kind of configuration. The judgments on them range from acceptable to fully unacceptable with coreference.

(15) a. <u>He</u> lied to me—something that <u>John</u> was rather fond of doing.
   b. ?Mary hit <u>him</u> before <u>John</u> had a chance to get up.
   c. ?People still regard <u>him</u> highly in <u>Carter's</u> home town.
   d. *<u>She</u>'ll have to move soon, since <u>Mary</u> has found a new job.
   e. *<u>She</u> marries Tom Cruise in <u>Kathleen Turner's</u> latest movie.

In general, unless there is a sharp intonation break between the two nominals—which would signal a shift in attention in the middle of the sentence—speakers tend to assume that the reference point's dominion includes everything that comes after it in the linear string. We can think of this as a kind of default assumption: In the absence of any cues to the contrary, one assumes that the reference point through which one "views" the sentence remains the same all the way to the end, and that having adopted a particular vantage point, one does not abandon it for no particular reason. (For some speakers, even an intonation break is insufficient to separate the parts of the sentence, and so none of the examples in [15] are acceptable.)

If the word order is rearranged, however, so that the prominent nominal (the reference point) comes later in the linear string, then there is much less reason to assume that the less prominent nominal must belong to its dominion. The less prominent nominal becomes more independent, and might even—by virtue of coming earlier in the linear sequence—be selected as the position in which to name the referent. This would happen not because it has prominence of the figure/ground or profile/base variety (the subject of the entire sentence is still the figure, and thus the most prominent nominal in the sentence), but simply because it comes earlier in the linear sequence, and because there is no robust connectivity to ensnare it in the dominion of the other nominal. This possible outcome is illustrated by the rephrasings in (16).

(16) a. <u>John</u> was my friend and <u>he</u> betrayed me.
    b. Before <u>John</u> had a chance to get up, Mary hit <u>him</u>.
    c. In <u>Carter's</u> home town, people still regard <u>him</u> highly.
    d. Since <u>Mary</u> has found a new job, <u>she</u>'ll have to move soon.
    e. In <u>Kathleen Turner</u>'s latest movie, <u>she</u> marries Tom Cruise.

In the section Point-of-View Effects, we saw POV effects that were often subtle, with judgments varying between speakers. In this section we see much more clear-cut judgments. The reason for the difference is simply that, when the relative degrees of prominence and the conceptual inter-connections between elements are spelled out explicitly, speakers have much less flexibility to choose alternate construals of a sentence. In the more subtle POV examples, much more is left to the conceptualizer's discretion, and so different speakers understand the sentence through different points of view.

SUMMARY

The Cognitive Grammar account of the pronoun facts, as presented here, makes more general claims about the way we understand language, aside from just the interpretation of nouns and pronouns. It starts from the idea of the Stage Model, in which words and sentences not only invoke concepts, but specifically locate those concepts in relationship to the imagined audience—the speaker and the addressee. Different linguistic forms signal the degree of closeness or distance between the conceptualizers and the people or things conceived. Every time a speaker refers to someone by a name, a descriptive phrase, or a pronoun, he or she is taking a particular view of that person, situating that person in a particular way in relationship to the speaker and the addressee.

We also find that a sentence (or larger discourse) is not understood as a static conception, but rather has a dynamic aspect to it. There is a sense of entering the sentence from a particular starting point, moving from point to point and understanding clumps of meaning in relationship to what has gone before. The conceptualizer follows a particular line of sight through the sentence, placing different facets of the imagined scene in the foreground or background, seeing some elements as peaks of prominence and others as valleys in their shadow. All along the way, both speaker and listener are guided by such fundamental notions as figure/ground organization, focus of attention, and temporal sequence.

This account differs from the standard c-command account in a number of ways. Not only does it provide conceptual semantic grounding for the coreference facts—as opposed to an unexplained list of rules stated on syntactic tree structures—but it provides a unified explanation for a large array of data for which the c-command accounts have no explanation. Discourse-level patterns of coreference are not explicable in terms of c-command, because syntactic tree structures encompass only one sentence at a time. The reference point model does generalize to the cross-sentential, discourse level. Within a discourse, the dominion of a reference point extends only until there is a conceptual break in the discourse, equivalent to an attentional shift. After the conceptual break (which, depending on the specific discourse genre, may consist of a scene change, a shift in topic, or a new narrative unit initiated by a character's taking action), referents who have previously been referred to via pronouns are reintroduced with names or descriptive noun phrases, as the former reference point is felt to be too distant to sanction the use of a pronoun. The reference point model thus encompasses the range of coreference patterns, from nominals contained within a single clause to nominals separated by many sentences in discourse, and provides a unitary set of principles for explaining the patterns that manifest at all of the different levels.

One of the most interesting findings is that the notion of a point-of-view, which may seem too vague and peripheral to be of any help in explaining the vast array of pronominal anaphora data, turns out to be a kind of prototype for the notion of a reference point. Looking into the sentence from the point-of-view of an individual means contextualizing the contents of the sentence within the mental space of his or her thoughts; looking into the sentence from the position of a reference point means contextualizing the contents of the sentence within the mental space of its dominion. Understanding complex expressions crucially involves creating relationships between the viewer and that which is viewed, following paths suggested by prominence and conceptual interconnections to understand each element in context.

REFERENCES

Ariel, M. (1990). *Accessing noun phrase antecedents.* New York: Routledge.

Barry, D. (1988). *Dave Barry's greatest hits.* New York: Random House.

Bolinger, D. (1979). Pronouns in discourse. In T. Givón (Ed.), *Syntax and semantics: Vol. 12. Syntax and discourse* (pp. 289–309). New York: Academic Press.

Brugman, C., & Lakoff, G. (1987, December). *The semantics of aux-inversion and anaphora constraints.* Paper presented at the annual meeting of the Linguistic Society of America, San Francisco, CA.

Druyan, A. (1977). *A famous broken heart.* New York: Stonehill Publishing.

Fauconnier, G. (1985). *Mental spaces: Aspects of meaning construction in natural language.* Cambridge, MA: MIT Press.

Fox, B. (1987). *Discourse structure and anaphora.* Cambridge, MA: Cambridge University Press.

Givón, T. (1989). *The grammar of referential coherence as mental processing instructions* (Technical Rep. No. 89-7). Eugene, OR: University of Oregon.

Givón, T. (1998). The functional approach to grammar. In M. Tomasello (Ed.), *The new psychology of language* (pp. 41–66). Mahwah, NJ: Lawrence Erlbaum Associates.

Kibrik, A. (1999). Reference and working memory: Cognitive inferences from discourse observations. In K. van Hoek, A. Kibrik, & L. Noordman (Eds.), *Discourse studies in cognitive linguistics* (pp. 29–52). Amsterdam: John Benjamins.

Langacker, R. W. (1985). Observations and speculations on subjectivity. In J. Haiman (Ed.), *Iconicity in syntax* (pp. 109–150). Amsterdam & Philadelphia: John Benjamins.

Langacker, R. W. (1987). *Foundations of cognitive grammar: Vol. 1. Theoretial prerequisites* (pp. 231–236). Stanford, CA: Stanford University Press.

Langacker, R. W. (1991). *Foundations of cognitive grammar: Vol. 2. Descriptive application* (p. 323). Stanford, CA: Stanford University Press.

Langacker, R. W. (1995). Viewing in cognition and grammar. In P. W. Davis (Ed.), *Alternative linguistics: Descriptive and theoretical models* (pp. 153–212). Amsterdam: John Benjamins.

Langacker, R. W. (1998). Conceptualization, symbolization and grammar. In M. Tomasello (Ed.), *The new psychology of language* (pp. 1–39). Mahwah, NJ: Lawrence Erlbaum Associates.

MacWhinney, B. (1977). Starting points. *Language, 53*, 152–168.

Reinhart, T. (1983). *Anaphora and semantic interpretation.* Chicago: University of Chicago Press.

Tomlin, R. S. (1987). Linguistic reflections of cognitive events. In R. Tomlin (Ed.), *Coherence and grounding in discourse* (pp. 455–479). Amsterdam & Philadelphia: John Benjamins.

van Hoek, K. (1995). Conceptual reference points: A cognitive grammar account of pronominal anaphora constraints. *Language, 71*(2), 310–340.

van Hoek, K. (1997). *Anaphora and conceptual structure.* Chicago: University of Chicago Press.

Chapter 7

On Explaining Language Universals

Bernard Comrie
Max Planck Institute for Evolutionary Anthropology

The study of language universals is the study of those properties that are necessarily common to all human languages. It is important to understand that by claiming that a particular property is a language universal, we are not merely claiming that it is true of all human languages that happen to be available to us—all the languages that are spoken today and all those for which we have historical records. Rather, we are making a claim about the human language potential: This is the way human languages have to be. A "thought experiment" will make this clearer. Let us suppose that all human languages other than English were to die out without trace. Under this set of circumstances, any arbitrary property of English, say the fact that the word for the domestic canine quadruped is *dog*, would be "universal" in the sense of being true of every accessible language, but clearly not universal in the more interesting sense of being an essential property of human language; with the knowledge currently at our disposal, we know, for instance, that it is possible for a language to have a different word for the domestic canine quadruped, such as French *chien*, Spanish *perro*, German *Hund*, Russian *sobaka*, Japanese *inu*, and so forth.

The question of how one establishes language universals in this interesting sense is a complex one, but one that I do not dwell on in this chapter.[1] Rather, I take for granted that certain language universals have been reasonably securely established—examples follow in the chapter—and ask a

---

[1]Reference may be made, for instance, to Comrie (1989) for my ideas on this score.

further question: Why do these language universals exist? Why is it that human language is bound by these universal principles?

There are various ways in which one might classify possible answers to this question, but it seems to me that the following dichotomy is a fruitful way of thinking about possible answers. (A third possibility is considered but discarded in the Monogenesis section.) First, some features of human language may necessarily be the way they are because that is the way human beings are constructed. An obvious example here would be the absence from the phonological system of human languages of sounds that require the speaker to articulate the tip of the tongue against the tip of the nose: Most humans are physically incapable of making this gesture, so this physical limitation militates against the inclusion of such a sound in a human language. This example is perhaps too obvious to be particularly interesting, so in the Structure-Dependence section I come back to some other examples that are more surprising, though nonetheless just as valid as language universals. Language universals of the first type are thus explained by means of the physical (including physiological and cognitive) limitations of human beings. A second kind of explanation considers not so much the form of language universals, relating them to formal properties of the human species, but thinks rather of the function of language, for instance as a means of communicating information and as a means of maintaining social contact. As a simple example here—again, not so interesting, I think, as the slightly more elaborate examples to be considered in the Reflexive Pronouns section—we might cite the existence in all human languages of greetings. Clearly, there is nothing in the physical makeup of people that forces languages to have greetings, rather the social constraints on interpersonal behavior militate in their favor: One of the essential functions of language is to enable members of a speech community to maintain social relations with one another, and greetings are a very straightforward way of doing this. Indeed, an appropriate social interchange may well consist entirely of greetings, without any communication of information content. In this chapter, I want to try and demonstrate that both kinds of explanations of language universals, the formal and the functional, are essential if we are to gain an overall understanding of the motivations underlying the existence of language universals.

STRUCTURE-DEPENDENCE

In English, as in many other languages of the world, one of the ways in which sentences can be related to one another is by changes in word order. Compare the corresponding statement and question in Examples (1) and (2), whose only grammatical difference is in word order:

(1) Albert can swim.

(2) Can Albert swim?

Given examples like (1) and (2), we might wonder about the precise formulation that would enable us to form questions from corresponding statements. As far as (1) and (2) are concerned, an answer that "works" might say that we form a question by inverting the first two words of the corresponding statement; this will certainly produce (2) from (1). However, if we apply this simple rule to other examples, we get the wrong result. For instance, applying this rule to (3) gives the ungrammatical sentence (4a) rather than the grammatical sentence (4b):[2]

(3) [The dog] can swim.

(4) a. *Dog the can swim?
    b. Can [the dog] swim?

(The function of the square brackets in these sentences is explained later.) In converting (3) to (4), we have rather to take the first two words and invert them with the third word. What is the overall generalization that covers these various cases? The crucial point is that, in order to change word order, it is necessary to identify pieces of grammatical structure and carry out processes involving those pieces of grammatical structure. One way of formulating the relation is as follows: Find the subject of the sentence and invert it with the auxiliary verb.[3] In (3), the subject is *the dog* (enclosed in

---

[2]It is usual in current linguistic work to preface ungrammatical sentences with an asterisk. Note that the distinction between "grammatical" and "ungrammatical" here does not refer to the prescriptions of traditional grammarians. Rather, it refers to the linguistic intuitions of native speakers. Native speakers of English, irrespective of whether or not they have had formal grammatical training, know that (4b) is right and that (4a) is wrong.

[3]This rule requires a certain amount of further refinement to cover all cases in English, although the general principle expressed in the text holds. For instance, if a statement contains more than one auxiliary verb, then it is only the first auxiliary verb that is inverted with the subject, as in (i) (with the string of auxiliaries *should have been*) and (ii):

(i)   [The boy] should have been singing.
(ii) Should [the boy] have been singing?

The formulation in the text also says nothing about a statement that contains no auxiliary verb, such as (iii); interestingly, here English requires the insertion of an auxiliary verb, *do*, in order to form the corresponding question, as in (iv):

(iii) [The dog] swam.
(iv) Did [the dog] swim?

brackets for clarity of exposition), the first auxiliary is *can*, and inverting them gives us (4b). The same rule applies in the case of (1); it just happens that the subject, *Albert*, is a single word. The subject noun phrase can in principle be indefinitely long, as is illustrated by Examples (5) and (6):

(5) [The professor who knows Sanskrit] can swim.

(6) Can [the professor who knows Sanskrit] swim?

In fact, the rule for forming questions from statements in English is a special case of a general property of the syntactic structure of human languages, namely that syntactic processes in human languages are *structure-dependent*. By this, we mean that syntactic processes require identification of pieces of syntactic structure, rather than of arbitrary sequences of words or sounds, with processes then being carried out on those identified pieces of syntactic structure.[4] We could easily imagine an artificial language that did not follow the principle of structure-dependence. Let us imagine a language exactly like English, called Anti-English, except that its rule for forming questions is: Invert the order of words in the corresponding statement. In Anti-English, the question corresponding to (5) would be (7):[5]

(7) Swim can Sanskrit knows who professor the?

The important difference between Anti-English and real English is that Anti-English does not require the identification of units of syntactic structure; Anti-English carries out changes on words quite irrespective of the

---

Notice that some other languages have slightly different versions of the English rule. Thus, German requires inversion of the subject and finite verb, irrespective of whether or not this is an auxiliary verb, so that the translations of (iii) and (iv) are (v) and (vi), respectively:

(v)   [Der Hund] schwamm.
(vi) Schwamm [der Hund]?

The German rule is still, in the terms introduced later in this section, structure-dependent, as it requires identification of pieces of syntactic structure (subject, finite verb). Proponents of different syntactic theories would, incidentally, formulate these rules somewhat differently, but all such formulations would bear the crucial hallmark of structure-dependence.

[4]Although, for ease of exposition, I speak throughout of "syntactic processes," this should not be interpreted as a commitment to a process view of syntax. In fact, what is crucial is rather the existence of systematic correspondences between different sentence types, such as statements and questions in English. Process terminology is simply a convenient way of speaking about these relationships.

[5]Sentence (7) is not preceded by an asterisk because it is a grammatical sentence of the imaginary language Anti-English. Of course, in a discussion of real English it would be preceded by an asterisk.

syntactic structures in which they participate. Anti-English is thus structure-independent.[6]

It should be emphasized that there is nothing a priori more plausible about structure-dependence in comparison with structure-independence. As a way of forming questions in an artificial language, not intended for direct human consumption, the left–right word order inversion of Anti-English is a perfectly good rule, a perfectly clear way of marking the difference between statements and questions. Indeed, in terms of the general theory of automata, the kind of inversion used by Anti-English is actually a very simple kind of system, known technically as a *pushdown storage device*. In a pushdown storage device, whatever was put in last will be on top of the store, and will therefore be the first item to be retrieved, with the result that items are retrieved in the opposite order to that in which they are inserted. By comparison, structure-dependent rules are formally much more complex types of rules. Why, then, does English, like indeed all other human languages, prefer structure-dependent rules?

The answer to this lies in a basic structural property of human cognition: Human cognition requires structure in order to be able to work with strings consisting of more than a few items. Examples of this abound in areas outside linguistics. For instance, when presented with longish strings of numbers, such as telephone numbers, people divide them into groups— 123-4567 rather than 1234567—thus imposing a structure that is quite unnecessary for the functioning of the telephone system. An even closer parallel to linguistic behavior can be seen in operations performed on strings. The following can be tried as an experiment: First, say the alphabet forwards. Then, try saying it backwards. Unless one has practiced saying the alphabet backwards, effectively learning the reverse alphabet alongside the regular alphabet, the procedure of reversing the all-too-familiar order of letters is fraught with difficulties. Production of the reverse alphabet is

---

[6]Note, incidentally that a left–right inversion of the words in a sentence does preserve the overall structure of the sentence, for example, in that words that belong together will remain together, as can be seen by comparing (i) and (ii):

(i) [The little dog] bit [the big cat]. (= [10])
(ii) [Cat big the] bit [dog little the].

This is contrast, for instance, to fronting the second-last word of the sentence, which will typically break up syntactic structure, as in the relation between (i) and (iii):

(iii) Big [the little dog] bit [the cat].

Thus, the crucial feature of structure-dependence versus structure-independence is the necessary reference to elements of syntactic structure in the former, not whether overall syntactic structure is retained.

much less fluent; mistakes are quite likely to occur, especially if any attempt at fluency is made; much of the disfluency is caused by "backtracking," that is, silently saying part of the alphabet forwards in order to determine what letter precedes the last letter pronounced. The alphabet is a prime example of an unstructured string, though one which most people, as a benefit of the educational system, have learned; however, attempting to apply structure-independent changes to this unstructured string stretches human cognitive capacity to and beyond its limitations. Thus, the inability to deal with structure-independent operations is a basic limitation of the human cognitive capacity, presumably determined by the physiology underlying the cognitive system.[7]

Two important conclusions emerge from this. One is that the grammar of human language is structure-dependent. The other is that this property of structure-dependence is not a specific property of language, but rather a general property of human cognition. I emphasize this second point because in at least one current approach to grammar, mainstream generative grammar, great emphasis is placed on the alleged uniqueness of the formal properties of language relative to other cognitive systems, even to the extent of positing a special "language faculty" or even "language organ." This strikes me as an unnecessary assumption. The stronger hypothesis is to assume that the formal properties of language are special cases of formal properties of cognition more generally, in the absence of compelling evidence to the contrary.

Before leaving the principle of structure-dependence, I would like to consider one further set of data to illustrate it, namely passive formation. To form the passive of an active sentence like (8), there are in principle a number of formulations that would work, including one that is largely structure-independent, along the following lines: Take the first word, move it to the end and place the preposition *by* in front of it; take the last word and move it to the front; take the verb, put it into the past participle form and place the appropriate form of the verb *be* in front of it.

(8) Brutus killed Caesar.

(9) Caesar was killed by Brutus.

---

[7]It should be emphasized that this limitation applies to strings presented in real time. If one can obviate the real-time limitation, for instance by writing down a string and then reading it backwards, then such a structure-independent operation poses no problem—though, of course, in reality no structure-independent operation is being performed: One is simply reading a string from right to left instead of from left to right! (This is, incidentally, how I created Example (7)—by looking at Example (5) and typing the words starting from the end of the sentence.) Language, in its basic manifestation as spoken language, is, of course, a real-time phenomenon.

However, just as in the case of question formation, consideration of more complex sentences shows that what is crucial is not identifying arbitrary units like the first word, but rather identifying syntactic units like the subject of the sentence (which is moved after the verb, with the preposition *by*) and the direct object of the sentence (which is moved into subject position). Compare the active sentence (10) with its passive counterpart (11):

(10) [The little dog] bit [the big cat].

(11) [The big cat] was bitten [by the little dog].

Exactly the same principle is operative in the passive in Russian, as can be seen in examples like (12) to (15), and indeed in their English translations. In (12) and (13) the relevant noun phrases happen each to be a single word, but (14) and (15) show that the principles required must be able to cover phrases consisting of several words:

(12) Raskol´nikov ubil Lizavetu.
     Raskolnikov killed Lizaveta.

(13) Lizaveta byla ubita Raskol´nikovym.
     Lizaveta was killed by Raskolnikov.

(14) [Geroj romana] ubil [sestru staroj zakladčicy].
     [The hero of the novel] killed [the sister of the old money-lender].

(15) [Sestra staroj zakladčicy] byla ubita [geroem romana].
     [The sister of the old money-lender] was killed [by the hero of the novel].

An interesting difference between English and Russian, however, is that in Russian the syntactic structure of the sentence is carried not so much by the order of words, but rather by the case inflections of noun phrases. Thus, in (12) and (14) the subjects, *Raskol´nikov* "Raskolnikov" and *geroj romana* "the hero of the novel" stand in the nominative case, whereas in the corresponding passives these noun phrases show up in the instrumental case; conversely, the direct objects *Lizavetu* "Lizaveta" and *sestru staroj zakladčicy* "the sister of the old money-lender" stand in the accusative case in (12) and (14), but these noun phrases show up in the nominative as subjects of the passive sentences (13) and (15). In Russian, then, the identification of syntactic units involves not so much the ordering of the words as the case morphology of the noun phrases.[8] But both Russian and English represent different instantiations of the general principle of structure-dependence.

Reflexive Pronouns

The data in this section concern reflexive pronouns, such as English *herself, himself, yourself* in sentences like (16) and (17).[9] A reflexive pronoun is a pronoun that is necessarily interpreted as being coreferential with (referring to the same entity—person or thing—as) some other noun phrase. Thus, in Example (16), *himself* must be interpreted as coreferential with another noun phrase, the only candidate being *David*. We adopt the convention of marking coreferential noun phrases by means of the same subscript index letter, as both are marked with i in (16). Where relevant, non-coreferential noun phrases are marked by means of different subscript index letters, for example, i versus j.

(16) David$_i$ hates himself$_i$.

(17) You$_i$ hate yourself$_i$.

(18) I$_i$ hate myself$_i$.

(19) David$_i$ hates him$_j$.

(20) David$_i$ hates me$_j$.

Examples (16) to (20) show that English has a distinction between reflexive and non-reflexive pronouns in each grammatical person, namely *me* versus *myself* in the first person, *you* versus *yourself* in the second person, and *him* versus *himself* in the third person masculine (with corresponding forms for other numbers and genders where relevant). At least in simple Subject–Verb–Object sentences like those presented above, the ordinary pronouns as direct objects will always be non-coreferential with the subject, while the reflexive pronouns will always be coreferential with the subject.

Russian shows precisely the same phenomenon, namely a distinction between reflexive and non-reflexive pronoun in each grammatical person, but with an interesting difference: The form of the reflexive pronoun does

---

[8]The English and Russian types can be given a single treatment if syntactic processes are stated neither in terms of word order nor in terms of morphological case, but rather in terms of "grammatical relations," such as subject, direct object: The direct object of an active sentence corresponds to the subject of the corresponding passive sentence. This approach is developed in one variety of formal grammar, namely Relational Grammar.

[9]In English, reflexive pronouns have the same form as emphatic pronouns, as in *David himself ate the banana*. Only reflexive pronouns are relevant to the discussion in this section.

not differ for person, so that, depending on the person (and number and gender) of the subject, *sebja* will translate into English now as 'myself,' now as 'himself,' and so on. But crucially, the form of the reflexive pronoun will always be distinct from that of the corresponding non-reflexive pronoun, as illustrated in (21) through (25):

(21) Onegin$_i$ nenavidit sebja$_i$.
Onegin$_i$ hates himself$_i$.

(22) Ty$_i$ nenavidiš' sebja$_i$.
You$_i$ hate yourself$_i$.

(23) Ja$_i$ nenavižu sebja$_i$.
I$_i$ hate myself$_i$.

(24) Onegin$_i$ nenavidit ego$_j$.
Onegin$_i$ hates him$_j$.

(25) Onegin$_i$ nenavidit menja$_j$.
Onegin$_i$ hates me$_j$.

A question that arises at this stage is whether it is necessary for a language to have such a distinction between reflexive and non-reflexive for all grammatical persons. The answer is in the negative. Indeed, a striking contrast to Modern English is provided by Old English (Anglo-Saxon): In Old English, there was no distinction between reflexive and non-reflexive pronouns in any grammatical person, as illustrated in (26) to (28):[10]

(26) Hē$_i$ slōh hine$_{i/j}$.
He$_i$ hit himself$_i$/him$_j$.

(27) Ic$_i$ slōh mē$_i$.
I$_i$ hit myself$_i$.

(28) Hē$_i$ slōh mē$_j$.
He$_i$ hit me$_j$.

---

[10]Traces of this earlier English system survive in some dialects, in sentences like (i):

(i)   I$_i$ bought me$_i$ a cat.

Note that (i) is grammatical in the relevant dialects, though not, of course, in the standard language.

Thus, the same direct object pronoun is used in both (27), with a reflexive interpretation, and (28), with a non-reflexive interpretation. Perhaps even more surprising, from the viewpoint of Modern English, is that (26) can be interpreted two ways: with the direct object coreferential with the subject, and with the direct object non-coreferential with the subject.

Yet another system is found in French.[11] As can be seen in Examples (29) through (34), French has a distinction between reflexive *se* and non-reflexive *le* (with corresponding feminine and plural forms) in the third person, but has no distinction between reflexive and non-reflexive forms in the first and second persons, with first-person *me* and second-person *te* serving in both functions.

(29) Satan$_i$ se$_i$ déteste.
Satan$_i$ detests himself$_i$.

(30) Tu$_i$ te$_i$ détestes.
You$_i$ detest yourself$_i$.

(31) Je$_i$ me$_i$ déteste.
I$_i$ detest myself$_i$.

(32) Satan$_i$ le$_j$ déteste.
Satan$_i$ detests him$_j$.

(33) Satan$_i$ te$_j$ déteste.
Satan$_i$ detests you$_j$.

(34) Satan$_i$ me$_j$ déteste.
Satan$_i$ detests me$_j$.

We have thus seen three types of systems for overt distinction between reflexive and non-reflexive pronouns, namely the first three types shown in (35). In this example, *yes* means that the language distinguishes reflexive and non-reflexive pronouns in that grammatical person, whereas *no* means that the language does not.

(35)

	Third person	First/Second person
English, Russian	yes	yes
Old English	no	no
French	yes	no
===	no	yes

---

[11]The system as in French is particularly widespread in Romance languages (and is found in their ancestor Latin) and in Germanic languages.

An obvious question is whether the fourth type, the inverse of the French type, is found in human languages (or, more accurately: whether it is possible in human language). On the empirical level, I am certainly not aware of any language that shows this system, and I would hypothesize that such a system is in fact impossible. We might call this fourth system Anti-French: It would involve a distinction between reflexive and non-reflexive in the first and second persons, but not in the third person. Formulated slightly differently, we can set up the following language-universal implication: If a language has distinct reflexive pronouns anywhere, it will have them in the third person. The next question is: Why should this generalization hold?

If one approaches the question from a purely formal point of view, there is, I believe, no answer. From a formal viewpoint, there is no reason for the system of Anti-French to be less preferred than that of real French: Either one makes the distinction only in the third person, or one makes it only in the other persons. Yet one system is allowed, the other apparently disallowed. But once one starts asking about the function of reflexive pronouns, a ready explanation appears. As is shown clearly by comparison of examples like (16) and (19), a distinct reflexive pronoun enables us to make a distinction between two kinds of situations, one where subject and object are coreferential, the other where they are non-coreferential. In the third person this is an extremely useful device, as third person pronouns can in principle refer to any entity other than the speaker (first person) and the hearer (second person), and in a discourse ranging over a number of topics it can be important to distinguish which one is being referred to at any particular point in the discourse. By contrast, for a given sentence there is normally only one speaker, only one hearer.[12] Thus, whether a language has distinct first- and second-person reflexives or not, the reference of first- and second-person pronouns is nearly always going to be clear from the speech situation, and does not require further elaboration in order to identify who is speaking or being spoken to. Thus a distinction between reflexive and non-reflexive is particularly useful in the third person, certainly more so than in the other persons.

It should be emphasized that I am not claiming that a language has to have a reflexive/non-reflexive distinction in the third person—Old English did not—nor that a language must lack this distinction in the first and second persons (Modern English and Russian have the distinction). Rather, the function of reflexive pronouns as a device for establishing presence versus absence of coreference is particularly useful in the third person, and that is where we expect to find it most well established cross-linguistically. Indeed, we find an excellent correlation between the function and distribution of the reflexive/non-reflexive distinction, making this a prime illustra-

---

[12]The hearer, and indeed the speaker, may, of course, be a group.

tion of the relevance of functional explanations for language universals. To reiterate the most important point: The fact that the reflexive/non-reflexive distinction is found most readily in the third person directly reflects the function of this distinction.

Earlier I suggested that, in general, there is no possibility of having two or more non-coreferential first-person referents or two or more non-coreferential second-person referents in a sentence, because speaker and hearer do not normally change in mid-sentence. However, under exceptional—almost pathological—circumstances, such shifts may be observed, although this phenomenon is certainly vastly rarer than the existence of two or more non-coreferential third-person referents in a sentence. Interestingly, such shifts in reference outside the third person are more plausible in the second person than in the first. Thus, the speaker may, in the same sentence, address two individuals in turn, using the pronoun *you* to address each of them, indicating the distinction by some extra-linguistic means, such as pointing or nodding toward the intended referent.[13] Under these circumstances, a sentence like *have you$_i$ been introduced to you$_j$?*, with non-coreferential *you*'s is conceivable. In the first person it is hard to imagine comparable examples; presumably even split personality does not provide them, assuming that the different personae of someone with a split personality are not aware of one another and therefore cannot interact in a single sentence. At best, one might get a shift of first-person referent where one person finishes off a sentence started by someone else. Certainly, it is more likely to have the (albeit marginal) phenomenon of non-third-person referent shift in the second person than in the first person. Given this, and given the functional explanation offered previously for the difference between third and non-third person reflexives, one might predict that there should be a similar, even if less marked, distinction between second person and first person, with the reflexive/non-reflexive distinction more likely with second person than with first person. And indeed there is evidence in support of this prediction.

The Gokana language, spoken in southern Nigeria, has a kind of co-reference-marking phenomenon known as logophoric reference, whereby in indirect speech a special form is used to show that a referent in the reported speech is coreferential with the subject of the verb of speaking (Hyman & Comrie, 1981). In Gokana sentence (36), therefore, it is clear that the person who fell is not the one who is reporting the event, whereas in (37) it is equally clear that someone is reporting the event of his own falling. Note that English has no equivalently compact way of making this distinction. The distinction is shown by a suffix, in the examples given -ɛ̀, on

---

[13]By "referent," I mean simply the person or thing that is referred to by the noun phrase (including pronoun) in question.

the verb of the subordinate clause, this suffix serving to mark coreference, its absence to mark non-coreference. In Gokana, the formal and semantic difference between (36) and (37) is absolutely strict:

(36) aè kɔ aè dɔ̀.
He$_i$ said that he$_j$ fell.

(37) aè kɔ aè dɔ-ɛ̀.
He$_i$ said that he$_i$ fell.

This strict distinction, however, applies only in the third person. In the first and second persons, the marking of coreference in this way is optional, as can be seen in the variants in (38) and (39):

(38) oò kɔ oò dɔ-ɛ̀/dɔ̀.
You$_i$ said that you$_i$ fell.[14]

(39) mm̀ kɔ mm̀ dɔ̀/dɔ-ɛ̀.
I$_i$ said that I$_i$ fell.

But what is particularly interesting is that in the second person, as in (38), it is preferred to use the marker of coreference, whereas in the first person, as in (39), it is preferred not to do so; the order of variants given in each of these examples thus represents the order of preference. In other words, the likelihood of its being necessary to distinguish among competing referents not only predicts the difference between third person and the other persons—the main point of this section—but also serves to make a correct prediction about the differential behavior of second person versus first person.

Monogenesis

There is a third possible kind of explanation for language universals that should not be rejected a priori, although I think there are in fact good reasons for not considering it a major factor in the explanation of language universals. Suppose all languages of the world were descended from a single common ancestor—a hypothesis that we may never be in a position to verify empirically—then it might be the case that language universals simply reflect properties of that ancestor language that have been retained, by chance, in all descendant languages, much as French *bon*, Spanish *bueno*, Portuguese *bom*, Italian *buono*, and Rumanian *bun*, all meaning "good," reflect a common inheritance from Latin *bonus* "good."

---

[14]If one wishes to express the special situation of non-coreferential hearers, then one must of course use (38) without the marker of coreference.

Unfortunately, there are some kinds of universals that cannot be inherited from ancestor language to descendant language in this way, namely implications, such as the generalization "if a language has distinct reflexive pronouns anywhere, it will have them in the third person." If there was a "Proto-World" language ancestral to all languages spoken nowadays, then it could have been of the English/Russian type, or of the Old English type, or of the French type (see (35)). But whichever one of those types it belonged to, it could at best have bequeathed that particular type to its descendants, not an abstract implication of the type "if a language has distinct reflexive pronouns anywhere, it will have them in the third person"; for crucially, no single language provides sufficient evidence to establish an implication: Either it has a particular feature or it does not, but it cannot in itself establish an implicational relation between different features.

It does not even help to assume that Proto-World somehow managed to combine the English/Russian, Old English, and French types, perhaps as stylistic variants, and that different descendant languages at some point picked different individual choices. This would only predict the observed distribution if one made the further assumption that no language can innovate a new type, as this assumption would be necessary to prevent a language from innovating the "Anti-French" type that is excluded by the implication. However, we know that languages can innovate: Modern English has innovated relative to Old English, shifting from a language that had no reflexive pronouns to a language that has reflexive pronouns in all grammatical persons.

Thus, monogenesis is not a viable explanation for at least certain kinds of language universals. In fact, we can generalize this observation by being a little more specific about the nature of language universals research. First, language universals research is concerned with specifying what features are necessary and what features are impossible in a human language. Second, it is concerned with the systematic study of cross-linguistic variation in the case of those features that are possible but not necessary in a human language, with the implication—justified, I believe, by language universals research over the last 40 years—that cross-linguistic variation is indeed systematic. Now, if the observed patterns of features found in all known languages, found in no known languages, and known to vary in known languages were simply the result of random inheritances from a presumed single ancestor language, then there would be no reason to expect that these patterns would be systematic. This is particularly so when one considers that known languages are separated from any possible common ancestor by at least tens of thousands of years, which, given known rates of linguistic change, would have been sufficient to disrupt almost any systematic pattern that might have obtained in that ancestor language. Monogenesis is thus not a plausible explanation for the bulk of linguistic universals, even if there was a common ancestor and even if there are particular isolated universal features that happen to have been inherited from that ancestor, given the systematicity of cross-linguistic variation. And of course it must also be borne in mind that the hypothesis of a single common ancestor is considered by most linguists to be well beyond the limits of demonstrability given current knowledge and methods.

CONCLUSION

In this chapter, I have argued that at least two rather different kinds of explanations must be entertained for the existence of language universals. First, some language universals reflect inbuilt constraints on human beings, in particular on their cognitive capacities; for such universals, we can essentially only say that language is the way it is because people are the way they are—though of course the question remains open why people are the way they are. But some other language universals find a more natural explanation in terms of the relation between linguistic structures and the functional uses to which they are put. In current linguistics, there is much friction between "formalists" and "functionalists." I hope to have shown that any overall understanding of language must pay due attention to both form and function (Darnell, Moravcsik, Newmeyer, Noonan, & Wheatley, 1999).

ACKNOWLEDGMENTS

Earlier versions of this chapter have been presented to numerous audiences, and I am grateful to all those who have provided feedback. I am especially grateful to the Department of Modern Languages in the College of Liberal Arts of the University of Mississippi, which invited me to present a version of this as the Christopher Longest Lecture at the University of Mississippi in October, 1991.

REFERENCES

Comrie, B. (1989). *Language universals and linguistic typology* (2nd ed.). Chicago: University of Chicago Press.

Darnell, M., Moravcsik, E., Newmeyer, F., Noonan, M., & Wheatley, K. (Eds.). (1999). *Functionalism and formalism in linguistics.* (Studies in Language Companion Series 41.) Amsterdam: John Benjamins.

Hyman, L. M., & Comrie, B. (1981). Logophoric reference in Gokana. *Journal of African Languages and Linguistics, 3,* 19–37.

Chapter 8

The Geometry of Grammatical Meaning: Semantic Maps and Cross-Linguistic Comparison

Martin Haspelmath
Max Planck Institute for Evolutionary Anthropology, Leipzig

THE PROBLEM OF MULTIFUNCTIONALITY IN GRAMMAR

A recurrent problem in linguistic analysis is the existence of multiple senses or uses of a linguistic unit. Although this affects all meaningful elements of language alike, content words as well as function words (such as prepositions and auxiliaries) and affixal categories (such as tense and case), it is particularly prominent with the latter two. Function words and affixes, which I group together as "grammatical morphemes" (or "grams" for short), have more abstract and general meanings and are thus more apt to be used in multiple ways than content words. Moreover, many linguists regard the study of grammar as more interesting and prestigious, so the grams have tended to occupy center stage in linguistic theory. A few examples of grammatical morphemes with multiple senses/uses are given in (1) to (3). Each English example is followed by a short label describing the use or sense. The specific item whose uses/senses are exemplified is highlighted by boldface.

(1) English preposition *on*
    a. *a cup **on** the table*   (support/vertical)
    b. *a fly **on** the wall*   (support/horizontal)
    c *keys **on** a hook*   (attachment/non-part)
    d. *leaves **on** a tree*   (attachment/part)

(2) English preposition *to*
a. *Goethe went **to** Leipzig as a student.* (direction)
b. *Eve gave the apple **to** Adam.* (recipient)
c. *This seems outrageous **to** me.* (experiencer)
d. *I left the party early **to** get home in time.* (purpose)

(3) English Past Tense[1]
a. *Goethe **wrote** a poem every day.* (past habitual)
b. *Goethe **wrote** Faust in 1808.* (past perfective)
c. *If she **wrote** to me tomorrow, I would
reply in time.* (hypothetical)

In this chapter, I use the term *multifunctionality* to describe situations like those in (1) to (3), and I mostly refer to different *functions* of an expression, rather than "senses" (= conventional meanings) or "uses" (= contextual meanings), because often it is not easy to tell whether we are dealing with different senses or just different uses. The term "function" is meant to be neutral between these two interpretations.

The optimal linguistic treatment of multifunctionality has long been a contentious issue. Idealizing considerably, three possible positions can be distinguished. The *monosemist* position claims that a grammatical morpheme has just a vague abstract meaning, and that all the various functions that can be distinguished are not linguistically significant because they arise from the interaction with the context. In other words, they are not different conventional senses, but only different uses. Thus, one might claim that the meaning of *to* in (2a) and (2b) is really the same (e.g., "abstract direction"), and that the idea of a recipient is an automatic consequence of the fact that *Adam* is animate. The intermediate *polysemist* position recognizes that there are different senses or meanings attached to each gram, but these meanings are related to each other in some fashion that needs to be specified, so that it is by no means an accident that the different senses have the same formal expression. At the other extreme, the *homonymist* position advocates totally separate meanings for each of the functions and recognizes different grams or lexemes for each different meaning.[2] These three positions are

---

[1]Names of morphological categories of particular languages are capitalized, following a convention first proposed by Comrie (1976). This helps avoid confusion between categories and meanings, because the traditional names of categories do not always describe their meaning well. In English, for instance, the Past Tense does not always describe past tense.

[2]From a semantic point of view, polysemy and homonymy are similar in that both involve different senses. The fundamental semantic problem has often been seen as that of distinguishing between *vagueness* (= monosemy) and *ambiguity* (= polysemy or homonymy). Important references are Zwicky and Sadock (1975), Geeraerts (1993), and Tuggy (1993). See also Croft (1998) for a broader perspective.

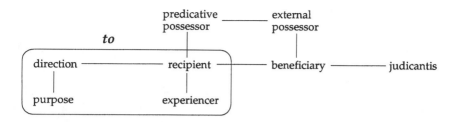

FIG. 8.1. A semantic map of typical dative functions/the boundaries of English *to*.

adopted only for particular analyses, and it is perfectly possible, for example, to propose a monosemic analysis for the functions of *on* in (1), but at the same time a polysemic analysis for the functions of *to* in (2). Or one might regard the verbal *to* in (2d) and the nominal *to* in (2a–c) as homonyms, while analyzing nominal *to* as polysemous or even monosemous. As the analysis of multifunctionality is controversial in many cases, I avoid the terms *sense, use,* and *polysemy,* preferring the more general terms *functions* and *multifunctionality.* Thus, when I talk about different *functions* of *on* and *to* and the Past Tense, I do not commit myself to a particular claim about which functions are part of the conventionalized linguistic knowledge and therefore constitute different senses, and which functions only arise in different utterances depending on the pragmatic context.

In this chapter I discuss *semantic maps,* a method for describing and illuminating the patterns of multifunctionality of grammatical morphemes that does not imply a commitment to a particular choice among monosemic and polysemic analyses. Semantic maps crucially rely on *cross-linguistic comparison,* as I explain in the next section. As a first example, consider Fig. 8.1 (cf. Haspelmath, 1999a), which shows a number of typical functions of dative cases in case-marking languages. A semantic map is a geometrical representation of functions in "conceptual/semantic space" that are linked by connecting lines and thus constitute a network. The configuration of functions shown by the map is claimed to be universal.

In addition to the nodes of the network (i.e., the labels of the various functions) and the connecting lines, Fig. 8.1 also shows a range of functions of English *to*: direction (cf. 2a), recipient (cf. 2b), experiencer (2c), and purpose (cf. 2d). Curved closed lines on the map indicate the boundaries of a language-particular gram in semantic space. Thus, we see in Fig. 8.1 that English *to* lacks some functions that dative cases often have in other languages, such as the predicative-possession function (**This dog is to me.* "This dog is mine"), the beneficiary function (*I'll buy a bike {for/*to} you.*), or the "judicantis" function (*dativus judicantis* "judger's dative"), as in German *Das ist mir*DAT *zu warm* "That's too warm {for/*to} me." Of course, English *to* has some other functions not represented in Fig. 8.1, which I ignore here.

The *semantic-map method* for representing grammatical meaning has several advantages over its rivals. In this section I mention only two prominent rivals, the *list method* and the *general-meaning method*, and I only summarize the main advantages here, deferring more detailed discussion to a later section, "The Advantages of Semantic Maps." The list method is the approach that is often used in descriptive grammars and is particularly well known from older school grammars of Latin and Greek, where the different uses or senses of morphological categories are simply listed, illustrated, and provided with labels such as *genitivus subjectivus, genitivus materiae, genitivus possessivus*, and so on. It is perhaps a bit unfair to mention this method as a "rival" here because it has never implied any theoretical claims, but it is clear that the semantic-map approach is superior in that it treats the set of functions of a particular gram not as an arbitrary list, but as a coherent chunk of a universal network.

The general-meaning method is the classical approach of structuralist analyses of grammatical meaning, going back to Jakobson (1936/1971). In this approach, grammatical meanings are typically identified on the basis of their contrasts with other elements in the system with which they are in opposition, and an attempt is made to formulate highly abstract meanings that subsume all the individual functions. Compared to the list method, the general-meaning method is thus in a sense at the other extreme of the scale, and it was originally developed as a reaction to this overly "atomistic" procedure. An example of an abstract formulation in this spirit is Van Hoecke's (1996) characterization of the Latin Dative case: "The dative serves as the limit of the predicate in the sense that it indicates the ultimate term towards which the action or process referred to tends" (p. 31). The problem with such formulations is that they are difficult to interpret and thus to apply in a consistent and objective fashion—What exactly is meant by "limit" and "ultimate term"? It seems quite impossible to derive the various functions of the Latin Dative case from such a description, unless one already knows what they are. Moreover, such general-meaning analyses are not particularly helpful if one wants to know in what way languages differ from each other. For instance, Burridge (1996) characterized the Dative in Middle Dutch as indicating "non-active involvement in an activity," and Barnes (1985) said about French: "The dative clitic always represents an oblique argument of the verb which is a 'theme' of the sentence, that is, the center of attention" (p. 161). It would be hard to infer from these descriptions that the Dative functions of Latin, Middle Dutch, and French overlap to a considerable extent. In the semantic-map method, by contrast, cross-linguistic comparison is straightforward. For instance, the functions of the French preposition *à*, although similar to English *to*, are not quite the same.

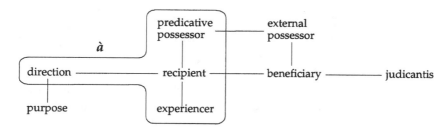

FIG. 8.2. The boundaries of French *à*.

The boundaries of French *à* in semantic space are shown on the same semantic map in Fig. 8.2.

The difference between French and English is that French *à* is not used for purpose (**J'ai quitté la fête tôt à arriver à la maison en bon temps.* "I left the party early to get home in time."), but that it may be used for predicative possession (*Ce chien est à moi.* "This dog is mine.").[3] Now an advocate of the general-meaning method might object that semantic maps do not tell us what the various functions of a gram have in common: The only thing shared by all the functions is that they are located in a similar region in semantic/conceptual space. But this is perhaps just as well: It is quite possible that the senses of a grammatical morpheme are related only by family resemblances and that there is no single schematic sense under which they could be subsumed.

HOW SEMANTIC MAPS WORK

In this section I explain the notational conventions of semantic maps in greater detail. The leading idea of the semantic-map method is that multifunctionality of a gram occurs only when the various functions of the gram are similar. (This presupposes, of course, that accidental homonymy, where formally identical elements have unrelated meanings, can be distinguished from polysemy in some way.)[4] Similarity is expressed topologically by close-

---

[3]Another salient difference between French *à* and English *to* is of course that only the former can be used to express static location (*Marie est à Bruxelles* "Marie is in Brussels"). The map in Figs. 8.1 and 8.2 could easily be extended to show the location function as well, but I arbitrarily limit the discussion here to the functions shown in Figs. 8.1 and 8.2.

[4]Here, too, cross-linguistic comparison can help. Consider the case of plural *-s* and genitive *'s* in English, and of directional and purposive *to*. A priori, one could claim for both of these that they are semantically similar and hence we have polysemy rather than accidental homonymy (cf. Leiss, 1997, for an attempt to spell out the semantic relation between the English plural and genitive), or that they are semantically so distinct that we need to posit homonymy. Now the cross-linguistic perspective helps us distinguish these two options, as was

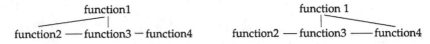

FIG. 8.3.   Two different semantic maps.

ness of nodes in representational space, which metaphorically can be thought of as mapping the possibilities of meaning, or "semantic/conceptual space." For the sake of clarity, closeness is formally shown not only by spatial adjacency, but also by a straight connecting line. Thus, Fig. 8.3a is not identical to Fig. 8.3b.

The difference between Fig. 8.3a and Fig. 8.3b could have been expressed by printing function1 and function2 more closely together in Fig. 8.3a, and function1 and function4 more closely in Fig. 8.3b, but in larger maps, connecting lines greatly help legibility. (However, in practice they are often omitted, cf., e.g., Anderson, 1982, 1986.) The simplest semantic map is one-dimensional and has the form "function1 – function2 – function3," but most of the more elaborate maps that have been proposed are two-dimensional. In the notation that I use here, neither the length of the connecting lines nor their spatial orientation (vertical/horizontal) are significant—these are purely a matter of representational convenience. Likewise, left–right or top–bottom orientation plays no role.

Ideally, a complete theory of grammatical meaning would allow us to derive deductively the functions that are needed for the world's languages and their relative position on the map. This is, of course, totally utopian, but we can take recourse to induction. That is, for each language examined, the functions are arranged in such a way that each gram occupies a contiguous area on the semantic map. As long as only one language is considered, this procedure is of course circular, and for the reasons mentioned in the previous section we could not be sure which functions to represent on the map in the first place. It is here that cross-linguistic comparison is of

---

noted by Haiman (1974) (he used "word" rather than "gram," but the point carries over to grammatical morphemes):

> If a word exhibits polysemy in one language, one may be inclined, or forced, to dismiss its various meanings as coincidental; if a corresponding word in another language exhibits the same, or closely parallel polysemy, it becomes an extremely interesting coincidence; if it displays the same polysemy in four, five, or seven genetically unrelated languages, by statistical law it ceases to be a coincidence at all. (p. 341)

Applying this method to English *to*, we find that in language after language, the same gram is used for direction and purpose (cf. Haspelmath, 1989). But genitive/plural polysemy is extremely rare outside of Indo-European, where -*s* was both a genitive suffix and a plural suffix in the proto-language. Thus, we can probably dismiss the genitive/plural multifunctionality of English *s* as an accidental homonymy.

crucial importance, both for choosing the relevant functions and for arranging the functions on the map.

First, selection of functions: A function is put on the map if there is at least one pair of languages that differ with respect to this function. Consider the distinction between direction and recipient in Fig. 8.1. Neither English nor French have different prepositions for these two functions, so these two languages provide no basis for distinguishing them. If we knew only these two languages, it could be that the direction–recipient distinction is only one that can be made a priori, but not one that is made by language (perhaps analogous to the distinction between "non-part" *on* in [1c] and "part" *on* in [1d], which is perhaps not reflected in any language). In order to justify this distinction on our semantic map, we need at least one language that has different formal expressions for the two functions. Of course, such a language is easy to find: German, for instance, uses *zu* or *nach* for direction, but the Dative case for recipient. This procedure is repeated as more languages are taken into account until no new functions are encountered.

Second, arrangement of functions: Here there is no mechanical procedure. The functions must be arranged in such a way that all multifunctional grams can occupy a contiguous area on the semantic map. When just one language is considered, three functions of a multifunctional gram can be arranged in three different ways. Let us look again at the example of English *to* and the three functions "direction," "recipient," and "purpose." In principle, these could be arranged in any of the three ways in (4).

(4) a. purpose – direction – recipient
    b. direction – purpose – recipient
    c. direction – recipient – purpose

As soon as data from French are added, the option (4b) can be eliminated, because French *à* expresses recipient (*à Adam*) and direction (*à Leipzig*), but not purpose. And when we also consider the German preposition *zu*, option (4c) can be eliminated, because *zu* expresses both purpose (*Anna ging zum Spielen in den Garten* "Anna went into the garden to play") and direction (*Ich gehe zu Anna* "I'm going to Anna's place."), but not recipient. Thus, only (4a) remains, which is of course a subnetwork of the map in Fig. 8.1.

Experience shows that it is generally sufficient to look at a dozen genealogically diverse languages to arrive at a stable map that does not undergo significant changes as more languages are considered. Of course, any new language can immediately falsify a map and require a revision, but the map method allows us to generate interesting hypotheses fairly soon. The configuration of functions on a semantic map is claimed to be universal, thus a

FIG. 8.4. A vacuous semantic map.

map makes predictions about possible languages that are easy to test on new languages.

Let us go back to our example (4a). What happens if we now find a language that expresses both recipient and purpose, but not direction, with the same gram? This would contradict (4a), and in order to resolve the contradiction, we would have to add a connecting line between recipient and purpose. The map would now look as in Fig. 8.4, and it would be compatible with all the data, but at a high price: In Fig. 8.4, all the functions have connecting lines with all other functions, so the map is vacuous. It excludes no possible language and is not particularly interesting (except that it shows that these three functions are closely related).

It may well turn out that in a number of functional domains non-vacuous maps are impossible to construct, but experience shows that there are many areas in which there are very strong universal restrictions, so that interesting maps can be drawn. As soon as more than three functions are considered, a vacuous map would have to involve crossing or curved connecting lines, that is, in fact more than two dimensions.[5] So it is a general rule that the fewer dimensions and the fewer connecting lines a map shows, the more predictions it makes and the more interesting it is.

A final point to make is that it is not uncommon for different grams of the same language to overlap in their distribution. For instance, in addition to the dative-like preposition *à*, French has a dative series of clitics (*me, te, lui, nous, vous, leur*), which has a somewhat different distribution. Dative clitics do not express direction (**Je lui vais* "I go to him") or predicative possession (**Ce livre m'est* "This book is mine"), but they can be used for the benefactive sense (*Je lui ai trouvé un emploi* "I found a job for her") and the external–possessor sense (*On lui a cassé la jambe* "They broke his leg"), where *à* is impossible (cf. Haspelmath, 1999a). Thus, the boundaries of French dative-like grams are as shown in Fig. 8.5. So strictly speaking, one does not even need cross-linguistic comparison to construct a semantic map, because all we need is different grams with an overlapping distribution. But of course such different grams are most easily found by examining different languages.

---

[5]Of course, there is no a priori reason why a semantic map should not be three-dimensional or indeed n-dimensional. But maps with more than two dimensions are difficult to read, and they are less interesting than one-dimensional or two-dimensional maps, so they are rarely used (cf. Haspelmath, 1997b, p. 106 for a rare example of a three-dimensional map).

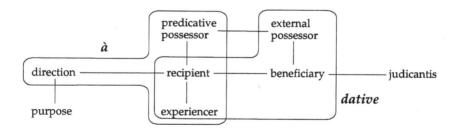

FIG. 8.5.   The boundaries of French *à* and dative.

Before moving on to more elaborate concrete examples of semantic maps, let me insert a note on terminology: Because the semantic-map approach is fairly recent,[6] there is no fully established term yet. The term *semantic map* is used in Kemmer (1993, p. 201), Stassen (1997, p. 578), and van der Auwera and Plungian (1998). Croft's (2001) term is *conceptual space.* Others have used the terms *mental map* (Anderson, 1986) or *cognitive map* (e.g., Kortmann, 1997, p. 177, 210), because it is hoped that the universal configuration of functions on the map directly corresponds to the cognitive structuring of meaning.[7] Haspelmath (1997a) used the term *implicational map* to highlight the fact that semantic maps express implicational universals (see later section "The Advantage of Semantic Maps"). Here I use *semantic map* because it is more transparent than *implicational map* and less ambitious than *cognitive map/mental map.* The only problem with this term is that the functions that we want to map are not necessarily differentiated only semantically. For instance, the function "predicative possession" in Figs. 8.1 and 8.2 also contains the syntactic component "predicative." Similarly, the "hypothetical" function of the English Past tense (cf. [3c]: *If she wrote to me tomorrow*) is restricted to the protasis (the *if*-clause) of a conditional construction, although the main-clause verb presumably also has hypothetical meaning. So sometimes the syntactic context must also be taken into account, and the term *semantic map* is thus not completely accurate. But as it is fairly well established, it seems best to continue using it.

---

[6]An early influential paper was Anderson (1982) (his approach was foreshadowed in Anderson, 1974), which was endorsed (but not applied further) by Bybee (1985, pp. 195–196). Applications in the 1980s include Anderson (1986, 1987), Croft, Shyldkrot, and Kemmer (1987), and Haspelmath (1987).

[7]Semantic maps are also similar to cognitive-grammar "networks" (e.g., Enger & Nesset, 1999; Lakoff, 1987; Langacker, 1988; Rudzka-Ostyn, 1996; Sandra & Rice, 1995), that is, spatial arrangements of the polysemy structure of an item in a particular language. However, these networks do not seem to imply anything about the universality of the spatial arrangement of the senses.

Croft (2001) made a useful terminological distinction between a *conceptual space* (i.e., the universal arrangement of functions) and a *semantic map* (i.e., the boundaries of particular elements in particular languages). But in fact we need terms for three different entities: (a) conceptual/semantic space (the object of study), (b) universal semantic maps or conceptual spaces (a particular linguist's hypothesis about a segment of (a) as represented geometrically), and (c) language-particular and gram-specific subdivisions of (b).

SOME FURTHER SEMANTIC MAPS

Let us now look at a few concrete cases of semantic maps that have been discussed in the literature.

Indefinite Pronouns

The first case to be mentioned here is the distribution of different series of indefinite pronouns (cf. Haspelmath, 1997a). English has three such series: the *some*-series (*someone, something, somewhere*, etc.), the *any*-series (*anyone, anything, anywhere*, etc.), and the *no*-series (*no one, nothing, nowhere, never*, etc.). In these series, I consider the first element (*some/any/no*) as the grammatical morpheme whose functions are to be mapped in semantic/conceptual space. But what are the relevant semantic or syntactic distinctions? Quirk, Greenbaum, Leech, and Svartvik (1985, p. 83) described the contrast between *some*-indefinites and *any*-indefinites in terms of the notion of "assertiveness." *Some*-indefinites occur in assertive contexts, that is, in propositions whose truth is asserted (cf. 5a-b), whereas *any*-indefinites occur in non-assertive contexts such as questions (6a), conditional protases (6b), and negative sentences (6c), which do not claim the truth of the corresponding positive statement.

(5) a. *Yesterday Mariamu met **someone** (/*anyone) from Botswana.*
    b. *At the DGfS conference I always meet someone (/*anyone) I know.*

(6) a. *Has **anything** happened while I was away?*
    b. *If I can help you **in any way**, please tell me.*
    c. *I didn't notice **anything** suspicious.*

But although a highly abstract notion such as "(non-)assertiveness" certainly captures important aspects of the semantics of *some*- and *any*-indefinites, it is not sufficient to predict all their functions. For instance, *any*-indefinites are not normally possible in imperatives (7a), and *some*-indefinites are also possible in questions and conditional protases (cf. 7b–c).

(7) a. *Please buy **something** (/??anything) for our son when you go to town.*
    b. *Has **something** happened while I was away?*
    c. *If I can help you **in some way**, please tell me.*

Moreover, many languages have a distinction among indefinites that is roughly comparable to that in English, but differs from it in subtle ways. For example, Russian has two indefinite series characterized by the markers *-to* (*kto-to* "someone," *čto-to* "something," *gde-to* "somewhere," etc.) and *-nibud'* (*kto-nibud'* "anyone," *čto-nibud'* "anything," *gde-nibud'* "anywhere," etc.). Like English *any*-indefinites, the Russian *-nibud'*-indefinites do not occur in positive declarative sentences such as (8a), but they do occur in questions and conditionals (e.g., 8b).

(8) a. ***Kto-to** (/*kto-nibud')* postučal v dver'.*
       "Someone (/*anyone) knocked at the door."
    b. *Esli **čto-nibud'** slučitsja, ja pridu srazu.*
       "If anything happens, I'll come immediately."

However, *-nibud'*-indefinites also occur in "assertive" contexts when *nonspecific* reference is intended, that is, the speaker has no particular referent in mind. For instance, whereas the English sentence *He wants to marry someone from Botswana* is ambiguous (he might have a fiancée who happens to be from Botswana, or being from Botswana might be a prerequisite for any future wife), Russian distinguishes these two readings. The *-to*-indefinite is used for specific reference, and the *-nibud'*-indefinite is used for nonspecific reference.

(9) a. *On xočet ženit'sja na **kom-to** iz Botsvany.*
       "He wants to marry someone [specific] from Botswana."
    b. *On xočet ženit'sja na **kom-nibud'** iz Botsvany.*
       "He wants to marry someone [non-specific] from Botswana."

In imperatives, reference to indefinite phrases is necessarily non-specific, so the *-to*-indefinite is impossible here:

(10) *Kupi **čto-nibud'** (/*čto-to) dlja našego syna.*
     "Buy something for our son."

The Russian distinction between *-to*-indefinites and *-nibud'*-indefinites is thus often characterized as consisting in the property of *(non-)specificity*, but just as (non)assertiveness cannot account for all functions of English *some/*

any, (non)specificity cannot account for all functions of Russian *-to/-nibud'*.
For instance, *-nibud'*-indefinites cannot occur in negative contexts such as
(6c), and again unlike *any*-indefinites, they cannot occur in the "freechoice" sense as in (11).

(11) **Anybody** *can solve this easy problem.*

Thus, English and Russian have two different grams in indefinite pronouns that overlap in their distribution, but do not coincide. Abstract labels
such as specificity and assertiveness do not capture the similarities between
the languages, and they are not sufficient to derive the exact range of functions of these types of indefinites. To describe the differences and similarities in the functions of indefinites in 40 languages, I developed a semantic
map in Haspelmath (1997a), shown in Fig. 8.6.

Here "irrealis non-specific" refers to non-specific functions such as (9b)
and (10), as opposed to other non-specific functions such as negation, free
choice, and so on. The distribution of English *some-/any*-indefinites and of
Russian *-to/-nibud'*-indefinites on the map is shown in Figs. 8.7 and 8.8. In
these figures, the connecting lines between the functions are omitted for
ease of legibility.

The functions "specific known," "indirect negation," and "comparative"
are all needed because some languages have indefinite pronoun series that
differ from each other precisely in this respect. Let me just give an example
for the need to distinguish "specific known" and "specific unknown": German *jemand* "someone" and *irgendjemand* "someone" differ in that
irgendjemand cannot be used when the referent's identity is known to the
speaker. Thus, *irgendjemand* is appropriate in (12a), but not in (12b).

(12) a. *Mein Handy ist weg, (**irgend**)**jemand** muss es gestohlen haben.*
        "My cell phone is gone, someone must have stolen it."
     b. **Jemand** */*irgendjemand* hat angerufen – rate mal wer.*
        "Someone called—guess who."

The semantic map in Fig. 8.6 has been tested for 40 languages in
Haspelmath (1997a), and no counterexamples have been found.

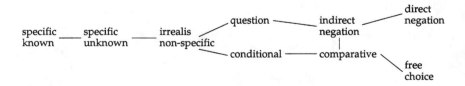

FIG. 8.6.   A semantic map for indefinite pronoun functions.

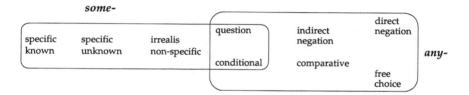

FIG. 8.7.   The boundaries of English *some*-indefinites and *any*-indefinites.

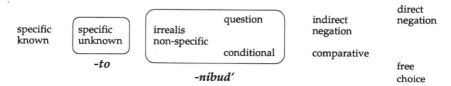

FIG. 8.8.   The boundaries of Russian *-to*-indefinites and *-nibud'*-indefinites.

Reflexives and Related Functions

My next example comes from the area of voice-marking on verbs. Quite a few languages have grammatical morphemes associated with the verb that express reflexive actions as well as a number of related senses that often involve intransitivization. A case in point is French, which uses its reflexive clitic (*se* "him/herself," *me* "myself," *te* "yourself," etc.) not only with fully transitive verbs such as "kill" (cf. 13a), where it corresponds to English *-self*, but also in a number of other cases (cf. 13b–13e).

(13) a. *Judas s'est tué.*   (full reflexive)
        "Judas killed himself."
     b. *Bathséba s'est lavée.*   (grooming)
        "Bathseba washed."
     c. *Mamoud s'est agenouillé.*   (body motion)
        "Mamoud kneeled down."
     d. *Elisabeth et Marie se sont rencontrées.*   (naturally reciprocal)
        "Elizabeth and Mary met."
     e. *La porte s'est ouverte.*   (anticausative)
        "The door opened."

In (13b) and with other verbs of grooming (shaving, combing, etc.), one can still construe *se* as "herself," because *Bathseba washed* can be paraphrased by "Bathseba washed herself," and such a construal is not totally impossible either in (13c). However, (13d) and (13e) are clearly no longer truly reflexive. Example (13d) is reciprocal, and (13e) expresses a spontaneous non-caused event ("anticausative"). Such non-reflexive functions of reflexive morphemes are often called (somewhat vaguely) "*middle voice*," following the terminology of classical scholars (cf. Kemmer, 1993). Another language that is similar to French in that its reflexive marker has a number of middle functions is Russian (reflexive marker *-sja/s'*):

(14) a. *Batseba umyla-s'.*   (grooming)
     "Bathseba washed."
   b. *Učitel' povernul-sja.*   (body motion)
     "The teacher turned around."
   c. *Elizaveta i Marija vstretili-s'.*   (naturally reciprocal)
     "Elizabeth and Mary met."
   d. *Dver' otkryla-s'.*   (anticausative)
     "The door opened."
   e. *Vopros obsuždal-sja komissiej.*   (passive)
     "The question was discussed by the committee."
   f. *Sobaka kusaet-sja.*   (deobjective)
     "The dog bites."

   In order to describe the range of meanings that reflexive markers may have, some linguists have attempted to formulate abstract general meanings or functions such as "derived intransitivity" (Cranmer, 1976), "nondistinct arguments" (Langacker & Munro, 1975), or "low degree of elaboration of events" (Kemmer, 1993). These abstract notions certainly capture significant aspects of the meaning components that are shared by the various middle functions, but they are not helpful for comparing languages, for example, for describing the difference between French and Russian. In order to do this, we need finer-grained functions. For instance, Russian *-sja* does not have the full reflexive function: The independent reflexive pronoun *sebja* must be used in the translation of French *Judas s'est tué* (13a):

(15) *Iuda ubil sebja.* (**Iuda ubil-sja*.)
     "Judas killed himself."

On the other hand, French does not have the "deobjective" function exemplified by Russian *Sobaka kusaet-sja* "The dog bites" (= 14f), and the passive function of French *se* is highly restricted.

   Again, a more profitable approach is the construction of a universal semantic map on which middle-like grams of individual languages occupy a contiguous area. A good approximation for our purposes is the map in Fig. 8.9 (cf. Haspelmath, 1987, p. 35, and Kemmer, 1993, p. 202; see also Geniušienė, 1987 for detailed discussion and a rich collection of relevant data).

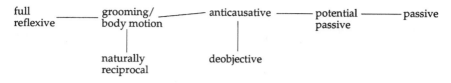

FIG. 8.9.   A semantic map for reflexive and middle functions.

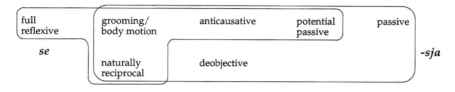

FIG. 8.10.   The boundaries of French *se* and Russian *-sja*.

The distribution of the French reflexive gram *se* (i.e. *me/te/se*, etc.) and the Russian verbal reflexive *-sja/-s'* is shown in Fig. 8.10.

"Potential passive" refers to a kind of passive construction with generic meaning and generally an obligatory adverbial phrase such as "easily" or "well." Some languages, for instance German, allow the reflexive gram in potential passives, but not in ordinary passives:

(16) a. *Der neue Roman von Grass verkauft **sich** gut.*
      "Grass's new novel sells well."
   b. *Humboldt liest **sich** nicht leicht.*
      "Humboldt doesn't read easily."
   c. **Das Fahrrad hat **sich** gestern repariert.*
      "The bike was repaired yesterday."

Naturally reciprocal events are clearly distinct semantically from naturally reflexive events such as grooming and body motion, and there are some languages in which reciprocal events are expressed differently. For instance, Turkish has the suffix *-In* for grooming and body motion (e.g., *giy-in-mek* "dress [oneself]"), but the suffix *-Iş* for naturally reciprocal events (e.g., *bul-uş-* "meet [each other]," *sev-iş-* "make love [to each other]," *döv-üş-* "hit each other"). Turkish also illustrates the case in which grooming and body motion is not expressed in the same way as the anticausative, which is marked by the suffix *-Il* (e.g., *aç-ıl-mak* "open [intr.]," cf. *aç-mak* "open [tr.]"). That the anticausative function must be closer to the passive than to the other functions is also illustrated by Turkish, because the suffix *-Il* also expresses the passive in this language:

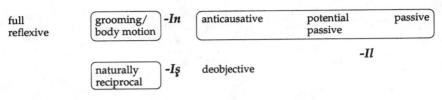

FIG. 8.11.   The boundaries of Turkish *-In*, *-Iş*, and *-Il*.

(17) Turkish passive
     Bu   iş-ler   makine-ler-le   yap-ıl-ır.
     these thing-PL machine-PL-INSTR make-PASS-AOR
     "These things are made with machines."

The boundaries of the three markers *-In, -Iş* and *-Il* are shown in Fig. 8.11. Reflexive-like markers have quite a few further functions in many languages, such as "emotion" (e.g., French *s'étonner* "be astonished"), "emotive speech action" (e.g., French *se lamenter* "lament"), and "cognition" (e.g., French *s'apercevoir* "become aware, notice") (cf. Kemmer, 1993, for detailed discussion). These would eventually have to be integrated into the semantic map, but because their occurrence is strongly lexically determined, cross-linguistic comparison is not easy. Quite generally, comparison by means of the semantic-map approach is straightforward for analytically expressed grams or inflectional grams with high lexical generality, but is difficult for derivational grams that occur only in a small number of lexemes.

Instrumentals and Related Functions

My third example again concerns prepositions and case markers, like the first example of typical dative functions in the first section. In this section I look at prepositions and case markers that express the instrumental role and related functions (cf. Michaelis & Rosalie, 2000). In English, the normal instrumental preposition *with* (cf. example 18a) also has the function of accompaniment (or *comitative*), as illustrated in (18b).

    (18) a. *Kanzi cracked the nut **with** a nutcracker.*
        b. *Sancho Pansa has arrived **with** Don Quijote.*

Comitative-instrumental polysemy is frequent in the world's languages (cf. Stolz, 1996; and Lakoff & Johnson, 1980, p. 134 on the kind of metaphorical transfer that is involved here), but it is by no means universal. For example, Russian uses its instrumental case (here the suffix *-om/-em*) to express instrument (cf. example 19a), but it requires the preposition *s* "with" for the comitative function (cf. example 19b).

(19) a. *Kanzi raskolol orex kamn-em.*
"Kanzi cracked the nut with a stone."
b. *Sančo Pansa prišel s Don Kixotom.*
"Sancho Pansa has arrived with Don Quijote."

Another common type of polysemy involves comitative(-instrumental) and conjunctive, that is, the coordinating notion "and." This particular polysemy is almost non-existent in European languages,[8] but it is widespread in other parts of the world, for instance in Africa. Thus, Nkore-Kiga (a Bantu language of Uganda) has the preposition *na* for instrument (20a), comitative (20b) and conjunction (20c).

(20) Nkore-Kiga (Taylor, 1985)
    a. (instrument)   *n' enyondo*   "with a hammer"
    b. (comitative)   *na Mugasho*   "(together) with Mugasho"
    c. (conjunctive)   *emeeza n' entebe*   "a table and a chair"

Probably as a result of influence from African substratum languages, many creole languages of the Atlantic and Indian Ocean with European lexifier languages also show this kind of polysemy (cf. Michaelis & Rosalie, 2000). For example, in Seychelles Creole, the preposition *ek* (from French *avec* "with") has a wide range of functions, including the three functions just exemplified from Nkore-Kiga (20a–c).

(21) Seychelles Creole (Michaelis & Rosalie, 2000)
    a. (instrument)   *Nou fer servolan, nou file ek difil.*
       "We made a kite, we let it fly with a string."
    b. (comitative)   *Mon 'n travay ek Sye Raim.*
       "I have worked with Mr. Rahim."
    c. (conjunctive)   *dan zil Kosmoledo ek Asonpsyon*
       "on the islands of Cosmoledo and Assomption"
    d. (passive agent)   *Mon 'n ganny morde ek lisyen.*
       "I have been bitten by dogs."

---

[8]However, Russian has a coordination-like construction in which the preposition *s(o)* "with" is used:

(a) *starik so staruxoj*   "the old man and (lit. 'with') the old woman"

  e. (source)   *Mon ganny pansyon **ek** gouvernman.*
                      "I get a pension from the government."
  f. (cause)   *Pa kapab reste laba **ek** moustik.*
                      "It was impossible to stay there because of
                      the mosquitoes."
  g. (recipient)   *Mon 'n donn larzan **ek** li.*
                      "I gave the money to him."

From the point of view of the European languages, this rampant polysemy of a single preposition may look unusual, but it is not difficult to find parallels for most of the functions. Thus, the Russian Instrumental case expresses both the instrumental role and the passive agent (e.g., *Orex byl raskolot Konstantin-**om*** "the nut was cracked by Konstantin"), and the German preposition *von* expresses both passive agent and source:

  (22) a. (source)   *Ich bekomme eine Pension **von** der Regierung.*
                          "I get a pension from the government."
       b. (passive agent) *Ich wurde **von** Hunden gebissen.*
                          "I have been bitten by dogs."

The French preposition *par* expresses both passive *agent* (*par des chiens* "by some dogs") and cause (*par hazard* "by accident"), and German *aus* expresses both source (*aus Paris* "from Paris") and cause (*aus Hass* "out of hatred"). Only the coincidence between comitative and recipient is somewhat special in that it is not found in European languages.

The various patterns of multifunctionality noted so far do not lend themselves easily to a description in terms of an abstract general meaning of the kind "non-assertiveness" or "non-distinct arguments," and they have not attracted much attention by theoreticians (but cf. Croft, 1991). Still, they are by no means random and can be captured by a universal map just like indefinite pronoun functions and middle functions. The map I propose here (based largely on Michaelis & Rosalie, 2000) is given in Fig. 8.12. The role "co-agent" refers to a comitative-like participant that takes active part in the action, as in *X fought with Y, X kissed with Y.* It is shown in parentheses in Fig. 8.12 because I have no good cross-linguistic evidence for its position as a linking element between comitative and recipient. However, semantically it seems to make sense, and expressions such as English *talk to/with somebody,* where a co-agent can alternatively be expressed like a comitative (*with*) or like a recipient (*to*), seem to confirm this view.

In Figs. 8.13–8.15, some of the prepositions and case-markers that we have seen so far are shown as they appear on the map.

In addition to the functions mentioned so far, the map also contains the function "beneficiary," linked to both "recipient" and "cause." The recipi-

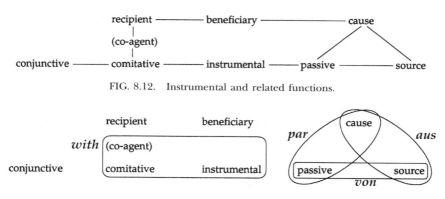

FIG. 8.12. Instrumental and related functions.

FIG. 8.13. The boundaries of some English, German, and French prepositions.

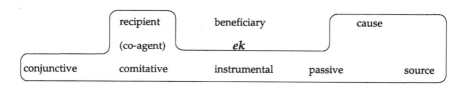

FIG. 8.14. The boundaries of Seychelles Creole *ek.*

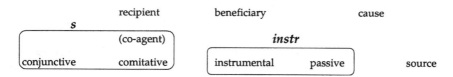

FIG. 8.15. The boundaries of the Russian instrumental and *s* "with."

ent–beneficiary link (which we already saw on the map in Fig. 8.1) is justified by many languages with a dative case that has both these functions (e.g., German and Latin), whereas the beneficiary–cause link is justified by prepositions like English *for* (beneficiary: *for my mother*; cause: *for this reason*) or Italian *per* (beneficiary: *per mia madre* "for my mother"; cause: *per questa ragione* "for this reason"; passive agent: *Questa noce è stata schiacciata per Kanzi* "This nut has been cracked by Kanzi.").

Through the linking element "beneficiary," this map has a circular shape, thus contrasting with the other maps that have so far been discussed in this chapter. However, there is nothing peculiar about this: Conceptual space is not infinite, and there are many different routes through it, so there is no reason why some paths should not lead back to where they started.

The overlap between Fig. 8.12 and Fig. 8.1, which share the subnetwork "recipient — beneficiary," raises the question of what the relation between two overlapping maps is. The answer is simple: Both maps represent just an arbitrary subnetwork of the "semantic universe." It would be possible to consolidate the two maps into one big map, just as it is always possible to split up a map into smaller submaps. What is significant is only the links and the (mostly semantic) substance of the functions, but the size and the extension of each map depends solely on the linguist's current purposes.

THE ADVANTAGES OF SEMANTIC MAPS

The semantic-map approach has a number of important advantages, some of which have already been mentioned and illustrated.[9] Semantic maps ensure cross-linguistic comparability, they allow us to avoid the problem of distinguishing between polysemy and vagueness, they help us detect universal semantic relationships, they generate a number of implicational universals as a side effect, and they lead to expectations about diachronic change. In this and in the next section I spell out these advantages in somewhat more detail.

In contrast to the structuralist general-meaning approach, semantic maps permit cross-linguistic comparisons. Jakobson (1936/1971), one of the founders of structuralism, observed himself that universal meanings cannot be formulated in his framework: "Man kann nicht universal und allezeit gültige und vom gegebenen System (bzw. Systemtypus) der Kasusgegensätze unabhängige Kasusbedeutungen aufstellen." [It is not possible to set up case meanings that are universally and always valid and independent of the given system (or system type) of case oppositions.] (p. 26). On the structuralist view, case meanings (and grammatical meanings more generally) exist only within particular systems and are derived from system-internal contrasts (cf. Bybee, 1988, for some discussion). But if this were the whole story, we would expect languages to differ much more radically from each other than we actually find. Empirical typological work has generally found that similar semantic distinctions are relevant in language after language, independently of genealogical or areal affinities, even though the grams of different languages (and often also different grams within the same language) carve up the space of possibilities in different ways. For instance, although many languages express direction and recipient in the same way (e.g., English and French, cf. Figs. 8.1–8.2), there are also many languages (such as German and Latin)

---

[9]To my knowledge, the earliest clear discussion of the advantages of the function-based method as opposed to the general-meaning approach is Ferguson (1970). However, Ferguson did not mention semantic maps.

that make a distinction between these two notions, reserving a separate gram for recipient and one for direction (cf. Croft, 1991, p. 157). On the Jakobsonian view, this is surprising—one would expect languages to carve up the direction–recipient space in numerous totally different ways. But the fact that the same distinctions occur again and again allows us to make a reasonably limited list of "atomic" constituents of conceptual space, the *functions*. Of course, no semantic domain has been studied in any detail for hundreds of languages, but the typical experience is that after a dozen languages have been examined, fewer and fewer functions need to be added to the map with each new language. On the structuralist view, we would expect every language to behave in a completely different way, so that each further language that is examined would force us to posit a plethora of new distinctions. But this is not what we observe in practice. The finding that languages are in fact so similar invites systematic cross-linguistic comparison, and semantic maps are an important tool for such studies.

Semantic maps describe the grammatical meaning(s) of a gram in a very concrete way that can easily be discussed, improved on, or proven wrong. In contrast, the general-meaning approach generally arrives at descriptions so abstract and vague that it is practically impossible to work with them. As Lakoff (1987) noted (for word meanings), a general meaning is "so devoid of real meaning that it is not recognizable as what people think of as the meaning of a word" (p. 416).

Semantic maps do not presuppose that we have found THE correct semantic analysis of a grammatical morpheme in a particular language. They simply sidestep the vexing problem of distinguishing between polysemy and vagueness. If there is one language whose grams distinguish between two functions, then these two functions must be added to the map. Thus, the fact that German *jemand* and *irgendjemand* differ with respect to the speaker's knowledge of the referent (cf. section "Indefinite Pronouns") forces us to distinguish a "known" function and an "unknown" function on the map. Now of course this implies nothing about the analysis of other languages. English *some*-indefinites are not sensitive to this distinction, but it does not seem reasonable to say that they therefore have two different senses—*some*-indefinites are simply vague with respect to this distinction. Thus, a gram that covers several functions on a map may have just a single sense and be vague with respect to the relevant distinctions, or it may be polysemous, and of course it may also be vague with respect to some of the distinctions, whereas others are distinct senses. But all this does not matter for the semantic map. This is an important advantage because semantic analysis of grammatical meaning is very difficult. Cross-linguistic comparison of grammatical meaning is easier: It only requires us to be able to identify functions across languages. This is not a trivial prerequisite either, but it is more manageable.

Similarly, the semantic-map perspective can help us avoid making unnecessary homonymy claims. For example, there is a long-standing debate on whether the different usage types of English *any* (cf. section "Indefinite Pronouns") can be subsumed under one general meaning, or whether two different *any*s have to be recognized, a "polarity-sensitive *any*" and a "freechoice *any*." The semantic map in Fig. 8.7 provides a way out of this dilemma: It shows the different functions of *any*, but it also shows that the different functions are close to each other on the map, so the fact that the "two *any*s" are not unrelated is captured as well. Likewise, it has sometimes been claimed that French has two different items *à*, a "preposition" *à* that expresses direction, and a "case marker" *à* that expresses recipient. Again, the semantic map in Fig. 8.2 expresses both the differences and similarities, so that we do not need to assume accidental homonymy here.

Semantic maps also do not require the identification of a central or prototypical function (or use or sense) of a grammatical item. It has often been suggested in recent years that polysemy networks are organized around a prototypical sense that is surrounded by more peripheral senses (Lakoff, 1987; Langacker, 1988). Such analyses are compatible with semantic maps: For instance, one might want to claim that the "direction" sense of English *to* is the central sense, and that the other functions (cf. Fig. 8.1) should be seen synchronically as extensions from this sense. However, in many other cases the identification of a central, prototypical sense is not straightforward (e.g., Seychelles Creole *ek*, Fig. 8.14), and probably it is not a good strategy to look for one single central sense in all cases. The semantic-map method is completely neutral in this respect.

Semantic maps not only provide an easy way of formulating and visualizing differences and similarities between individual languages, but they can also be seen as a powerful tool for discovering universal semantic structures that characterize the human language capacity. Once a semantic map has been tested on a sufficiently large number of languages (i.e., at least a couple of dozen) from different parts of the world, we can be reasonably confident that it will indeed turn out to be universal, and even if a map is based only on a handful of languages, the map can serve as a working hypothesis to be tested by further evidence. Thus, every semantic map can be interpreted as making a universal claim about languages that can be falsified easily. By showing that there exists at least one language with a pattern of multifunctionality that cannot be accommodated by the map, a map is falsified and needs to be abandoned or at least modified. So for every sub-chain of three functions "function1 — function2 — function3" (where function3 is not linked directly to function1), the claim is made that if a language has a multifunctional gram with the functions "function1" and "function3," then that gram also has "function2." That is, each semantic map embodies a series of implicational universals (hence Haspelmath's [1997a] term "implicational map"). These universals emerge as an automatic side effect of the construction of a map that allows the representation of cross-linguistic similarities and differences.

Because multifunctionality of grammatical morphemes presumably occurs only when the different functions are similar, semantic maps provide objective evidence for which meanings or functions are perceived as similar by speakers. In this sense, our semantic maps can indeed be taken as a direct representation of the relationships between meanings in speakers' minds ("mental maps," "cognitive maps"). In Croft's (2001) words, they represent "the geography of the human mind, which can be read in the facts of the world's languages in a way that the most advanced brain scanning techniques cannot ever offer us" (p. 364). However, semantic maps only show the relative closeness or distance of relations, not the exact nature of the relations within semantic space. So semantic maps cannot replace cognitive–semantic analyses, but they can supplement them and constrain them in various ways.

SEMANTIC MAPS AND DIACHRONIC CHANGE

In addition to summarizing the synchronic relationships between different grammatical meanings, semantic maps can also be an important tool for diachrony, in particular grammaticalization studies. The simplest way in which semantic maps make predictions about diachronic change is by showing that some changes presuppose others. For example, given the mini-map "direction – recipient – predicative possessor" (a sub-map of Figs. 8.1–8.2), it is predicted that if a direction marker (such as Latin *ad* "to," which later gave rise to French *à*) is extended to additional functions and comes to express predicative possession, it must have been extended to "recipient" before. This is really a trivial consequence of the synchronic implicational relations: Just as synchronically each gram covers a contiguous area, so diachronically a gram cannot arbitrarily "jump" to a distant function, but must be extended step by step (or "incrementally," Croft, Shyldkrot, & Kemmer, 1987).

But we can say more than this, because diachronic change is typically directed, and this directionality can be encoded easily on semantic maps by turning the neutral connecting lines into directed arrows. A diachronic version of the map in Figs. 8.1 and 8.2 would look as in Fig. 8.16.

An arrow between two function labels means that a gram can extend its meaning only in the direction shown. For instance, direction markers are typically extended to the purpose function (Haspelmath, 1989) and to the recipient function (the latter has happened both to English *to* and French *à*, from Latin *ad*), but the reverse development, from purpose or recipient

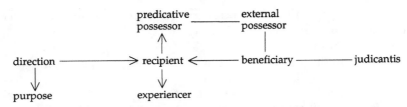

FIG. 8.16.   A semantic map of typical dative functions, with directionality.

to direction, is unattested. Evidence for directionality comes from attested diachronic changes, and as the diachronic data are far more difficult to obtain than the corresponding synchronic data, the possible directions of change are not always known. For instance, it is not clear to me whether there are any restrictions for the direction of change for the functions of external possessor and judicantis, simply because of insufficient data. (Thus, Fig. 8.16 shows simple connecting lines rather than arrows for these functions.) We can be really certain that a change is unidirectional only if there are numerous attested cases and no counterexamples.

Often, however, a further strong indication of unidirectionality comes from the substance of the meanings involved: The most common type of grammatical change, grammaticalization, generally entails a unidirectional bleaching and extension of meaning, that is, the loss of specific, concrete meaning elements, increasing abstractness, generalization to new contexts, and loss of pragmatic emphasis.[10] The changes from "direction" to "recipient" and from "direction" to "purpose" illustrate bleaching quite well, because in both cases, the concrete spatial meaning component is lost and the gram is extended to new contexts.

Some semantic maps show a systematic directionality of semantic change across a range of functions and can therefore be likened to sloping territory in semantic space. A good example is the map of reflexives and middles (section "Reflexives and Related Functions," Figs. 8.9–8.11). In Fig. 8.17, a somewhat modified version of this map with arrows is given.

Figure 8.17 is simplified in that "naturally reciprocal" and "deobjective" are omitted, for which diachronic data are insufficient. To the left, the function "emphatic reflexive" is added, that is, the function of English *-self* as in *The mayor herself opened the exhibition*. Such emphatic reflexives are usually the source of (full) reflexive markers (as in *The mayor admires herself*) (cf. König, 2001). Figure 8.17 is a good example of a "slope" because grammatical morphemes can only acquire new meanings from left to right on this figure. In Fig. 8.18, the boundaries of (originally) reflexive grams in several

---

[10]Cf. Lehmann (1995), Heine et al. (1991), Hopper and Traugott (1993), and Bybee et al. (1994) for the nature of semantic change in grammaticalization, and Haspelmath (1999b) for an explanation of the unidirectionality of grammaticalization.

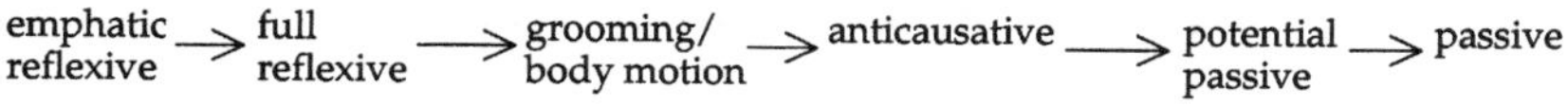

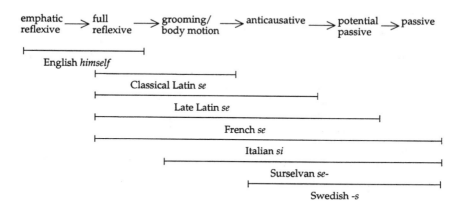

emphatic reflexive → full reflexive → grooming/body motion → anticausative → potential passive → passive

FIG. 8.17. A semantic map for reflexive and middle functions, including directionality.

FIG. 8.18. The boundaries of reflexive/middle grams in seven languages.

languages are shown that illustrate the unidirectional diachronic development (cf. Croft et al., 1987; Kemmer, 1993, for more discussion).[11]

Particularly instructive is the comparison of Classical Latin, Late Latin, and French, because these three represent three successive stages of the same language. Whereas Classical Latin *se* was restricted to full reflexives (e.g., *se videt* "sees himself") and grooming/body motion (e.g., *se movet* "moves [himself]"), Late Latin texts already show *se* extended to the anticausative function (e.g., *cludit se* "closes [intr.]"). French allows *se* in the potential passive construction (*Son livre se vend bien* "Her book sells well"), and Italian has extended *si* even further (*Si è evitata una tragedia* "A tragedy was avoided.")

But a gram cannot go on acquiring new functions indefinitely. When a gram has taken on a certain number of abstract functions, chances are that speakers will prefer a novel expression for the more concrete or more emphatic functions that stand at the beginning of the slope. Thus, Latin *se* very early lost the original emphatic reflexive sense (which it must have had at some point), and *ipse* "same, self" was used as a new emphatic reflexive marker. In Surselvan Romansch,[12] the marker *se-* (which has become a pre-

---

[11]A completely analogous figure for indefinite pronouns is given in Haspelmath (1997a, p. 149).

[12]Surselvan Romansch is one of the "Rhaeto-Romance" varieties of the canton of Graubünden, Switzerland. It is discussed by Kemmer (1993, pp. 166–175), following the original work by Stimm (1973).

fix in this language) has lost the full reflexive function, for which the rein-
forced reflexive *sesez* is used (*vesa el sesez* "he sees himself"). The corresponding Swedish suffix *-s* does not, of course, descend from Latin *se*, but its
history is completely analogous (Kemmer, 1993, pp. 182–193). Going even
further than Surselvan, Swedish *-s* has lost also the grooming and body motion functions, for which the full reflexive pronoun *sig* is used (e.g., *vaska
sig* "wash [oneself]"), and it is restricted to the anticausative and passive
functions (e.g., *förändra-s* "change [intr.]," *hata-s* "be hated"). For such
slope-like semantic maps, we can thus summarize the diachronic development by the following metaphor: A grammatical morpheme is like a window that opens the view onto part of semantic space. The window gradually
moves in one direction over the map, and as new functions come into view
on one side, some old functions disappear on the other side.

Figures such as Fig. 8.17 are well-known from grammaticalization studies. They are variously called "grammaticalization channels" (Lehmann,
1995), "grammaticalization paths" (Bybee, Perkins, & Pagliuca, 1994), or
"grammaticalization chains" (Heine, Claudi, & Hünnemeyer, 1991, p. 220).
However, as van der Auwera and Plungian (1998) have stressed recently,
they are really completely equivalent to semantic maps, with arrows added
to indicate directionality.

In a grammaticalization path, a newly grammaticalized item normally
comes in at one margin and is then gradually extended to some of the more
central functions. However, occasionally a new form may come to express a
function in the middle of the map and "oust" a gram from this function that
still expresses a number of adjacent functions. A simple concrete example
comes from the domain of tense and aspect. A very rudimentary map links
the functions "habitual," "progressive," and "future" as in (23).

(23) habitual ——— progressive ——— future

The English Progressive (*I'm leaving*) can express progressive and future,
the Spanish Present (*Juan canta* "Juan sings/is singing") expresses habitual
and progressive, and the German Present can express all three (*ich spiele* "I
play/I'm playing/I'll play"). Now if a language with the German multifunctionality pattern develops a new progressive form that ousts the old
form in its progressive function, the old form may end up with just the two
functions "habitual" and "future" (cf. Haspelmath, 1998, for detailed discussion). This appears to have happened in Turkish, where the old present
tense (e.g., *okut-ur* "teaches/will teach") is now restricted to habitual and future, whereas the progressive is obligatorily expressed by the new progressive form (*okut-uyor* "is teaching"). As a result, the Turkish old present tense
no longer expresses a coherent area on the semantic map, but rather a region in the form of a doughnut, with a hole in the middle (cf. Croft et al.,
1987, p. 190; van der Auwera & Plungian, 1998, p. 113). If this phenome-

non turned out to be widespread, the idea that grammatical morphemes generally express a coherent region on a map would be jeopardized, and constructing semantic maps would become more complicated. This is thus an area where further research is needed most urgently.

SOME FURTHER ISSUES

So far in this chapter I have limited myself to semantic maps that represent the mutual relationships of grammatical meanings. However, the problem of multifunctionality arises in the same way with lexical meanings, so for the sake of completeness I give one example here. It involves various senses or uses of words for "tree" and "wood," and it comes from Hjelmslev (1963, p. 53), an important theoretical work of European structuralism. Hjelmslev compared just four languages (Danish, German, French, Spanish) and found that five different functions have to be distinguished: "tree," "firewood," "wood (stuff)," "small forest," and "large forest." The semantic map is one-dimensional, so the boundaries of the lexemes in the four languages can be conveniently represented together (as in Fig. 8.19):

Being a structuralist, Hjelmslev used this example to show how different languages carve up the semantic space in radically different ways, but from the present perspective, the differences are not all that great. One could easily imagine the differences to be such that no non-trivial universal semantic map can be drawn. Thus, Hjelmslev's own example can be used to make a very different point, not for relativism, but for universalism of meaning.

Another topic that should briefly be mentioned is the relationship between semantic (or implicational) maps and *implicational hierarchies*, because the two are occasionally confused. The two concepts are related in that both stand for a series of implicational universals, but implicational hierarchies are much stronger statements. A simple example of an implicational hierarchy of lexical items comes from numerals. If a language has a

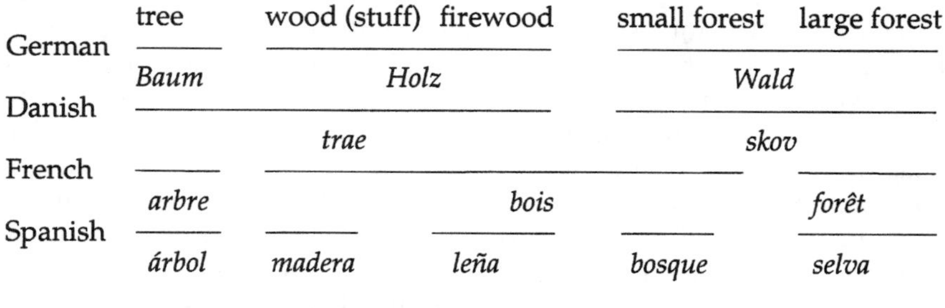

	tree	wood (stuff)	firewood	small forest	large forest
German	—	—	—	—	—
	Baum	*Holz*		*Wald*	
Danish	—	—		—	
		trae		*skov*	
French	—	—		—	
	arbre		*bois*		*forêt*
Spanish	—	—	—	—	—
	árbol	*madera*	*leña*	*bosque*	*selva*

FIG. 8.19. A semantic map for "tree"/"wood," and the boundaries of four languages.

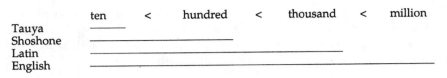

FIG. 8.20.   An implicational hierarchy of numerals, and four exemplifying languages.

word for a high number, it also has words for all lower numbers. Thus, there are languages like Tauya (New Guinea) that have a word for "ten" but none for "hundred," languages like Tümpisa Shoshone (Nevada), which has "ten" and "hundred," but not "thousand," and so on (cf. Fig. 8.20).

Figure 8.20 is somewhat similar to Figs. 8.18 and 8.19, but there are important differences. The most salient one is of course that implicational hierarchies do not involve multifunctionality, but merely the existence of several different words (or more generally, patterns). More interestingly, implicational hierarchies differ from implicational maps in that the existence of one item makes a prediction about all items up to the beginning of the hierarchy, not just about an arbitrary part of the hierarchy. For example, there could be no language that has words for "thousand" and "million," but not for "hundred" and "ten." As a result, an implicational hierarchy allows far fewer language types and thus makes stronger predictions than an implicational map.

CONCLUSION

Semantic maps are a powerful methodological tool for cross-linguistic and diachronic semantic studies, but they are also highly relevant for semantics itself. Semantics is difficult, because unlike phonetic substance, semantic substance cannot be measured or observed objectively. At least at the present stage of our knowledge, it is questionable whether one could motivate a structuring of semantic space that is independent of linguistic expression. Linguists have long been aware of this problem, and they have mostly shied away from speculation about universal semantic structures, concentrating instead on the semantic analysis of particular expressions in particular languages. By doing this, they are on much safer ground than by reasoning about a priori possibilities, but this self-restraint also means that the study of meaning is confined to the historically accidental structures of particular languages. The semantic-map approach takes us a step further: It is firmly rooted in empirical observation of individual languages, but through systematic cross-linguistic comparison we can arrive at well-motivated structural patterns in universal conceptual space.[13]

From the psychologist's point of view, a further natural question to ask is about the mental reality of the universal semantic structures discovered by this method, or indeed merely the mental reality of the language-particular structures that are represented by boundaries on the map. But this is a question that cannot be answered with the linguist's tools, that is, the observation of the behavior and distribution of expressions in naturally occurring texts and speakers' intuitions. As Croft (1998) and Sandra (1998) have emphasized, linguists have a tendency to claim more than their evidence warrants. In particular, they are vulnerable to both the "generality fallacy" (Croft) and the "polysemy fallacy" (Sandra). They can be guilty of the generality fallacy when they claim that a generalization that they have made (e.g., a monosemic analysis) is also the speakers' generalization. Thus, whereas a linguist would be tempted to claim that the spatial sense of *in* (e.g., *in Leipzig*) and its temporal sense (e.g., *in February*) are closely related or even constitute two contextual uses of a single monosemous sense, there is no basis for claiming that this generalization is also found in speakers' mental representations.[14] On the other hand, linguists who favor polysemic analyses (in particular cognitive linguists) may make a multitude of sense distinctions (e.g., those in [1a–d]) that are (explicitly or implicitly) attributed to speakers' mental representations. When no evidence for distinguishing these senses is cited (apart from the linguist's imagination), this may be a case of the polysemy fallacy.

But cross-linguistic comparison allows us to go one step further. Whereas someone who only looks at English has a hard time deciding whether the preposition *on* in *a fly on the table* and *a fly on the wall* are mentally represented as the same item or as different item, a cross-linguistic perspective immediately reveals that some languages use different prepositions for this case (e.g., German *auf* vs. *an: eine Fliege auf dem Tisch* vs. *eine Fliege an der Wand*). The fact that there are such languages makes an analysis in terms of separate representations much more plausible. Conversely, if no language uses different expressions for two supposedly distinct senses, this may serve as a warning against an analysis in terms of separate representations. Thus, although semantic maps are not a method for arriving directly at mental representations, they can give linguists some guidance in avoiding the Scylla of the generality fallacy and the Charybdis of the polysemy fallacy.

---

[13]Another approach that uses cross-linguistic comparison to arrive at semantic universals is that of Goddard and Wierzbicka (1994), which is, however, quite different in other respects.

[14]Cf. Sandra and Rice (1995) for relevant experimental evidence that points toward homonymy rather than polysemy or monosemy in this case.

For psychologists, they provide a useful summary of what linguists know about the mutual relations between the various senses of multifunctional expressions.

ACKNOWLEDGMENTS

This chapter is dedicated to Ekkehard König on the occasion of his 60th birthday, and to the memory of Andreas Blank (1962–2001).

I am grateful to Bill Croft and Vladimir Plungian for detailed comments on an earlier version, as well as Mike Tomasello, Susanne Michaelis, and Hans-Olav Enger.

REFERENCES

Anderson, L. B. (1974). Distinct sources of fuzzy data: Ways of integrating relatively discrete and gradient aspects of language, and explaining grammar on the basis of semantic fields. In R. W. Shuy & C.-J. N. Bailey (Eds.), *Towards tomorrow's linguistics* (pp. 50–64). Washington, DC: Georgetown University Press.

Anderson, L. B. (1982). The 'perfect' as a universal and as a language-particular category. In P. Hopper (Ed.), *Tense-aspect: Between semantics and pragmatics* (pp. 227–264). Amsterdam: Benjamins.

Anderson, L. B. (1986). Evidentials, paths of change, and mental maps: Typologically regular asymmetries. In W. Chafe & J. Nichols (Eds.), *Evidentiality: The linguistic encoding of epistemology* (pp. 273–312). Norwood, NJ: Ablex.

Anderson, L. B. (1987). Adjectival morphology and semantic space. *Chicago Linguistic Society, 23*, 1–17.

Barnes, B. K. (1985). A functional explanation of French nonlexical datives. *Studies in Language, 9*(2), 159–195.

Burridge, K. (1996). Degenerate cases of body parts in Middle Dutch. In H. Chappell & W. McGregor (Eds.), *The grammar of inalienability* (pp. 679–710). Berlin: Mouton de Gruyter.

Bybee, J. L. (1985). *Morphology: A study of the relation between meaning and form.* Amsterdam: Benjamins.

Bybee, J. L. (1988). Semantic substance vs. contrast in the development of grammatical meaning. *Berkeley Linguistics Society, 14*, 247–264.

Bybee, J. L., Perkins, R. D., & Pagliuca, W. (1994). *The evolution of grammar: Tense, aspect, and modality in the languages of the world.* Chicago: The University of Chicago Press.

Comrie, B. (1976). *Aspect.* Cambridge: Cambridge University Press.

Cranmer, D. J. (1976). *Derived intransitivity: A constrastive analysis of certain reflexive verbs in German, Russian and English.* Tübingen, Germany: Niemeyer.

Croft, W. (1991). *Syntactic categories and grammatical relations. The cognitive organization of information.* Chicago: The University of Chicago Press.

Croft, W. (1998). Linguistic evidence and mental representations. *Cognitive Linguistics, 9*(2), 151–173.

Croft, W. (2001). *Radical Construction Grammar: Syntactic theory in typological perspective.* Oxford: Oxford University Press.

Croft, W., Shyldkrot, H. B.-Z., & Kemmer, S. (1987). Diachronic semantic processes in the middle voice. In A. G. Ramat, O. Carruba, & G. Bernini (Eds.), *Papers from the 7th International Conference on historical linguistics* (pp. 179–192). Amsterdam: Benjamins.

Enger, H.-O., & Nesset, T. (1999). The value of Cognitive Grammar in typological studies: The case of Norwegian and Russian passive, middle and reflexive. *Nordic Journal of Linguistics, 22,* 27–60.

Ferguson, C. (1970). Grammatical categories in data collection. *Working Papers in Language Universals,* 4. Stanford, CA: Stanford University.

Geeraerts, D. (1993). Vagueness's puzzles, polysemy's vagaries. *Cognitive Linguistics, 4*(3), 223–72.

Geniušienė, E. (1987). *Typology of reflexives.* Berlin: Mouton de Gruyter.

Goddard, C., & Wierzbicka, A. (Eds.). (1994). *Semantic and lexical universals: Theory and empirical findings.* Amsterdam: Benjamins.

Haiman, J. (1974). Concessives, conditionals, and verbs of volition. *Foundations of Language, 11,* 341–359.

Haspelmath, M. (1987). *Transitivity alternations of the anticausative type.* (Arbeitspapiere, N. F. 5) Cologne, Germany: University of Cologne.

Haspelmath, M. (1989). From purposive to infinitive—A universal path of grammaticization. *Folia Linguistica Historica, 10*(1–2), 287–310.

Haspelmath, M. (1997a). *Indefinite pronouns.* Oxford: Oxford University Press.

Haspelmath, M. (1997b). *From space to time: Temporal adverbials in the world's languages.* Munich: Lincom Europa.

Haspelmath, M. (1998). The semantic development of old presents: New futures and subjunctives without grammaticalization. *Diachronica, 15*(1), 29–62.

Haspelmath, M. (1999a). External possession in a European areal perspective. In D. Payne & I. Barshi (Eds.), *External possession* (pp. 109–135). Amsterdam: Benjamins.

Haspelmath, M. (1999b). Why is grammaticalization irreversible? *Linguistics, 37*(6), 1043–1068.

Heine, B., Claudi, U., & Hünnemeyer, F. (1991). *Grammaticalization: A conceptual framework.* Chicago: The University of Chicago Press.

Hjelmslev, L. (1963). *Prolegomena to a theory of language.* Madison, WI: University of Wisconsin Press.

Hopper, P., & Traugott, E. (1993). *Grammaticalization.* Cambridge: Cambridge University Press.

Jakobson, R. (1936). Beitrag zur allgemeinen Kasuslehre: Gesamtbedeutungen der russischen Kasus [Contribution to the general study of case: General meanings of the Russian cases]. *Travaux du Cercle Linguistique de Prague, 6,* 240–288. (Reprinted from R. Jakobson, 1971, *Selected writings, Vol. 2,* pp. 22–71. The Hague: Mouton)

Kemmer, S. (1993). *The middle voice.* Amsterdam: Benjamins.

König, E. (2001). Intensifiers and reflexive pronouns. In M. Haspelmath, E. König, W. Oesterreicher, & W. Raible (Eds.), *Language typology and language universals: An international handbook* (pp. 747–760). Berlin: Mouton de Gruyter.

Kortmann, B. (1997). *Adverbial subordination: A typology and history of adverbial subordinators based on European languages.* (EALT, 18.) Berlin: Mouton de Gruyter.

Lakoff, G. (1987). *Women, fire, and dangerous things.* Chicago: The University of Chicago Press.

Lakoff, G., & Johnson, M. (1980). *Metaphors we live by.* Chicago: The University of Chicago Press.

Langacker, R. (1988). A usage-based model. In B. Rudzka-Ostyn (Ed.), *Topics in cognitive linguistics* (pp. 127–161). Amsterdam: Benjamins.

Langacker, R. W., & Munro, P. (1975). Passives and their meaning. *Language, 51,* 789–830.

Lehmann, C. (1995). *Thoughts on grammaticalization.* Munich: Lincom Europa.

Leiss, E. (1997). Synkretismus und Natürlichkeit [Syncretism and naturalness]. *Folia Linguistica, 31*, 133–160.

Michaelis, S., & Rosalie, M. (2000). Polysémie et cartes sémantiques: Le relateur *(av)ek* en Créole Seychellois [Polysemy and semantic maps: The relator *(av)ek* in Seychelles Creole]. *Études Créoles, 23*(2), 79–100.

Quirk, R., Greenbaum, S., Leech, G., & Svartvik, J. (1985). *A comprehensive grammar of the English language.* London: Longman.

Rudzka-Ostyn, B. (1996). The Polish dative. In W. Van Belle & W. Van Langendonck (Eds.), *The dative: Vol. 1. Descriptive studies* (pp. 341–394). Amsterdam: Benjamins.

Sandra, D. (1998). What linguists can and can't tell you about the human mind: A reply to Croft. *Cognitive Linguistics, 9*, 361–378.

Sandra, D., & Rice, S. (1995). Network analyses of prepositional meaning: Mirroring whose mind—The linguist's or the language user's? *Cognitive Linguistics, 6*, 89–130.

Stassen, L. (1997). *Intransitive predication.* Oxford: Oxford University Press.

Stimm, H. (1973). *Medium und Reflexivkonstruktionen im Surselvischen* [Middle and reflexive constructions in Surselvan]. Munich: Verlag der Bayerischen Akademie der Wissenschaften.

Stolz, T. (1996). Some instruments are really good companions—some are not: On syncretism and the typology of instrumentals and comitatives. *Theoretical Linguistics, 23*(1–2), 113–200.

Taylor, C. (1985). *Nkore-Kiga.* London: Croom Helm.

Tuggy, D. (1993). Ambiguity, polysemy, and vagueness. *Cognitive Linguistics, 4*(3), 273–290.

van der Auwera, J., & Plungian, V. A. (1998). Modality's semantic map. *Linguistic Typology, 2*(1), 79–124.

Van Hoecke, W. (1996). The Latin dative. In W. Van Belle & W. Van Langendonck (Eds.), *The dative: Vol. 1. Descriptive studies* (pp. 3–37). Amsterdam: Benjamins.

Zwicky, A., & Sadock, J. (1975). Ambiguity tests and how to fail them. In J. Kimball (Ed.), *Syntax and semanatics: Vol. 4* (pp. 1–36). New York: Academic Press.

Chapter 9

Regularity and Idiomaticity in Grammatical Constructions: The Case of *Let Alone**

Charles J. Fillmore
Paul Kay
Mary Catherine O'Connor
University of California, Berkeley

1. BACKGROUND

This chapter advocates an approach to grammar that differs from most current approaches in several ways. The overarching claim is that the proper units of a grammar are more similar to the notion of construction in traditional and pedagogical grammars than to that of rule in most versions of generative grammar. This is not to say that the generative ideal of explicitness is foregone; nor is the necessity of providing for recursive production of large structures from smaller ones set aside. Constructions on our view are much like the nuclear family (mother plus daughters) subtrees admitted by phrase structure rules, EXCEPT that (1) constructions need not be limited to a mother and her daughters, but may span wider ranges of the sentential tree; (2) constructions may specify, not only syntactic, but also lexical, semantic, and pragmatic information; (3) lexical items, being mentionable in syntactic constructions, may be viewed, in many cases at least, as constructions themselves; and (4) constructions may be idiomatic in the sense that a large construction may specify a semantics (and/or pragmatics) that is distinct from what might be calculated from the associated semantics of the set of smaller constructions that could be used to build the same morphosyntactic object.

Not all current approaches to grammar in the broad generative tradition, in which the current effort situates itself, differ from Construction Grammar in each of the respects detailed above; for example, various forms

---

*This chapter is reprinted, in slightly modified form, from *Language, 64*(3), pp. 501–538. Copyright © 1988 by the Linguistic Society of America. Used by permission.

of phrase structure grammar take as their basic unit a syntactic-semantic rule pair, thus integrating semantic and syntactic modeling. But no framework in this tradition, so far as we are aware, agrees with the approach advocated here in all of these details. For instance, no current formal approach to grammar countenances direct pragmatic interpretation of syntactic structures, not mediated by the proposition expressed.

All of the many competing accounts of the workings of language draw a distinction in one way or another between what it is that speakers know outright about their language and what it is that they have to be able to figure out. For example, speakers of English have to know what *red* means and that it is an adjective, and they have to know what *ball* means and that it is a noun. They have to know that adjectives can co-occur with nouns in a modification structure (as in a phrase like *red ball*), and they have to know the proper strategies for giving a semantic interpretation to such adjective-noun combinations. But they do not have to know separately, or to be told, what the phrase *red ball* means. That is something which what they already know enables them to figure out.

Current formal models of grammar take a severe view of the distinction between knowing and figuring out: they assign as much work as possible to the computing or figuring out part of knowing how to use a language, and they attempt to keep at a minimum those aspects of linguistic competence that have to be represented as stored or known. Briefly, the standard idealization of the workings of a grammar goes something like this:

(a) The speakers of a language have, first of all, knowledge of the WORDS in their language. This knowledge comprises information about what kinds of words they are, in what environments they can appear and how they function in the language's phrases and sentences, what they mean, and how they are pronounced.

(b) Secondly, speakers know one or more sorts of fairly elementary GRAMMATICAL RULES in their language, rules by which simple phrases are constructed, by which these are combined into larger and more complex structures, and by which they are selected or modified according to their position in the larger structures.

(c) Thirdly, they know the basic SEMANTIC INTERPRETATION PRINCIPLES by which the meanings of phrases and sentences can be constructed out of the meanings of their constituent words and phrases. These principles of compositional semantics are such that speakers do not in general need to know in advance the meanings of complex structures (i.e., phrases and sentences); rather, the meanings of such larger structures simply follow from the knowledge of forms and rules that speakers have to know independently.

(d) Fourthly, in knowing how to use their language, speakers know how to create and recognize associations between semantically interpreted sentences and particular types of situations. Such PRAGMATIC knowledge uses but does not contribute to semantic interpretation. The notion of the 'literal meaning' of an expression does not, in short, incorporate information about the uses to which the expression can be put, beyond (perhaps) the pairing of conventional speech act forces with particular sentence types, such as the imperative and the interrogative.

There is vast disagreement in matters of detail, but most current formal models of grammar assume a limited categorial base and a limited set of configuration types upon which the rules of semantic interpretation are allowed to do their work. A commonly accepted categorial base is confined to the categories Sentence, Noun, Verb, Adjective, Adverb, Adpositon (i.e., Preposition or Postposition), their phrasal projections (the categories for which the named elements are heads), and a small number of associated trappings of these, such as complementizers. In general, the permitted primary set of configuration types is limited to what in phrase-structural terms can be spoken of as the nuclear family: a configuration consisting of a structural category, the mother node, and its immediate constituents, the daughter nodes.

The picture just sketched gives us an atomistic view of complex linguistic objects: generative syntax and compositional semantics provide the principles by which words whose meanings we know, arranged according to grammatical structuring principles whose semantic force we know, figure in the construction of an unlimitedly large set of possible meanings. Under the idealization just discussed, any sentence in a language can be resolved into configurations containing only constituents of the designated types, arranged according to the standard rules, and yielding interpretations which follow from regular principles of compositional semantics.

It should be noticed that the natural and intuitively simple notion of grammatical construction plays a limited part in the workings of this model. Traditional grammars are likely to have descriptions of the use and meaning of, say, negative questions, under the supposition that such structures might have certain properties of their own, as wholes. (An utterance of *Didn't you like the salad?* does more than ask a yes/no question.) In the atomistic view, which would not provide for a separate negative question construction, there is no way to treat the distinct semantic and pragmatic properties that emerge when negative and interrogative syntax are combined in an English sentence. (Moreover, there is evidence from the domain of negative contraction that negative questions are syntactically, as well as semantically and pragmatically, distinct from other inverted negative structures; see Green 1985, Kay 1987:33 fn.)[1]

---

[1]Our purpose here was not to give an accurate sketch of current frameworks, but to point up the absence of a place within most of them to deal with the complexities of the sort we are examining here—phenomena which we hold to be central to any grammar, not peripheral. In

1.1. Idiomaticity and Its Dimensions

As useful and powerful as the atomistic schema is for the description of linguistic competence, it doesn't allow the grammarian to account for absolutely everything in its terms. As anyone knows who has worked with practical grammar-writing or with detailed text analysis, the descriptive linguist needs to append to this maximally general machinery certain kinds of special knowledge—knowledge that will account for speakers' ability to construct and understand phrases and expressions in their language which are not covered by the grammar, the lexicon, and the principles of compositional semantics, as these are familiarly conceived. Such a list of exceptional phenomena contains things which are larger than words, which are like words in that they have to be learned separately as individual whole facts about pieces of the language, but which also have grammatical structure, structure of the kind that we ordinarily interpret by appealing to the operation of the general grammatical rules. This list is not merely a supplement to the lexicon: it contains information about fully productive grammatical patterns, including what have been variously referred to as 'minor sentence types', 'special constructions', and the like.

This 'Appendix to the Grammar' can be thought of as the repository of what is IDIOMATIC in the language. One of our purposes in this paper is to suggest that this repository is very large. A second is to show that it must include descriptions of important and systematic bodies of phenomena which interact in important ways with the rest of the grammar, phenomena

---

particular, we wish to emphasize that when constructions are interpreted as the products of maximally general rules, no place remains in the grammar for spelling out the non-predictable semantics and pragmatics that is frequently conventionally associated with particular constructions such as those we will describe.

Our rather sweeping sketch of the atomistic model is of course more appropriate as a characterization of some current frameworks than others. There are a number of individuals who do not subscribe to the atomistic model and who have contributed to work in the vein we argue for here. These include Dwight Bolinger, George Lakoff, Anna Wierzbicka, Igor Mel'chuk, and others. With these people, we also maintain that pragmatics pervades grammar, i.e. is not confined to a few lexical items with associated conventional implicatures. Wierzbicka in particular has invested a great deal of time in spelling out in detail the range of implications or meanings of the patterns she describes, such as the tautological construction exemplified by the fixed phrase *Boys will be boys* (see Wierzbicka 1987).

One particularly important focus illuminated by Wierzbicka's work in this area is the question of derivation: are the semantico-pragmatic forces associated with particular constructions to be thought of as arbitrary? Or are they interpretable on the basis of universal maxims of conversational behavior, augmented by contextual factors? We feel that a unified answer to this question does not exist, and that some constructions will, in a process similar to the semantic drift and freezing of certain lexical items, become non-transparent and apparently arbitrary. In any case, important as this issue is, our emphasis is somewhat different. We wish to call attention particularly to the range of ways in which constructions may have obligatory pragmatic and semantic attachments.

whose proper understanding will lead us to significant insights into the workings of language in general. A third is to make the case for a model of linguistic competence in which phenomena of the sort we have in mind are not out of place.

At this point we offer a brief survey of concepts from the domain of idiomaticity. We think of a locution or manner of speaking as idiomatic if it is assigned an interpretation by the speech community but if somebody who merely knew the grammar and the vocabulary of the language could not, by virtue of that knowledge alone, know (i) how to say it, or (ii) what it means, or (iii) whether it is a conventional thing to say. Put differently, an idiomatic expression or construction is something a language user could fail to know while knowing everything else in the language.

1.1.1. Encoding Versus Decoding Idioms.   Following Makkai 1972, we begin by recognizing an important distinction between IDIOMS OF ENCODING and IDIOMS OF DECODING.[2] A decoding idiom is an expression which the language users couldn't interpret with complete confidence if they hadn't learned it separately. With an encoding idiom, by contrast, we have an expression which language users might or might not understand without prior experience, but concerning which they would not know that it is a conventional way of saying what it says. (Anything which is a decoding idiom is also an encoding idiom, by these definitions, but there are encoding idioms which are not decoding idioms.) The expressions *kick the bucket* and *pull a fast one* are examples of both decoding and encoding idioms; expressions like *answer the door, wide awake,* and *bright red* are examples of encoding idioms only. That is, while it is likely that each expression of the latter group could be understood perfectly on first hearing, someone who did not know that they were conventional ways of saying what they say would not be able to predict their usability in these ways.[3]

1.1.2. Grammatical Versus Extragrammatical Idioms.   Idioms can further be divided into those which have words filling proper and familiar grammatical structures, and those which have words occurring in constructions which the rest of the grammar cannot account for. The so-called GRAMMATI-

---

[2]The distinction between decoding and encoding idioms is an important one, since a frequent objection to our claims about the extent of idiomaticity in the productive apparatus of the language is the suggestion that speakers should be able to interpret the intent of the expressions we discuss by making use of analogies from their linguistic knowledge or by depending on cognitive abilities not properly a part of the language faculty. It needs to be emphasized that linguistic competence is composed of two parts, not only the part that enables us to figure out what other people have said to us, but also the part that enables us to talk to them.

[3]What we have here is actually a gradient or cline rather than a simple two-way distinction. At one extreme we find idioms in which every element is fixed, such as *It takes one to know one.*

CAL IDIOMS include *kick the bucket, spill the beans, blow one's nose,* etc., where verbs and noun phrases show up just where you would expect them. But expressions like *first off, sight unseen, all of a sudden, by and large, so far so good,* etc., have anomalous structures. Nothing we know about the rest of the grammar of English would enable us to predict that these expressions are sayable in our language. Such expressions have grammatical structure, to be sure, but the structures they have are not made intelligible by knowledge of the familiar rules of the grammar and how those rules are most generally applied. These, then, are the EXTRAGRAMMATICAL IDIOMS.

1.1.3. Substantive Versus Formal Idioms.   Yet another distinction that we need to make is that between SUBSTANTIVE or LEXICALLY FILLED IDIOMS and FORMAL or LEXICALLY OPEN IDIOMS. The examples of idioms given so far have all been substantive idioms: their lexical make-up is (more or less) fully specified. Formal idioms, by contrast, are syntactic patterns dedicated to semantic and pragmatic purposes not knowable from their form alone. It is the formal idioms which raise the most serious theoretical issues, and which hold our main interest in this paper.

A fact which sometimes obscures the difference between substantive and formal idioms is that formal idioms can serve as host to substantive idioms. For example, there is a general syntactic pattern illustrated by such sentences as (1):

(1) The more carefully you do your work, the easier it will get.

While (1) may be a novel creation using the syntactic pattern in question, (2) is a set expression that uses the same form.

(2) The bigger they come, the harder they fall.

1.1.4. Idioms With and Without Pragmatic Point.   We find that in many cases idiomatic expressions have special pragmatic purposes associated with them. A large number of substantive idioms have obvious associated pragmatic practices (e.g. *Good morning, How do you do?, once upon a time*), but there are many more which serve more contextually neutral purposes (as with *all of a sudden, by and large,* and the like). In the case of formal idioms, we find the *the X-er the Y-er* type to be more or less free of pragmatic commitments, while oth-

---

Close to that extreme are idiomatic expressions in which everything is specified except what Pawley & Syder 1983 refer to as inflection: In *trip the light fantastic,* the actual form of *trip* can vary (*trips, tripping,* etc.); in *blow one's nose,* the 'nose possessor' can vary (*I blow my nose, you blow your nose*); and so on. The best examples of formal idioms are special syntactic patterns whose use is not predictable from the 'regular' grammatical rules, as in expressions fitting the pattern *Him, be a doctor?* But even here we find lexically limited means of 'expansion' (Pawley & Syder 1983), allowing, say, *What? Him, be a doctor?*

ers, like the type exemplified in *Him be a doctor?* (Akmajian 1984), appear to exist in the service of specific pragmatic or rhetorical purposes.

1.2. A Typology of Idiomatic Expressions

The contrasts and distinctions we have just named provide us with the means for constructing a typology of idiomatic expressions. The difference between encoding and decoding idioms will not figure in the classification (though it is important for other reasons), since the question of whether an interpreter could figure out what an expression meant on first encountering it cannot be established on general grounds. We will include examples of substantive idioms in each of the three categories we develop, but our major interest will be in the formal idioms. In the end the formal idioms will be absorbed into the category of grammatical constructions.

1.2.1. Unfamiliar Pieces Unfamiliarly Arranged.
As our first category, we consider the case of idioms which contain unfamiliar pieces which are (necessarily) unfamiliarly combined—'necessarily' because, if the pieces are themselves unfamiliar or unique, there can be no standard principles for arranging them in larger patterns. In the case of lexical idioms, the unfamiliar pieces are words which appear only in the idiom in question, as in *kith and kin, with might and main,* and the like.

As an example of a formal idiom, or grammatical construction, which fits this category, we can return to our *the X-er the Y-er* construction seen in (1) and (2) above. This structure is used for expressing a correlation between an independent variable and a dependent variable. The propositions participating in the statement of correlation can be derived from the lexico-syntactic form of the sentence's two main components. In a syntactic representation of Example (1), shown in Fig. 9.1, we see that the degree expression *the more carefully* is linked with the gap in *you do your work* [__], and the degree expression *the easier* is linked with the gap in *it will get* [__]. The interpretation, then, is paraphrasable as something like 'The degree to which you do your work carefully will determine the degree to which your work gets easy'.

This use of the comparative construction is unique; the use of the definite article that we find in this construction is not, so far as we can tell, found generally elsewhere in the language;[4] nor is the two-part structure uniting the two atypical *the*-phrases found in any of the standard syntactic forms in English.

---

[4]Historically, the definite article in this construction has an instrumental demonstrative (Old English *θy*) as its source. The same definite article + comparative adjective sequence is found in a few other formulae (pointed out to us by L. Talmy); such as *The better to see you with*; *all the more reason to . . .* ; *so much the better*; etc. (*Footnote continues . . .*)

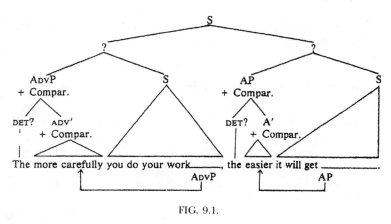

FIG. 9.1.

In spite of the fact that it is host to a large number of fixed expressions, the form has to be recognized as fully productive. Its member expressions are in principle not listable: unlimitedly many new expressions can be constructed within its pattern, their meanings constructed by means of semantic principles specifically tied to this construction.

With respect to the question of whether the expressions that instantiate this construction can be handled by the regular grammar, it is hard enough to believe that the familiar rules of English can so much as provide us the terms needed for describing the construction and labeling its parts. Do we, indeed, have the right to describe the *the* here as the definite article? Combined in what way with what? What is the constituent structure of either half

---

It has been suggested to us that synchronically this use of the definite article is related to that found in superlative expressions: *the best, the brightest,* etc. Many aspects of this construction are suggestively similar to parts of other constructions. However, when the syntax and semantics of these are examined in detail, no predictable relationships emerge, at least nothing which speakers could use to encode these meanings if they were ignorant of the construction. The existence of a diachronic relationship or a partial synchronic similarity between two constructions does not release the language learner from the obligation to acquire the construction as such. The notion of encoding idiom is particularly important here. Suggestive partial similarities among constructions may help the decoder who is ignorant of a particular construction guess at what a token of it is intended to convey, but our notion of a construction is precisely what a speaker has to know, independent of whatever else he knows about the language, in order to encode correctly an utterance of this form, meaning and use.

One reviewer suggested that this construction could profitably be seen as an instance of a more general 'paired parallel phrases' construction, as exemplified by the proverbs *Cold hands, warm heart; Scratch a Russian, find a Tartar; Garbage in, garbage out;* etc. The more general construction could presumably be said to encode the implicational relationship between the two parallel phrases, thus providing an account of the implicational semantics in examples like *The more the merrier.* Such family resemblances may facilitate the decoding of such conventional structure/meaning pairings. However, this more general paired parallel phrase construction still must be listed as having a conventional pairing of structure and meaning.

of the construction? Is the antecedent of the first gap *the more carefully* (as indicated) *more carefully* or simply *carefully*? Once we decide on one or another constituent structure grouping of the elements, to what syntactic categories can we assign each of these constituents? If the whole sentence is made up of the two parts, what syntactic category is represented by each of the parts? If we ever decide what syntactic category each of the paired *the*-phrases belongs to, can we be satisfied to say that the only grammatical rule in which the category figures is one which allows the construction of a sentence by juxtaposing exactly two of these?

In describing the pieces as unfamiliar we must recognize that they are not all completely unfamiliar: for example, the portions which follow the comparative phrase have some of the ellipsis properties of the complements of true comparative phrases. But they differ from ordinary comparative constructions in a number of ways. For example, these do not occur with the complementizer *than*, but can sometimes occur with *that* (*the more that I eat, . . .*). The level at which the structure is most clearly unfamiliar (in the sense of not being represented elsewhere in the language) is the level of the paired *the*-phrases and their mode of combination.

1.2.2. Familiar Pieces Unfamiliarly Arranged.

The second type of idiomatic expression includes those which are made up of familiar pieces which are unfamiliarly combined. Here, too, the semantic interpretation is necessarily novel, since the principles of combination used for general semantic interpretations cannot serve us here. Substantive idioms which fit this category include phrases like *all of a sudden* and *in point of fact*. Some idioms in this category are of the 'encoding only' type. That is, they require special syntactic and semantic rules, but the hearer of an expression embodying these rules who was not familiar with them might nonetheless guess the meaning successfully. An example is the occurrence of the bare noun *home* in contexts calling for locative or directional complements.

(3) She went/called/stayed/is/*has/*loves home.

An interesting formal idiom of this kind is the one which allows us to construct cousin terms, as in *second cousin three times removed*. We consider now some of the properties of this construction.

The regular grammar of English provides for plural noun phrases lacking determiners, and when the head nouns or N-bars of these phrases denote symmetrical predicates, it provides an appropriate and general syntax and semantics for sentences with conjoined subjects and copular verbs, such as Examples (4) through (6):

(4) Jane and Mary are *best friends*.

(5) Harry and Joe are *acquaintances of long standing.*

(6) Marge and Sue are *bitter enemies.*

Expressions for kinship relations are standard examples of noun phrases that may fill this role and other NP roles in the regular grammar:

(7) Jane and Sue are *sisters.*

(8) Harry and Sue are *cousins.*

(9) Jane is Sue's *sister.*

(10) Harry is Sue's *cousin.*

Many kinship expressions that can fill such slots are not lexical (like *cousin* and *sister*), but phrasal. Moreover, neither the morphosyntactic rules required to generate these phrases nor the semantic rules required to interpret them are predictable from knowledge of the general grammar; they have to be learned separately for the construction and interpretation of these particular phrases by the learner of English. Some subsets of these kinship phrases are of finite cardinality and so could be listed in the lexicon, although in so doing the grammarian would pass up an opportunity to extract a generalization. The expressions *mother-in-law, father-in-law, sister-in-law, brother-in-law, son-in-law,* and *daughter-in-law* exemplify such a finite set. But there are other sets of kinship expressions that are in principle of nonfinite cardinality and hence unlistable, for example the series exemplified in (11)–(12):

(11) grandmother, great grandmother, great great grandmother, . . . ;
     grandfather, great grandfather, great great grandfather, . . . ;
     grandson, . . .

(12) first cousin once removed, first cousin twice removed; . . . ; second
     cousin once removed, second cousin twice removed, . . . ; . . .

The morphosyntactic properties of the infinite set of phrases indicated in (12) may be summarized by the formula

(13) nth cousin m times removed,

where n is a positive integer and m is a non-negative integer. (The expression 'nth' in the formula is intended to abbreviate 'the English word for the ordinal number corresponding to the positive integer n'.) Note that nth *cousin* has the grammatical structure of *fourth chapter*, that *m times* has the grammatical structure of *two ways*, and that *removed* has that of *rewritten*. The regular syntactic machinery does not, however, provide us with the resources

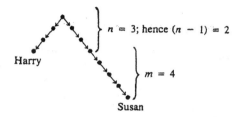

Harry is the second cousin four times removed of Susan.
Susan is the second cousin four times removed of Harry.
Harry and Susan are second cousins four times removed.

FIG. 9.2.

to assemble a nominal expression of the type *fourth chapter three ways rewritten.* This is the kind of situation we have in mind when, in speaking of n*th cousin* m *times removed*, we talk about familiar pieces unfamiliarly combined.

Standard morphological rules operate within these expressions to reduce *one times* to *once* and *two times* to *twice.* A morphosyntactic rule special to this construction realizes 'zero times removed' as the phonetically null string. The semantic rule associated with this phrasal construction produces a semantic form whose properties may be described as follows: Two distinct people X and Y are nth cousins m times removed iff (1) X and Y have a common ancestor, (2) the common ancestor closest to either X or Y is $n - 1$ generations removed from that person and (3) either X or Y is m generations further removed from the closest common ancestor than the other is.

This semantic rule is illustrated in Fig. 9.2 for the expression *second cousin four times removed*; the downward arrow represents the relation 'parent-of'.

As we have indicated, the internal syntax and semantics of such phrases require a special mini-grammar embedded within the general grammar, whose properties are not deducible from those of the larger grammar. Externally, such expressions behave as normal syntactic and semantic objects in the sentences in which they occur.

1.2.3. Familiar Pieces Familiarly Arranged.
The third type of formal idiom is made up of familiar pieces combined according to familiar combinatorial principles, but to which idiomatic interpretations are assigned. Substantive idioms meeting these conditions include *hang/tie one on* (in the sense of 'get drunk'), *pull someone's leg,* and *tickle the ivories.* Formal idioms in this category include fate-tempting expressions of the kind seen in *now watch me drop it* said by someone who has just picked up a tray of drinks, as well as rhetorical questions that convey negative messages: *Who's gonna make me?, Am I invisible?, When did I say you could do that?,* and so on.

2. FORMAL IDIOMS: THE CASE OF *LET ALONE*

We are interested in investigating formal idioms. The formal idioms which interest us are of both the grammatical and the extragrammatical kinds, and of both the encoding and the decoding varieties. They include the *the X-er the Y-er* case mentioned earlier, but also the constructions underlying such expressions as those in (14):

(14) a. There goes Charlie again, ranting and raving about his cooking.
     b. Look who's here!
     c. what with the kids off to school and all
     d. Why not fix it yourself?
     e. He's not half the doctor you are.
     f. Much as I like Ronnie, I don't approve of anything he does.
     g. He may be a professor, but he's an idiot.
     h. Him be a doctor?
     i. What do you say we stop here?
     j. It's time you brushed your teeth.
     k. One more and I'll leave.
     l. No writing on the walls!
     m. That's not big enough of a box.
     n. It satisfied my every wish.

In claiming that each of these expressions exemplifies a special grammatical construction or formal idiom, we claim that for each of them both of the following questions can be answered in the negative. (1) Does the expression exhibit properties that are fully predictable from independently known properties of its lexical makeup and its grammatical structure? (2) Does the expression deserve to be listed in a general phrasal lexicon of the language, and treated as a fixed expression? It is probably unnecessary to point out that it's sometimes difficult to know how to answer these two questions.

Consider Example 14h, illustrating what we may refer to as the Incredulity Response Construction. This particular sentence exemplifies an indefinitely large set of English sentences (*Your brother help me? Her write a novel about the Spanish Inquisition?*, . . .), discussed at length in Akmajian 1984, which consist of a main clause sentence whose subject is in the objective case and whose verb is in the bare-stem form. If a person spoke English perfectly except for never having encountered a sentence from this indefinitely large set, he could obviously not acquire its members one by one but would have to learn a general rule pairing a particular syntactic form (notably featuring a non-nominative subject and a non-finite main verb) with a specific pragmatic force. (Roughly, such sentences must be used to challenge or question a proposition just posed by an interlocutor.) No finite number of additions to the lexicon or phrasicon would do the trick. It is this sort of rule that we refer to as a 'formal idiom' or 'special grammatical construction'.

2.1. Preliminaries

Our central goal in this paper is to illustrate the analysis of grammatical constructions in their pragmatic, semantic, and syntactic aspects, using that grammatical device in English that incorporates the phrase *let alone*. Our aim in exploring the properties of the *let alone* construction is, of course, to discover whether they comprise a good example of the kind of semi-autonomous grammatical construction that interests us. *Let alone* expressions have properties shared by many other construction types and lexical items in the language, so the argument about whether they can be seen as instantiating an autonomous grammatical construction needs to be conducted with care. It is our impression that *let alone* sentences possess a collection of properties that is unique to this particular family of expressions, and that they must therefore be given treatment as the kind of formal idiom or special construction we have been discussing.

Examples of sentences exhibiting the *let alone* construction, with preceding context provided, include the following:[5]

(15) A: Did the kids get their breakfast on time this morning?
B: I barely got up in time to EAT LUNCH, let alone COOK BREAKFAST.

(16) A: I know that Louise is a picky eater, but I bought the kids some squid for dinner.
B: I doubt you could get FRED to eat SHRIMP, let alone LOUISE SQUID.

(17) A: You remember the battle of Verdun, don't you?
B: I was too young to serve in World War Two, let alone World War ONE.

(18) A: Do you think anyone will mind if I take my clothes off before I jump into this quaint little water hazard?
B: Look, around here you can get arrested for going BAREFOOT, let alone for walking around NAKED.

---

[5]Although these are a Paired Focus Constructions (about which more later), capital letters are not intended to indicate what is in focus. Rather, they are intended to indicate which constituents or elements sound most natural to us when rendered as prosodically prominent. Sometimes the prosodically focused element is a member of the focused constituent; sometimes it is the entire focus. For a discussion of the prosodic realization of focused VPs vs. NPs vs. Ss, and prosodic concomitants of paired foci, see Selkirk 1984.

(19) A: For Janey's birthday party I'm thinking of serving Coca Cola, but I'm afraid little Seymour's parents will be annoyed. They seem like health-oriented types.
     B: Don't worry. Little Seymour's parents let him drink WHISKEY, let alone COKE.

As a first approximation we can talk about *let alone* as a coordinating conjunction, each of whose conjuncts contains a focused element. To provide a notation for developing the arguments offered below, we propose analyzing any *let alone* sentence as a syntactic structure of either of the following two types:

(20) a. F <X A Y let alone B>
       'I doubt you could get FRED to eat squid, let alone LOUISE.'
    b. F <X A let alone B Y>
       'I doubt you could get FRED, let alone LOUISE, to eat squid.'

Here A and B are coordinated, prosodically focused, and contrasting constituents. X and Y are the neighboring, non-contrasting parts of the clause in which the coordination occurs. The type of coordination is that by which the phrase *let alone B* is seen as parenthetical (to be discussed further below). As we will discuss at length below, *let alone* appears to be a negative polarity item, and F at this point can be loosely designated as a negative polarity trigger which has the rest of the sentence in its scope. (The entire construction, F <X A Y *let alone* X B Y>, can of course occur embedded within a larger structure, the contents of which are not relevant to this analysis, e.g.: *My observations warrant the inference that* [*Fred will not eat shrimp, let alone squid*].)

In demonstrating the division just named, we can examine sentence (21):

(21) [I doubt [he made COLONEL in World War II],
      F   X   A   Y
       let alone [GENERAL.]]
                B

In (21), F is *I doubt*, X is *he made*, Y is *in World War II*, A is *Colonel*, and B is *General*.

We will have more to say about the operator F below. Here we will simply point out that this element may be external (in surface structure) to the portion of the sentence yielding the <X A Y *let alone* B> element, but that it may also occur clause-internally, as the simple negative does in (22):

(22) He doesn't like SHRIMP, let alone SQUID.

In fact, the element F must be understood abstractly enough to correspond in certain sentences to a grammatical property distributed throughout a sentence, such as the semantico-grammatical property of being a rhetorical question:

(23) Who could IMAGINE such a thing, let alone DO it?

The syntactic schemata given in (20) and (21) can be taken as corresponding to the semantic schema in (24), where F' is a semantic predicate derived from the syntactic element F.

(24) F' <X A Y> and F' <X B Y>

A second semantic requirement of a *let alone* sentence is that the two semantic structures of the schema above represent points on a scale, in a way to be described below. This background affects the illocutionary strength of the two clauses, so that F' <X B Y> is being posed with greater force than F' <X A Y> and for the very reason that the latter is posed. If I doubt that he made colonel, I doubt all the more that he made general.

The pragmatic function of a *let alone* sentence is to enable the speaker to respond to a situation in which an expression of the meaning F' <X B Y> is RELEVANT, but in which expression of the meaning F' <X A Y> is more INFORMATIVE. The construction, in other words, is pragmatically sensitive to a conflict between two Gricean maxims, the maxim of informativeness (or Quantity) and the maxim of relevance (or Relation). It presents the more informative proposition first.

As the examples above illustrate, the use of the *let alone* construction allows the speaker to simultaneously address a previously posed proposition,[6] and to redirect the addressee to a new proposition which will be more informative.

The context proposition plays an important role in our understanding of the construction, since it is the denial of the informativeness of this con-

---

[6]Of course, the posed proposition may simply be part of the unspoken, pragmatically given context. Uttering a *let alone* sentence in an 'out of the blue' fashion simply causes hearers to expand their shared base of presuppositions. If hearers don't already realize that the content of the second conjunct is somehow given by the non-linguistic context, they accommodate (Lewis 1979) by adding it to their store of shared assumptions. An example of accommodation is readily available: in the context for ex. 17, readers who did not know that the Battle of Verdun took place in World War I will automatically have inferred that it did after they understand B's *let alone* utterance.

text proposition that determines what can and what cannot count as the syntactic operator F and its semantic projection F′.

2.2. The Syntax of *Let Alone*

Syntactically, *let alone* can be characterized as follows: it is a kind of conjunction; constructions containing it are examples of PAIRED FOCUS CONSTRUCTIONS; the post-*let alone* part of a sentence of this type is a particular type of sentence fragment; *let alone* appears to be a negative polarity item of a particularly tolerant type, which permits under certain contextual conditions (to be discussed below) utterances of sentences such as 18–19; and the construction creates special syntactic problems from the fact that it permits multiple paired foci in a single sentence. Each of these points will be taken up in turn.

2.2.1. Let Alone *as a Coordinate Conjunction.*   The expression *let alone* (generally) pairs two grammatically equivalent constituents. The interpretation of the sentence as a whole depends on constructing two sentences, each of which needs to be given an evaluation. (That is, if the sentence is an assertion, both the version containing A and the version containing B need to be true.) Its conjuncts comprise (at least) two paired foci, elements by which the two sentences being compared differ from each other.

The phrase *let alone* functions like a coordinating conjunction, in that it occurs in a wide variety of sentential environments where ordinary coordinating conjunctions occur. Consider Examples (25)–(30):

(25) a. I don't even want to read an article ABOUT, let alone a book written BY, that swine.
      b. I don't want to read an article about, or a book written by, that swine.

(26) a. You couldn't get JOHN to TOUCH it, let alone LUCILLE to EAT it.
      b. I want John to write it and Lucille to recite it.

(27) a. Max won't eat SHRIMP, let alone SQUID.
      b. We'll need shrimp and squid.

(28) a. Max won't TOUCH the SHRIMP, let alone CLEAN the SQUID.
      b. I want you to cook the shrimp and clean the squid.

(29) a. They couldn't make JOHN eat the SHRIMP, let alone LUCILLE the SQUID.
      b. They made John eat the shrimp and Lucille the squid.

(30) a. He wouldn't give A NICKEL to his MOTHER, let alone TEN DOLLARS to a COMPLETE STRANGER.
      b. He gave a nickel to me and a dollar to my sister.

We find in these examples many of the properties associated with coordinating conjunctions: coordinating conjunctions join like categories (illustrated above with VPs, clauses, and NPs), and they permit right node raising, gapping, stripping, conjunction reduction, various sorts of nonconstituent conjunction, etc. Yet we also find in these and other *let alone* sentences some properties that are not found in proper coordinate conjunction.[7]

For example, there is little reason to believe that the entire sequence *A let alone B* is a constituent. The following examples might lead us to assume that *let alone* does not conjoin phrases. Consider the asymmetry between true phrasal coordination and a *let alone* phrase with respect to topicalization:

(31) a. Shrimp and squid Moishe won't eat.
     b. *Shrimp let alone squid Moishe won't eat.
     c. *Shrimp Moishe won't eat and squid.
     d. Shrimp Moishe won't eat, let alone squid.[8]

WH-extraction from one side of a *let alone* phrase is also sometimes easier than similar extraction from a coordination containing *and*. Although 32b is not unexceptionably grammatical, it seems better to us than 32a.[9]

(32) a. *a man who Mary hasn't met or ridden in his car
     b. ?a man who Mary hasn't met, let alone ridden in his car

IT-clefting is possible with the full constituent of a coordinate construction, but not with *let alone*. Notice 33 and 34:

---

[7]We are aware that the semantics, pragmatics, and syntax of proper coordinate conjunctions are themselves not perfectly understood, and so specifying in complete detail the departures of *let alone* from this norm would be well beyond the scope of the present work.

It may be that some of the syntactic peculiarities of *let alone* correlate with certain aspects of its semantics and pragmatics according to regularities that we have not yet discovered. To the extent that this is the case, the account given here of the *let alone* construction could be reduced as such discoveries were made and the more general properties discovered assigned to distinct, perhaps more abstract, constructions.

[8]It has been suggested to us that 31b might be bad for a reason unrelated to the constituency or non-constituency of a sequence of the form *A let alone B*, namely that in 31b *let alone* occurs outside the scope of the entitling negation. This hypothesis can be checked by considering cases in which there is no entitling surface negative, the negative polarity trigger consisting only of the pragmatic denial of the context proposition. Under these circumstances the hypothesis according to which 31b is bad on account of *let alone* appearing outside the scope of negation predicts that topicalized *A let alone B* sequences should be okay. But they are not. On this hypothesis, (iii) should be just as good as (ii) in a discourse context that permits (i).

(i)   They've broken up Penutian, let alone Macro-Penutian.
(ii) Penutian they've broken up, let alone Macro-Penutian.
(iii) *Penutian, let alone Macro-Penutian, they've broken up.

(33) *It's shrimp let alone squid that Max won't eat.

(34) It's shrimp and squid that Max won't eat.

Some properties of the kinds of sentence fragments available in the second conjunct of a *let alone* sentence show them to be similar to the *than*-clause of a comparative construction, as seen in (35)–(38):

(35) Max won't eat shrimp, let alone Rabbi Feldstein.

(36) Max ate more shrimp than Rabbi Feldstein.

(37) Minnie wasn't born by 1941, let alone Meg.

(38) Minnie was born much earlier than Meg.

VP ellipsis, possible with coordinated constructions and comparative clauses, is not possible with *let alone*.

(39) Max will eat shrimp more willingly than Minnie will.

(40) Max won't eat shrimp but Minnie will.

(41) *Max won't eat shrimp let alone Minnie will.

In many of its uses, the *let alone* conjunction has much in common with what we might speak of as parenthetically used conjunctions. These form a constituent with their second conjunct, appearing either next to their first conjunct with parenthesis intonation, or extraposed to the end of their clause. Examples of such parenthetical conjunctions can be seen in (42)–(46):

(42) a. John'll do it for you, or maybe Bill.
     b. John won't do it for you, let alone Bill.

---

[9]On the other hand, there are cases in which extraction from a true coordinate structure is unexceptionable (cf. Lakoff 1986 and the literature cited therein) while extraction from the corresponding *let alone* sentence is impossible. Compare (i) and (ii):

(i)   That's the kind of adventure that you don't go home and tell your mother about.
(ii) *That's the kind of adventure that you don't go home let alone tell your mother about.
(iii) That's not the kind of movie that you get scared and have nightmares about.
(iv) ?That's not the kind of movie that you get scared let alone have nightmares about.

The difference in relative acceptability within the pair (i)–(ii) from that within the pair (iii)–(iv) has much to do with semantic differences between *and* and *let alone*. Lakoff's explanation of the constraint on non-across-the-board extraction with *and* hinges on the type of interpretative scenario evoked by the entire conjunction of verb phrases.

(43) a. John was there, and Louise (too).
   b. John wasn't there, let alone Louise.

(44) a. I wanted Fred to do it, rather than Sue.
   b. I didn't want Fred to do it, let alone Sue.

(45) a. Louise surely understood it, if not Susan.
   b. Louise surely didn't understand it, let alone Susan.

(46) a. I bet Louise, not to mention Susan, could pass that test.
   b. I bet Louise, let alone Susan, couldn't pass that test.

***2.2.2. Let Alone** as a Paired Focus Construction.* The *let alone* construction has several features in common with what are sometimes called FOCUS CONSTRUCTIONS (see Prince 1981 for a review of the unique aspects of each construction). Pseudoclefts, clefts, leftward movement constructions like Topicalization, and Yiddish Movement are commonly held to have the function of foregrounding a particular element, the Focus constituent. Each of these has its own prosodic and syntactic characteristics which, together with its particular semantics and pragmatics, differentiate it from the others in its class. Similarly, in the class of constructions we describe here, each has idiosyncrasies and particularities which distinguish it from the others. However, just as the constructions cited above can be characterized as a group by the appearance of some phrasal constituent at the leftmost point of an English sentence, so these can be grouped on the basis of several structural features. Some examples:

(47) He doesn't get up for LUNCH, let alone BREAKFAST.

(48) He doesn't get up for LUNCH, much less BREAKFAST.

(49) She didn't eat a BITE, never mind a WHOLE MEAL.

(50) She didn't eat a MEAL, just a SNACK.

(51) She beat SMITH at chess, not to mention JONES.

Each of these examples contains a complete clause, followed by a connective of some sort, followed by a fragment.[10] The fragment bears a certain relationship to some part of what we have called the context sentence. The fragment and the constituent that it corresponds to are both in focus (in a way to be discussed below at length), as is shown by the prosody typically as-

---

[10]A classical transformational analysis would describe these fragments as having undergone deletion under identity with material in the preceding clause by some process that shares characteristics of Stripping (Hankamer 1971). A nontransformational analysis could have recourse to a process that would copy the functional structure of the context sentence onto the fragment (Levin 1982). Our analysis does not depend on the form of the solution.

sociated with them, and their pragmatic status (also to be discussed below). In these double focus constructions, the unmarked prosodic shape consists of prominence on both the first and the second focused elements. Thus:

(52) She doesn't get up for LUNCH, let alone BREAKFAST.

All of these constructions allow the speaker (1) to make an assertion or contradict some proposition implied or asserted by another speaker, by focussing on a particular constituent of that proposition; and (2) to reset the value of that constituent, as it were.[11]

***2.2.3. Sentence Fragments and the Complement of* Let Alone** (deleted) discusses the fact that finite inflection associated with the negative polarity trigger F cannot occur after *let alone.*

2.2.4.* Let Alone *as a Negative Polarity Item (deleted) discusses the fact that most attested cases of *let alone* indicate that it is a negative polarity item, as illustrated in (i):

(i)   a. He didn't make lieutenant, let alone captain.
     b. ?? He made captain, let alone lieutenant.
     c. ?? He made lieutenant, let alone captain.

2.2.5. Multiple Paired Foci: A Syntactic Puzzle (deleted) deals with syntactic issues surrounding sentences with multiple occurrences of *let alone,* such as the synonymous sentences in (ii):

(ii) a. You couldn't get a poor man to wash your car for ten dollars, let alone a rich man to wax your truck for five dollars.
     b. You couldn't get a poor man, let alone a rich man, to wash your car, let alone wax your truck, for ten dollars, let alone five dollars.

2.3 The Semantics of *Let Alone*

We saw that syntactically a *let alone* sentence allowed an initial analysis into the components F <X A *let alone* B Y>, with the proper adjustments in case there is more than one pair of elements which the construction puts into contrast. The process of constructing a semantic interpretation of a *let alone* sentence begins with building (for each contrasting pair of As and Bs) two

---

[11]The *let alone* construction shares certain prosodic and semantic properties with other paired focus constructions, such as Gapping and Comparative Subdeletion (Selkirk 1984).

sentences, one with A and one with B, in which the syntactic F element is represented by the semantic F' element, in the formula F' <X A Y>.

In the simplest case, the case in which the F constituent is simply grammatical negation, we can say that the sentence simply asserts both 'not<X A Y.>)' and 'not<X B Y>'. (That is, from *He didn't make colonel, let alone general* we derive two propositions—that he did not make colonel and that he did not make general.) The general effect of the construction is to assert the first and to suggest that the second necessarily follows, and so the relation between the two parts, 'not(X A Y)' and 'not(X B Y)', is one of entailment. ('He didn't make colonel; a fortiori, he didn't make general.') But it is not simply an entailment relation. In particular, the entailment in this case must be against the background of a presupposed semantic scale. The interpretation of any *let alone* sentence requires seeing the two derived propositions as points on a scale. A second and essential step in the interpretation of a *let alone* sentence, then, requires the construction of a scale in which the A proposition and the B proposition are distinct points.

The discussion in this section will concentrate on (1) the interpretation of the sentence fragment containing or constituting the B constituent; (2) the nature of the entailment relation that holds between the A part and the B part; (3) the dimensions and scalar relations presupposed by a use of the construction; (4) the special case of complex scales (corresponding to the use of the construction with multiple paired foci); and (5) the roles of negative and positive polarity in the interpretation of the entailment relationship.

2.3.1. The Interpretation of Sentence Fragments.

It is our job here to present the salient syntactic and semantic facts about the *let alone* construction and to suggest their relevance for grammatical theory generally. While among these suggestions will be a claim that some of these facts are not readily accommodated within existing grammatical theories, we do not attempt to present a new formal framework of our own. Consequently, it should not be surprising that we come upon facts whose certain designation as syntactic versus semantic is not intuitively given and must wait upon a fully explicit treatment that establishes this distinction formally, if such a formal distinction is justified. We will continue here to use the idiom of the older form of transformational grammar as a heuristic, descriptive device, without intending any theoretical commitment regarding the issue of whether the phenomena we consider are really syntactic or semantic.

It will be recalled that a *let alone* sentence containing *n* pairs of foci may contain any number of tokens of *let alone* between 1 and *n* (the interpretation of such an expansion being, however, contingent on the independence of the dimensions, as discussed with respect to Example (78)). In the simplest case, *n* of course equals 1. It will be further recalled that any sentence containing more than one token of *let alone*, such as (75), means the same as another *let alone* sentence that contains just one instance of *let alone*, such as (74). In general, given the restriction to independent dimensions, any *let alone* sentence containing n paired foci belongs to a set of $2^{n+1} - 1$ synonymous *let alone* sentences containing these same paired foci. The members of the set differ of course in the number and placement of tokens of *let alone* (as well as in semantically irrelevant details regarding whether various non-focused elements occur more than once on the surface or are deleted under identity after their initial occurrence). Thus, when we have specified the semantics of an n-focus *let alone* sentence containing a single token of *let alone*, we have specified the semantics of every other member of the set of sentences syntactically derivable from this one by the process described in §2.2.5. If we take the process of syntactic derivation described in §2.2.5 literally, we are accounting for the relations of intersentential synonymy thereby specified with a syntactic as against an interpretive process. Our need here, however, is merely to establish that these relations of synonymy exist, and we abjure any position on the issue whether a fully explicit theory should provide a syntactic or a semantic account of these relations. What we need to establish for present purposes is no more than the following: a semantic account of all the sentences containing a single token of *let alone* is a semantic account of all *let alone* sentences. Consequently, for the remainder of this section 2.3, we may use the expression '*let alone* sentence' as a shorthand for '*let alone* sentence containing a single token of *let alone*' without loss of generality.

The interpretation of a *let alone* sentence of the form in (88) proceeds first by restoration of any X element on the right of the *let alone* that may have been deleted, yielding the abstract form in (89):

(88) $F[X_1A_1 \ldots X_nA_nX_{n+1} \text{ let alone } (X_1)B_2 \, (X_n)B_n(X_{n+1})]$

(89) $F[X_1A_1 \ldots X_nA_nX_{n+1} \text{ let alone } X_1B_1 \ldots X_n \, B_nX_{n+1}]$

For example, from an actual sentence such as (90) an abstract structure is reconstructed that can be represented by (91):

(90) You could never get Fred to eat SHRIMP at Jack-in-the-Box let alone SQUID.

(91) You could never get (Fred to eat shrimp at Jack-in-the-Box let alone Fred to eat squid at Jack-in-the-Box).

In the preceding example the abstract structure happens to correspond closely to an acceptable surface sentence, but in other cases this is not so, as when the F element is simple negation. For example, reconstruction of (92) yields (93):

(92) Fred won't eat shrimp at Jack-in-the-Box, let alone squid.

(93) Not (Fred will eat shrimp at Jack-in-the-Box let alone Fred will eat squid at Jack-in-the-Box).

Succeeding stages of the interpretation of a *let alone* sentence involve obtaining propositional interpretations P_1 and P_2 of the sentences of the form $X_1A_1 \ldots X_nA_nX_{n+1}$ and $X_1B_1 \ldots X_nB_nX_{n+1}$, respectively; and obtaining from F the semantic operator F′ in such a way that the form of the meaning of the full sentence is as in (94):

(94) $F'(P_1); F'(P_2)$

We now proceed to a description of these processes and the constraints they exhibit.

2.3.2. The Entailment Relation: Presupposed Dimensions and Scales (deleted) makes two major semantic points. First, the scales involved with *let alone* are contextually determined. Utterance of

(iii) I'll be surprised if Fred orders shrimp, let alone Louise, squid.

might, depending on context, evoke (1) a two dimensional scale in which Louise is more fastidious than Fred and squid are more distasteful than shrimp, or (2) one in which Louise is more miserly than Fred and squid are more expensive than shrimp, or (3) Louise is more health-conscious than Fred and squid are more toxic than shrimp, or . . .

Secondly, the unilateral entailment presupposed between the two semantic clauses of a *let alone* sentence must derive from a scalar model (briefly characterized below). A sentence like

(iv) Fred doesn't have an odd number of books, let alone seventy-five.

is anomalous, despite the fact that not having an odd number of books entails not having seventy-five books in any context. Imagine now a scalar context containing a lottery in which every odd numbered ticket gets a small prize and ticket number seventy-five gets the grand prize. Since now the unilateral entailment is based on a scale (value of prize) a sentence like v is readily interpretable:

(v) Fred didn't get an odd numbered ticket let alone seventy-five.

This long section goes on to develop the notion of *scalar model*, an n-dimensional matrix of propositions, subject to a particular pattern of unilateral entailment. Each dimension of the model corresponds to an n-tuple of alternative foci, e.g. (<Fred, Louise>, <shrimp, squid>), and each proposition in the model represents a distinct parameterization of a constant propositional function, e.g., X won't eat Y.

2.3.3.* Barely *as the F Element (deleted) discusses complications which arise when the F element is *barely*.

2.3.4. Complex Scales (deleted) relates the syntax of multiple focus and multiple *let alone* sentences to the scalar model semantics introduced in section 2.3.2.

2.4. The Pragmatics of *Let Alone*

A description of the pragmatic conventions associated with the *let alone* construction must mention the two speech acts which utterance of a *let alone* sentence confronts—namely, the stronger A part F' <X A Y> and the weaker B part F' <X B Y> and their separate evaluations as informative (satisfying the Gricean Quantity maxim) and relevant (satisfying the Relevance maxim), respectively. In addition, a pragmatic description must mention the manner in which the utterance of a *let alone* sentence fits its conversational context. Briefly, the essential pragmatic conditions on the felicitous utterance of a *let alone* sentence are the following:

(a) By way of the raising of what we may call the CONTEXT PROPOSITION, the immediately preceding context has created conditions under which a speech act represented by the weaker B clause is an appropriate or relevant response.
(b) The weaker B clause of the *let alone* sentence specifically accepts or rejects the context proposition.
(c) In either case, the speaker, while committing himself emphatically to the B clause, indicates that limiting himself to it would not be cooperative, since there is something even more informative to be said: the stronger A clause.

Thus the *let alone* construction, with its two parts, can be seen as having the function of meeting simultaneous and conflicting demands of Relevance and Quantity. The weaker clause answers to the demands of Relevance, either reasserting or denying the context sentence, according to the dictates of Quality. In either case, the stronger clause satisfies the demands of Quantity by saying the most informative thing the speaker of the *let alone*

sentence knows to be true. The effect of the whole, of course, is to emphasize the strength of the speaker's commitment to the B part.

It is important to notice a potential confusion regarding the notion of
strength. When we say that the A clause is stronger, we mean that it is more
informative, in the sense that it asymmetrically entails the B clause; but the
speaker's and hearer's attitude to the B clause can be said to be stronger in
the sense that it is uttered in greater confidence, being supported by the A
clause. The A clause (given the presupposed background) is more informative; the speech act performed through the B clause is more certain, more
emphatic.

It is not surprising that the word *even* fits comfortably into the A clause of
a *let alone* sentence, since *even* is used fittingly with expressions of propositions which are stronger than some contextually present or imagined proposition. Thus sentences like *He even made general* and *He didn't even make colonel* are usable in contexts in which, respectively, a lesser or greater
achievement may be presumed. The word *even* appears to have the function
of indicating that the sentence in which it occurs is somehow stronger than
another sentence with which it can be compared. (See Karttunen & Peters
1979 and the literature cited therein. The Appendix to the present paper
gives a formal definition of informativeness in terms of the wider concept
'scalar model'.)

As we have noticed, the expression *let alone* belongs to a family of phrasal
conjunctions with somewhat similar functions, these including *if not, in fact,
much less, not to mention, never mind*, and others. While constructions built
around these conjunctions differ from each other in a number of ways, what
is common to them all is the presupposition that the two propositions which
they confront identify distinct points on a scale. If we see the two points F' <X
A Y> and F' <X B Y> as points on a scale of certainty, the intent of the construction can be described as claiming that since some quantity has reached
the point represented by F' <X A Y>, then it has, ipso facto and a fortiori,
reached the point represented by F' <X B Y>. Expressed informally, we find
that *let alone* sentences can be paraphrased, this time with the clauses in the
order B–A, as in these three examples: *I wouldn't pay five dollars for it, let alone
ten dollars.* ('You want to know whether I'd pay ten dollars for it? Well, I'll
have you know that I wouldn't even pay five dollars for it'); *I don't let my children drink beer, let alone whiskey.* ('You ask if I permit my children to drink whiskey? Well, I don't even permit my children to drink beer'); *He could persuade
people that he's a duke, let alone a baron.* ('Could he persuade them that he's a
baron? Why, he could persuade them that he's a duke'). There are of course
conjunctive constructions which present the conflicting elements in the
more 'natural' order. That is, while *let alone*, together with *much less* and *not to
mention*, presents the stronger statement first, such conjunctions as *in fact* and
if not present the stronger point second.

(130) He didn't make general; in fact, he didn't even make colonel.

(131) He did make colonel; in fact, he even made general.

(132) I believe he made colonel, if not general.

As with many lexical items and grammatical constructions having pragmatic presuppositions, here too the presupposed scale underlying the construction's felicitous use does not need to be part of the speaker's world, but can be attributed to the source of reported speech or thought. Thus, we might be representing General Shotwell's feelings more faithfully than our own in (133):

(133) General Shotwell said that in the Grenada affair not enough Cubans were wiped out to make it worthwhile to open a bottle of champagne, let alone put on a proper banquet for the Joint Chiefs of Staff.

3. CONCLUSION

We hope to have demonstrated in the preceding pages that, in the construction of a grammar, more is needed than a system of general grammatical rules and a lexicon of fixed words and phrases. Those linguistic processes that are thought of as irregular cannot be accounted for by constructing lists of exceptions: the realm of idiomaticity in a language includes a great deal that is productive, highly structured, and worthy of serious grammatical investigation. It has come to seem clear to us that certain views of the layering of grammatical operations are wrong. We have in mind that view of the interaction of syntax and semantics by which the semantic composition of a syntactically complex phrase or sentence is always accomplished by the iteration of atomistic local operations, and that view of pragmatics by which semantically interpreted objects are invariably first situated in contexts and then given their contextualized construals. It has seemed to us that a large part of a language user's competence is to be described as a repertory of clusters of information including, simultaneously, morphosyntactic patterns, semantic interpretation principles to which these are dedicated, and, in many cases, specific pragmatic functions in whose service they exist. The notion of literal meaning should perhaps be anchored in what is common to the understanding of expressions whose meaning is under consideration; and that might necessarily bring in information that goes beyond considerations of truth conditions. Further, certain lexical items and constructions, such as *let alone*, may have literal meanings that determine (in part) truth conditions on the utterances of sentences in which they occur, but not on the sentences themselves. A language can associate semantic information with structures larger than elementary lexical items and can associate semantic interpretation principles with syntactic configurations larger and more complex than those definable by means of single phrase structure rules.

It appears to us that the machinery needed for describing the so-called minor or peripheral constructions of the sort which has occupied us here will have to be powerful enough to be generalized to more familiar structures, in particular those represented by individual phrase structure rules. A phrase structure rule characterizes a structure whose external category is identified with the category indicated on the left-hand side of an arrow (in the traditional notation) and whose constituent categories are those indicated on the right-hand side of the arrow; the semantic interpretation of such a construction is the semantic rule associated with that phrase structure rule. (In general, such constructions do not have associated pragmatic rules.) It can be hoped that the structure-building principles of the so-called core and the machinery for building the phraseological units of the kind discussed in this paper may be of a uniform type, the former being a degenerate instance of the latter.

[An appendix, SCALAR MODELS (deleted), presents a model-theoretic definition of scalar model along with an extended illustrative example.]

REFERENCES

Akmajian, Adrian. 1984. Sentence types and the form-function fit. Natural Language and Linguistic Theory 2.1–23.

Allwood, Jens. 1972. Negation and the strength of presuppositions. (Logical grammar report 2.) Gothenburg: University of Goteborg.

Anscombre, Jean-Claude, and Oswald Ducrot. 1983. L'argumentation dans la langue. Brussels: Mardaga.

Baker, C. Leroy. 1970. Double negatives. LI 1.169–86.

Bresnan, Joan. 1975. Comparative deletion and constraints on transformations. Linguistic Analysis 1.25–74.

Clark, Herbert. 1974. Semantics and comprehension. Current trends in linguistics 12, ed. by Thomas A. Sebeok, 1291–428. The Hague: Mouton.

Cresswell, Max J. 1976. The semantics of degree. Montague grammar, ed. by Barbara H. Partee, 280–91. New York: Academic Press.

Ducrot, Oswald. 1973. La preuve et le dire. Paris: Mame.

Fauconnier, Gilles. 1975a. Pragmatic scales and logical structure. LI 6.353–75.

——. 1975b. Polarity and the scale principle. CLS II.188–99.

——. 1976. Etude de certains aspects logiques et grammaticaux de la quantification et de l'anaphore en français et en anglais. Doctorat d'Etat, Université de Paris VII.

Fraser, Bruce. 1970. Vice versa. LI 1.277.

Gazdar, Gerald. 1979. Pragmatics: Implicature, presupposition, and logical form. New York: Academic Press.

Green, Georgia. 1985. The description of inversions in Generalized Phrase Structure Grammar. BLS 11.117–45.

Hankamer, Jorge. 1971. Constraints on deletion in syntax. Yale University dissertation.

Horn, Laurence. 1972. On the semantic properties of logical operators in English. UCLA dissertation.

Karttunen, Lauri, and Stanley Peters. 1979. Conventional implicature. Syntax and semantics 11: Presupposition, ed. by Choon-Kyu Oh and David A. Dinneen, 1–56. New York: Academic Press.

Kay, Paul. 1987. EVEN. Berkeley Cognitive Sciences Report No. 50. Berkeley: University of California. [To appear in Linguistics and Philosophy.]

Klima, Edward. 1964. Negation in English. The structure of language, ed. by Jerry A. Fodor and Jerrold J. Katz, 246–323. New York: Prentice Hall.

Lakoff, George. 1986. Frame semantic control of the coordinate structure constraint. Papers from the Parasession on Pragmatics and Grammatical Theory (CLS 22:2), 152–67. Chicago.

Levin, Lori S. 1982. Sluicing: A lexical interpretation procedure. The mental representation of grammatical relations, ed. by Joan Bresnan, 590–654. Cambridge, MA: MIT Press.

Lewis, David. 1979. Scorekeeping in a language game. Semantics from different points of view, ed. by R. Bauerle, Urs Egli, and Arnim von Stechow, 172–87. Berlin: Springer-Verlag.

Linebarger, Marcia. 1981. The grammar of negative polarity. Bloomington: Indiana University Linguistics Club.

Makkai, Adam. 1972. Idiom structure in English. The Hague: Mouton.

Mandel, Mark. 1974. When things don't happen. Berkeley Studies in Syntax and Semantics 1.XIX:1–3.

McCawley, James D. 1976. The annotated respective. Grammar and meaning, ed. by James D. McCawley, 121–32. New York: Academic Press.

Partee, Barbara H. 1977. Comments on the paper by Bresnan. Formal syntax, ed. by Peter Culicover, Thomas Wasow, and Adrian Akmajian, 197–206. New York: Academic Press.

Pawley, Andrew, and Frances Syder. 1983. Two puzzles for linguistic theory: Nativelike selection and nativelike fluency. Language and communication, ed. by Jack C. Richards and Richard W. Schmidt, 191–225. London: Longman.

Prince, Ellen F. 1981. Topicalization, focus movement and Yiddish movement: A pragmatic differentiation. BLS 7.249–64.

Selkirk, Elizabeth O. 1984. Phonology and syntax: The relation between sound and structure. Cambridge, MA: MIT Press.

Wierzbicka, Anna. 1987. Boys will be boys: 'Radical semantics' vs. 'radical pragmatics'. Lg. 63.95–114.

Author Index

A

Aissen, J., 50, *85*
Akmajian, A., 249, 254, *269*
Allwood, J., *269*
Anderson, J. M., 152, *165*
Anderson, L. B., 216, 219, *240*
Anscombre, J-C., *269*
Ariel, M., 48, 53, 55, 56, 65, 79, 81, *85*, 173, *193*
Ashby, W. J., 48, 55, 62, 63, *85, 86*, 138, *140*
Auer, P., 120, *140*

B

Baker, C. L., *269*
Baldwin, G., *12*, 14
Barnes, B. K., 214, *240*
Barry, D., 175, *193*
Bates, E., 81, *85*
Bentivoglio, P., 63, *85*
Biber, D., 3, *13*, 121, *140*
Bickerton, D., 149, *165*
Boas, F., 50, *85*
Bolinger, D., 9, *13*, 187, *193*
Bowerman, M., 89, *116*
Boyland, J. T., 153, 155, *165*

Braine, M., 12, *13*
Bresnan, J., *269*
Brooks, P., 12, *13*
Browman, C. P., 146, *165*
Brugman, C., 187, *193*
Burridge, K., 214, *240*
Bybee, J. L., 11, 12, *13*, 94, *116*, 119, 120, *140*, 146, 149, 152, 153, 156, 157, 160, *165*, 219, 230, 234, 236, *240*

C

Call, J., 89, *118*
Carlin, E., *116*
Chafe, W. L., 4, *13*, 48, 52, 53, 54, 55, 62, 65, 66, 70, 79, 81, 82, *85*, 122, 126, 127, *140*
Chomsky, N., 2, 9, 12, *13*, 151, *165*
Clahsen, H., 9, *13*
Clancy, P. M., 55, 56, *85*
Clark, E. V., 92, *116*
Clark, H. H., 53, 66, *85*, 120, 138, *140, 269*
Claudi, U., 146, 151, 152, 160, 161, 162, *166*, 234, 236, *241*
Comrie, B., 89, 92, *116, 117*, 195, 206, *209*, 212, *240*
Conrad, S., 3, *13*
Cranmer, D. J., 224, *240*

Cresswell, M. J., *269*
Croft, W., 1, 5, 7, *13*, 99, *117*, 135, *140*,
        212, 219, 220, 228, 231, 233, 235,
        236, 239, *240*, *241*
Cullicover, P., 10, *13*
Cumming, S., 54, 55, *86*, 139, *140*

D

Dahl, Ö., 131, *140*
Darnell, M., 209, *209*
DeLancey, S., 8, *13*
Dixon, R. M. W., 135, *140*
Dodson, K., 12, *13*
Druyan, A., 187, *193*
Dryer, M., 1, 5, *14*
Du Bois, J. W., 48, 52, 53, 54, 55, 60, 61,
        62, 63, 67, 69, 71, 74, 77, 81, 82, 83,
        85, *86*, 139, *140*
Ducrot, O., *269*
Durie, M., 71, *86*
Dutra, R., 63, *86*

E

Edelman, G. M., 120, *140*
Enger, H.-O., 219, *241*
Englebretson, R., 136, *140*

F

Faltz, L., 100, *117*
Fauconnier, G., 177, *193*, *269*
Ferguson, C., 90, *117*, 230, *241*
Ferris, D. C., 135, *140*
Fillmore, C. J., 9, *14*, 19, 55, 82, *86*, 122,
        140
Firbas, J., 77, *86*
Ford, C. E., 3, 55, *86*, 125, 126, *141*
Fox, B. A., 3, 4, *14*, 48, 55, 81, *86*, 128,
        129, 131, 134, *141*, 175, 190, *193*
Fraser, B., *269*
Fujii, N., *141*

G

Gazdar, G., *269*

Geeraerts, D., 212, *241*
Geluykens, R., 138, *141*
Geniušiene, E., 224, *241*
Givón, T., 6, *14*, 48, 55, *86*, 97, 110, *117*,
        121, 128, *141*, 160, 163, *165*, 173,
        193, *194*
Goddard, C., 239, *241*
Goldberg, A. E., 9, 10, *14*, 55, *86*, 97, *117*
Goldstein, L. M., 146, *165*
Goodwin, C., 120, 124, 125, 135, *141*
Goodwin, M. H., 120, 135, *141*
Green, G., 245, *270*
Greenbaum, S., 121, 135, *142*, 220, *242*
Greenberg, J. H., 89, 99, *117*
Güldemann, T., 148, *166*

H

Haiman, J., 102, 103, 110, 112, 113, *117*,
        120, *141*, 153, *165*, *166*, 216, *241*
Hankamer, J., 261, *270*
Harris, Z. S., 47, *86*
Haspelmath, M., 152, 159, *166*, 213, 216,
        218, 219, 220, 222, 224, 232, 233,
        234, 235, 236, *241*
Haviland, J., 107, *117*
Hayashi, M., 129, 131, 133, 134, 135, *141*
Heath, J., 99, *117*
Heine, B., 91, 92, 94, *117*, 146, 148, 149,
        151, 152, 160, 161, 162, 163, 164,
        166, 234, 236, *241*
Heritage, J. C., 120, *141*
Hinds, J., 130, *141*
Hjelmslev, L., 237, *241*
Hopper, P. J., 4, *14*, 48, 55, *86*, 94, 98, *117*,
        119, 120, *141*, 146, 155, 156, 160,
        161, *166*, 234, *241*
Horn, L., *270*
Hünnemeyer, F., 146, 151, 152, 160, 161,
        162, *166*, 234, 236, *241*
Hutchison, J. P., 107, *117*
Hyman, L. M., 206, *209*

I

Iwasaki, S., 133, *141*, *142*

J

Jackendoff, R., 9, 10, *14*
Jakobson, R., 82, *86*, 214, 230, *241*
Janzen, T., 149, *166*
Jasperson, R., 129, 131, 134, *141*
Jefferson, G., 124, 128, 133, 139, *142*
Johnson, M., 226, *241*

K

Karttunen, L., 267, *270*
Kawanishi, Y., 135, *143*
Kay, P., 9, *14*, 245, *270*
Kaye, P., *14*
Kemmer, S., 92, 100, 104, 105, 109, 110,
    111, *117*, 219, 224, 226, 233, 235,
    236, *241*
Kibrik, A., 173, *194*
Kilian-Hatz, C., 148, *166*
Kimura, D., 153, *166*
Klima, E., *270*
König, E., *241*
Kortmann, B., 219, *241*
Kumagai, Y., 62, *86*
Kumpf, L. E., 48, 55, 62, 63, *86*
Kuno, S., 77, *86*, 130, *142*

L

Lakoff, G., 2, 8, *14*, 97, *117*, 158, *166*, 187,
    193, 219, 226, 231, 232, *241*, 260,
    270
Lambrecht, K., 9, *14*
Langacker, R. W., 10, 11, *14*, 51, 82, *86*,
    87, 89, 99, 110, *117*, 119, 120, *142*,
    172, 173, 180, 182, 183, 188, *194*,
    219, 224, 232, *241*
Leech, G., 121, 135, *142*, 220, *242*
Lehmann, C., 146, *166*, 234, 236, *241*
Leiss, E., 215, *242*
Lerner, G. H., 124, *142*
Lessau, D. A., 148, *166*
Levin, L. S., 261, *270*
Lewis, D., 257, *270*
Lewis, L., 12, *13*
Lieberman, P., 153, *166*
Lieven, E., 12, *14*
Lightfoot, D., 165, *166*

Linebarger, M., *270*
Lord, C., 160, *166*

M

MacWhinney, B., 81, *85*, 180, *194*
Makkai, A., 247, *270*
Mandel, M., *270*
Mandler, J. M., 89, 98, *117*
Matsuda, K., 131, *142*
Matsumoto, K., 63, *87*
Maynard, S., 130, *142*
McCawley, J. D., *270*
McGregor, W. B., 62, *87*
McNeill, D., 53, 55, 66, *87*
Meillet, A., 146, *166*
Michaelis, L., 9, *14*, 226, 227, 228, *242*
Miller, J., 4, *14*
Moravcsik, E., 209, *209*
Mossé, F., 159, *166*
Mowrey, R., 146, *166*
Mulac, A., 55, *87*, 163, *167*
Munro, P., 224, *241*

N

Nesset, T., 219, *241*
Newmeyer, F., 209, *209*
Nichols, J., 48, *87*
Noonan, M., 120, 121, *142*, 209, *209*
Nunberg, G., 9, *14*

O

Ochs, E., 138, *142*
O'Connor, M., *14*
Olson, D., *14*
Ono, T., 130, 131, *141, 142*

P

Pagliuca, W., 94, *116*, 120, *140*, 146, 149,
    152, 153, 156, 157, *165, 166*, 234,
    236, *240*
Paolino, D., 54, 55, *86*, 139, *140*
Partee, B. H., *270*
Pawley, A., 11, *14*, 94, *117*, 248, *270*

Payne, D. L., 62, *87*
Perkins, R., 94, *116*, 120, *140*, 149, 152, 153, 156, 157, *165*, 234, 236, *240*
Peters, S., 267, *270*
Pine, J., 12, *14*
Pinker, S., 9, 12, *14*
Plank, F., 165, *166*
Plungian, V. A., 219, 236, *242*
Pomerantz, A., 127, 135, *142*
Prince, E. F., 261, *270*

Q

Quirk, R., 121, 135, *142*, 220, *242*

R

Reh, M., 146, 149, 163, *166*
Reinhart, T., 170, 171, 187, *194*
Reppen, R., 3, *13*
Rice, S., 98, *117*, 219, 239, *242*
Roberg, H., 148, *166*
Romaine, S., 149, *166*
Rosalie, M., 226, 227, 228, *242*
Rosch, E., 158, *166*
Roth, A. L., 120, *141*
Rudzka-Ostyn, B., 219, *242*

S

Sacks, H., 123, 124, 127, 128, 129, 133, 139, *142, 143*
Sadock, J., 212, *242*
Sag, I., 9, *14*
Sandra, D., 219, 239, *242*
Sankoff, G., 149, *166*
Sapir, 101
Saussure, F., 50, 51, *87*
Savage-Rumbaugh, S., 89, *118*
Schachter, P., 135, *142*
Schegloff, E., 120, 122, 124, 128, 129, 133, 139, *142, 143*
Scheibman, J., 11, *13*, 131, *143*
Schieffelin, B., 138, *142*
Schiffrin, D., 51, *87*
Schladt, M., 148, *166*
Schuetze-Coburn, S., 54, 55, 61, *86, 87*, 139, *140*

Selkirk, E. O., 255, 262, *270*
Shanker, S. G., 89, *118*
Shibatani, M., 130, *143*
Shyldkrot, H. B.-Z., 219, 233, 235, 236, *241*
Sinclair, J., 3, *14*
Slobin, D. I., 98, *118*
Smith, C. S., 151, *167*
Smith, W., 62, *87*
Stahlke, H., 163, *167*
Stassen, L., 97, *118*, 219, *242*
Stimm, H., 235, *242*
Stolz, T., 148, *166*, 226, *242*
Strauss, S., 135, *143*
Styles, N., 99, 101, *118*
Sullivan, T. D., 99, 101, *118*
Suzuki, R., 131, *142*
Svartvik, J., 121, 135, *142*, 220, *242*
Svorou, S., 152, *167*
Sweet, H., 159, *167*
Sweetser, E., 127, *143*
Syder, F., 11, *14*, 248, *270*

T

Talmy, L., 15, 17, 21, 23, 26, 31, 34, 38, 42, 46, 89, 92, 93, 94, 105, *118*
Tanaka, H., 130, 131, 133, 135, *143*
Tao, H., 121, 122, 133, 138, *142, 143*
Taylor, C., 227, *242*
Taylor, J. R., 158, *167*
Taylor, T. J., 89, *118*
Thompson, S. A., 3, 4, 12, *13, 14*, 48, 55, 74, 81, *86, 87*, 98, *117*, 126, 127, 130, 131, 135, 136, *141, 142, 143*, 163, *167*
Timberlake, A., 48, *87*
Tomasello, M., 2, 11, 12, *13, 14*, 68, *87*, 89, *118*
Tomlin, R. S., 190, *194*
Traugott, E. C., 94, *117*, 146, 155, 156, 160, *166, 167*, 234, *241*
Tuggy, D., 212, *242*

U

Uhmann, S., 135, *143*
Underhill, R., 99, 101, *118*

V

van der Auwera, J., 219, 236, *242*
Van Hoecke, W., 214, *242*
van Hoek, K., 173, 185, 187, *194*
Velazquez, M., 91, 110, *118*

W

Wasow, T., 9, *14*
Weber, E., *143*

Weber, T., 120, *143*
Weinert, R., 4, *14*
Weinreich, U., 151, *167*
Wetzer, H., 135, *143*
Wheatley, K., 209, *209*
Wierzbicka, A., 93, *118*, 239, *241*, 246, *270*
Wilkes-Gibbs, D., 138, *140*

Z

Zwicky, A., 212, *242*

Subject Index

A

Argument structure, 55–65, 73–75
  constraint, 75–78
  pattern, 78–80
  pragmatics, 65–70
  predicates, 58–61
  referential form, 56–58
Attention
  distribution of, 38–39

C

Cognitive typology, 90–95
Clauses, 95–98, 159–161

D

Discourse, 50–54
  and grammar, 47–50, 55, 70

G

Grammar, 5–10
  and discourse, 47–50, 55, 70
  assessments, 135–137

constructions, 98–109
  iconicity, 112–114
idiomaticity, 246–254
  formal idioms, 254–255
  "let alone," 255–268
interaction, 119–123, 127–129
multifunctionality, 211–215
referents, 137–138
repair, 129–135
syntactitization, 5–7
Grammaticalization, 146–154, 161–165
  emancipation, 154–157
  habituation, 157–159

I

Idioms, 246–255

L

Language
  event structure, 109–112
  frequency, 10–12
    rule-list fallacy, 11
  grammatical, 15–16, 21–22
  lexical, 15–16
  monogenesis, 207–209

Language *(cont.)*
   path windowing, 39–41
      in motion events, 41–45
   spoken, 3
      spontaneous spoken speech, 3–5
   structure, 196–202
   units of, 8–10
   written, 3–4

N

Nouns, 172–176, 183

P

Prepositions, 226–230
Pronominal anaphora, 169–172
   Point-of-view effects, 177–181
      connectivity, 186–192
      reference point, 181–186
Pronouns, 172–176, 202–207, 220–223

S

Schematic systems, 16
   causality, 31–34
   force dynamics, 26–30
   perspective, 34–38
      distance, 35–36
      location, 34–35
      motility, 36–37
      sequentializing, 37–38
      synopticizing, 38
Semantic maps, 215–220, 230–233, 237–238
   and diachronic change, 233–237
Space-time configuration, 16–17
   Figure-ground organization, 17–20
   topological properties
      fictive motion, 22–25
      paths, 23–25
      frame-relative motion, 25

V

Verbs, 223–226

DATE DUE

		JAN 1 6 2006
Oct 24 /10		OCT. 2 6 2010 8:30

CARR McLEAN, TORONTO FORM #38-297